Independent India, 1947–2000

Independent India, 1947–2000

Wendy Singer

**Longman
is an imprint of**

Harlow, England • London • New York • Boston • San Francisco • Toronto • Sydney • Singapore • Hong Kong
Tokyo • Seoul • Taipei • New Delhi • Cape Town • Madrid • Mexico City • Amsterdam • Munich • Paris • Milan

PEARSON EDUCATION LIMITED

Edinburgh Gate
Harlow CM20 2JE
United Kingdom
Tel: +44 (0)1279 623623
Fax: +44 (0)1279 431059
Website: www.pearson.com/uk

First edition published in Great Britain in 2012

© Pearson Education Limited 2012

The right of Wendy Singer to be identified as author
of this work has been asserted by her in accordance
with the Copyright, Designs and Patents Act 1988.

Pearson Education is not responsible for the content of third-party internet sites.

ISBN: 978-0-582-41494-5

British Library Cataloguing in Publication Data
A CIP catalogue record for this book can be obtained from the British Library

Library of Congress Cataloging in Publication Data
Singer, Wendy.
  Independent India, 1947-2000 / Wendy Singer.
    p. cm.
  Includes bibliographical references and index.
  ISBN 978-0-582-41494-5 (pbk.)
  1. India--History--1947---Textbooks   2. India--Politics and
government--1947---Textbooks.   I. Title.
  DS480.84.S5473 2012
  954.04--dc23
                                        2011027676

10   9   8   7   6   5   4   3   2   1
15   14   13   12   11

Set by 35 in 10/13.5pt Berkeley Book
Printed in Malaysia (CTP-PPSB)

Introduction to the series

History is narrative constructed by historians from traces left by the past. Historical enquiry is often driven by contemporary issues and, in consequence, historical narratives are constantly reconsidered, reconstructed and reshaped. The fact that different historians have different perspectives on issues means that there is also often controversy and no universally agreed version of past events. *Seminar Studies* was designed to bridge the gap between current research and debate, and the broad, popular general surveys that often date rapidly.

The volumes in the series are written by historians who are not only familiar with the latest research and current debates concerning their topic, but who have themselves contributed to our understanding of the subject. The books are intended to provide the reader with a clear introduction to a major topic in history. They provide both a narrative of events and a critical analysis of contemporary interpretations. They include the kinds of tools generally omitted from specialist monographs: a chronology of events, a glossary of terms and brief biographies of 'who's who'. They also include bibliographical essays in order to guide students to the literature on various aspects of the subject. Students and teachers alike will find that the selection of documents will stimulate discussion and offer insight into the raw materials used by historians in their attempt to understand the past.

Clive Emsley and Gordon Martel
Series Editors

Dedicated to Aaron and Elizabeth Lynn

Contents

Acknowledgements

I began this book in the Cambridge University library in 2004, when I was a By-Fellow at Churchill College and so it benefited from the time I spent with South Asia colleagues, such as Priyavada Gopal, Christopher Bayly, and Raj Chandravarkar (who we sadly lost two years later) and the other fellows and administrators at Churchill. In addition I am grateful for comments on chapters early on from Shuchi Kapila and Meena Khandelwal. Also I had useful feedback from former students, Richa Jha and Elizabeth Beckman, who read portions of this and a series of HIST 156 – History of India classes at Kenyon College, who tested it out. Special thanks are due to Christopher V. Hill, Dana Lightstone Bernstein, and Kailash Chandra Jha, who were all kind enough to read through the manuscript and make valuable suggestions. Also editors at Pearson Longman provided careful reading and essential feedback.

I had support from Kenyon College for travel and research in India and, through Kenyon, from the National Endowment for Humanities.

Finally, I am grateful for the patience of my family and, particularly, David Lynn throughout this process.

Publisher's acknowledgements

We are grateful to the following for permission to reproduce copyright material.

Documents

Documents 1, 2, 3 and 4 from http://parliamentofindia.nic.in/ls/coi.web/welcome.html. This information is downloaded from the website of Ministry of Law and Justice (Legislative Department); Document 6 (a) from Lalita, K., Kannabiran, V., Melkote, R.S., Maheshwari, U., Shatrugna, V., Tharu, S., *We Were Making History: Life Stories of Women in the Telangana People's Struggle*, Zed Books: New Delhi, (1989), pp.160–171; Document 11 from Parliament of India website, http://parliamentofindia.nic.in; Document 31 from Economic and Political Weekly, 24 June 1978; Document 33 from *Documents of the Communist Movement in India, XVII*, National Book Agency: Calcutta (1998), pp. 77–91; Document 37 from *Reservations for Backward Classes: Mandal Commisssion Report of the Backward Classes Commission*, Akalank Publications: Delhi, (1980); Document 39 from Narasimha Rao, P.V., *Ayodhya 6 December 1992*, Viking, (2006), pp. 155–6, 159, 165.

Maps

Map 1 from ePhotoPix.com; Map 3 from *The World Factbook 2009*. Washington, DC: Central Intelligence Agency, 2009.

Picture Credits

The publisher would like to thank the following for their kind permission to reproduce their photographs:

Plate 1 Copyright image courtesy of Tyeb Mehta Foundation, Mumbai, India. Image reproduced with kind permission by the Estate of Tyeb Mehta c/o

Vadehra Art Gallery; Plate 4 Copyright © 1996–2010, Kamat's Potpourri. All Rights Reserved; Plate 5 © FLC/ADAGP, Paris and DACS, London 2011; Plate 6 from The Times of India, Copyright © 2011, Bennett, Coleman & Co. Ltd. All Rights Reserved; Plate 7 from the National Gallery of Modern Art, New Delhi.

Every effort has been made to trace the copyright holders and we apologise in advance for any unintentional omissions. We would be pleased to insert the appropriate acknowledgment in any subsequent edition of this publication.

Chronology

1947   (15 August) Independence, Nehru becomes the first prime minister

1947   Mass migrations as a result of Partition (from 10 to 20 million people displaced)

1947   (October) Maharaja of Kashmir Accedes to India

1947   (November) Nizam of Hyderabad signs Standstill Agreement with Government of India.

1948   (30 January) Mahatma Gandhi's assassination

1948   Indian Army forces accession of Hyderabad

1948   Government revives production of documentaries and newsreels under its own film division

1949   (1 January) UN monitored cease-fire in Jammu and Kashmir, after 15-month war with Pakistan.

1950   (26 January) Constitution of India enacted

1950   (March) Planning Commission established to advance economic development

1951   (March) First Asian Games held at New Delhi (11 nations attended)

1951   (July) First Five-Year Plan initiated

1951   Formation of the Central Board of Film Censors (B. N. Sircar, Bengali film producer, represented the industry)

1951   Film Federation of India set up with Chadulal J. Shah as first President

1952   (21 February) First General Election (began 25 October 1951)

1952   Atomic Energy Establishment set up in Bombay

1953   (29 December) The States Reorganization Commission appointed to create linguistic states

1954   Bimal Roy's film 'Do Bigha Zamin' gets special mention at Cannes

1954   (April) India concludes treaty with China (Panchsheel)

1954   (July) Nehru inaugurates Bhakhra Dam

1955   Nehru plays important role at Bandung Conference of Asian and African Nations

1956   Second Five-Year Plan (more sweeping)

1956   Pather Panchali wins President's Gold Medal and award at Cannes for 'Best Human document'

1957   (24 February–9 June) Second General Election

1957   (March) Legislative Assembly Election in Kerala; Communist Party of India wins majority of seats.

1957   Mehboob's 'Mother India' massive box office hit and nominated for an Oscar for best foreign film

1958   (February) Finance Minister T. T. Krishnamachari resigns following Mundhra LIC share scandal

1959   Le Corbusier produces 'Statute of Land' for Chandigarh

1959   (March) Dalai Lama flees to India

1959   (October) Military confrontation with China in Aksai Chin

1960   Meeting of Afro-Asian Conference in New Delhi

1961   Indian troops enter Goa

1962   Satyajit Ray makes first colour film 'Kanchenjunga'

1962   (16 February–6 June) Third General Election

1962   Goa officially incorporated into India

1962   (October) Indo-China War

1964   (May 27) Jawaharlal Nehru dies

1964   (June 9) Lal Bahadur Shastri becomes prime minister

1965   (April) Pakistani Tanks enter India

1965   (1 September) War with Pakistan

1966   (January 4–10) Tashkent Conference between Pakistani and Indian leaders

1966   (11 January) Lal Bahadur Shastri dies

1966   (24 January) Indira Gandhi becomes prime minister

1967   (15–28 February) Fourth General Election

1971   Indian film industry, producing 432 films per year, becomes largest in world

1971   (1–13 March) Fifth General Election

1971   (December) War with Pakistan/Formation of Bangladesh

1972   Pakistan and India sign Shimla Accord

1972   Monsoon failure causes drought

1974   (May) Jaya Prakash Narayan begins Citizens for Democracy Movement

1974   George Fernandes, labour leader and politician, initiates strike of Railway Workers, affecting 1.5 million workers

1974   (December) Publication of *Towards Equality* – the Report of the Committee on the Status of Women in India, which met from 1971–74.

1975   Sikkim joins India

1975   (12 June) Justice Jag Mohan Sinha's (Allahabad High Court) verdict declared Indira Gandhi's election to the Lok Sabha as void.

1975   (24 June) In response to Indira Gandhi's appeal, Justice Krishna Iyer gave a conditional stay allowing her to remain a member of Parliament, but disallowing her to take part in the proceedings of the Lok Sabha.

1975   (25–26 June) The Emergency declared

1975–1977   Emergency suspension of civil liberties, 20-point programme

1975   (August) 'Sholay,' top grossing Indian film, first released

1976   India–Pakistan re-establish diplomatic relations for the first time since 1971 war.

1977   (18 January) Opposition politicians, jailed during the Emergency, are released

1977   The coalition Janata Party formed to contest elections

1977   (16–20 March) Sixth General Election – first time non-Congress government takes power – Morarji Desai is prime minister

1979   (19 June) Morarji Desai resigns after Janata Split

1980   (January) Seventh General Election

1980   Indira Gandhi becomes prime minister again

1980   (23 June) Sanjay Gandhi dies in plane crash

1980   (for about a decade) Sikh Separatist Movement in Punjab

1981   (February) Maruti Udyog set up (cooperative industry with Suzuki) to produce small Indian car

1982   (December) Ninth Asian Games – held in New Delhi

1983   (25 June) India wins the Cricket World Cup

1983   (6 October) Indira Gandhi imposes President's Rule in Punjab

1984   (5 June) Operation Blue Star (army attacks Golden Temple – 300 casualties)

1984   (31 October) Indira Gandhi assassinated

1984   Rajiv Gandhi becomes prime minister

1984   (24–28 December) Eighth General Election – Congress victory

1985   Narmada Bachao Andolan begins, protest Sardar Sarovar Dam

1985   (July) Rajiv Gandhi signs Punjab Accord

1986   (October) V.P. Singh elected president of Janata Dal (opposition party)

1986–1988   Series 'Ramayan' runs on television with great popularity

1987 (May) Bofors deal with Sweden

1988 (July) INSAT-IC launched (satellite)

1988 (22 August) The Darjeeling Accord – Ghurkha Hill Council

1989 (22–26 November) Ninth General Election: Congress Loses

1989 V.P. Singh becomes prime minister

1990 Mandal Commission Report debated in Parliament

1990 (September) L. K. Advani begins Rath Yatra to promote the Ayodhya issue

1991 (May and June) Tenth General Election (second phase postponed by Rajiv's assassination)

1991 (May) Rajiv Gandhi assassinated by LTTE during election campaign

1991 (September) Konkan Railway launched

1992 (6 December) Babri Masjid destroyed

1993 (March) 300 people killed in bomb blasts in Mumbai

1993 (30 September) The Latur earthquake hits central India

1994 (21 September) Outbreak and containment of pneumonic plague in Surat

1994 Aishwarya Rai wins Miss World and Sushmita Sen wins Miss Universe

1996 (27 January) Prithvi missile test-fired

1996 (27 April–21 May) Eleventh General Election – Atal Bihari Vajpayee becomes prime minister; BJP could not form government

1996 May Janata Party (with United Front) forms government – H. D. Deve Gowda becomes prime minister

1996 (November) Controversy and protest over Miss Universe Pageant, Bangalore

1997 (21 April) Government fails and I. K. Gujral becomes prime minister

1997 (May) Sotheby's first all Indian art sale, London

1997 (15 August) 50th anniversary of independence celebrations

1997 (5 September) Mother Teresa dies

1997 (27 November) Femina Miss India, Diana Hayden wins Miss World 1997

1997 (29 December) Sonia Gandhi enters politics

1998 (19 March) BJP-led Alliance sworn in to power. Vajpayee becomes prime minister

1998 (28 March)–2004 BJP alliance survives No-Trust vote. Telegu Desam Party and Jayalalithaa of Tamil Nadu work from behind the scenes

1998 (11 May) India tests nuclear explosives at Pokhram Range in Rajasthan

1998 (9 June) Cyclone in Gujarat kills 1000 people in 6 days

1998 (29 June) Three new states added Uttaranchal, Chattisgarh, and Jharkhand

1999 (February) Kargil Conflict – military hostilities between India and Pakistan

1999 Twelfth General Election

Who's who

Advani, L. K. (1927–): Leader and former President of the Bharatiya Janata Party; known as party ideologue and advocate of Hindutva philosophy; led Rath Yatra in 1990 to call attention to the Ayodhya issue.

Ambedkar, B. R. (1891–1956): A key author of India's constitution, he earned a PhD from Columbia University and practiced law in Bombay (now Mumbai) in the 1920s; an outspoken leader of the Depressed Classes, later known as Scheduled Classes and now as Dalits, he clashed with Gandhi over strategies for alleviated social (caste) discrimination; in the first cabinet, he was Law Minister from 1947–51; a member of the Mahar (a Scheduled Class) community himself, he converted to Buddhism (encouraging his followers to do the same) in 1950.

Desai, Morarji (1896–1995): A Gandhian and Freedom Fighter, who was a member of Nehru's first government after independence; a pro-business conservative, who was often at odds with Nehru; because of his strength in the Congress Party, he served as Deputy Prime Minister under Indira Gandhi in 1967, but lost power in the party split that established Indira Gandhi as leader in 1969; jailed during the Emergency, Desai became Prime Minister under the Janata government of 1977.

Gandhi, Indira (1917–1984): Third Prime Minister of India, from 1966 to 1977 and again from 1980 to 1984; led India to victory against Pakistan in the Bangladesh War and presided over the Green Revolution movement, which made India self sufficient in agriculture; known for ruling with an iron hand and surrounding herself with loyalists, she instituted the Emergency from 1975–77, a period of martial law, which defaced Indian democracy. She was assassinated in 1984. Daughter of the first Prime Minister, Jawaharlal Nehru, she was not related to Mahatma Gandhi).

Gandhi, Mohandas Karamchand (1869–1948): Internationally renown champion of non-violent resistance and major leader of India's freedom movement one; studied law in England and was called to the Bar in 1889; the British acknowledged him as the major force and symbol of Indian nationalist ambitions; assassinated in 1948, his death was seen as a martyrdom for the cause of communal – Hindu/Muslim – co-existence; he remains a powerful symbol in Indian politics. Known as Mahatma Gandhi – Great Soul – in respect to the spiritual basis of his political leadership.

Gandhi, Rajiv (1944–1991): Elder son of Indira Gandhi and a reluctant entrant into Indian politics; originally had a career as a pilot; married Sonia Gandhi an Italian woman he met when he was at Cambridge University; became a Member of Parliament in 1980 and Prime Minister from 1984–88, when he was known for emphasizing further modernization and technology; he was assassinated in 1991.

Gandhi, Sanjay (1946–1980): Younger son of Indira Gandhi and her main lieutenant during the Emergency; although he was not elected to office, he became his mother's most trusted advisor; his policies comprised some of the worst excesses of the Emergency, including forced sterilizations and destructions of homes in slums in the interest of beautification. Died in a plane crash in 1980.

Hussain, M. F. (Maqbool Fida) (1915–2011): Important modern artist who received international acclaim both for his paintings and his films; always living near or in Mumbai (formerly, Bombay), he studied at the J. J. School of Art. His work is displayed around the world and in major museums in India. In 1966 he was awarded the Padmashree, the highest award for an artist given by the Indian Government.

Jayalalithaa Jayaram (1948–): An actress turned politician, Jayalalithaa, as she is known, is the powerful chief of the AIADMK party in Tamil Nadu; she took over leadership of the party from her political mentor and former co-star M. G. Ramachandran in 1988 after his death; very controversial both for her political prowess and suggestions of corruption for which she spent a brief time in jail. She was adept at using her regional strength to influence political decisions in Delhi.

Kapoor, Raj (1924–1988): Famous Bollywood actor/director known for films that captured the struggle of an underdog hero; his RK Studios, which he founded in 1948, was one of the sources of prominent commercial films for decades; he was celebrated for pushing the limits of Bollywood formula films, but thereby not always achieving financial success.

Le Corbusier (1887–1965): The modernist architect, who designed the city of Chandigarh in India; born Charles-Edouard Jeanneret, Le Corbusier was a pseudonym, adopted in 1929 in Paris from a version of the name of his maternal grandfather's; through the construction of Chandigarh and employing many young Indian architects, Le Corbusier influenced a generation of Indian architectures.

Mayawati (1956–): Leader of the Bahujan Samaj Party, which supports the rights of Dalits, she comes from the Jatav (a Dalit) community; having completed her law degree, she worked as a teacher before entering politics, when in 1995 she became Chief Minister of Uttar Pradesh. She was the first Dalit to become Chief Minister of an Indian state.

Mehboob Khan (1907–1964): Pioneering Hindi film director and producer, whose 'Mother India,' (1957) became an iconic nationalist symbol and model for industry.

Mukherjee, Meera (1925–1998): Sculptor, whose use of tribal forms and techniques to create modern images, departed from the trends toward Western techniques popular among her contemporaries. Powerful figures of strong women challenging the viewer characterized her work.

Namboodiripad, E. M. S. (1909–1998): Leader of the Communist Party in Kerala, who presided over the first democratically elected communist government (which took place in the state in 1957). He served as Chief Minister at that time and again as Chief Minister in 1969.

Narayan, Jaya Prakash (JP) (1902–1979): Gandhian and Freedom Fighter from the state of Bihar, who dedicated his life after independence to support land rights for the most economically depressed populations; a socialist by conviction, he left the socialist party in India to turn to activism. In the 1970s he promoted what he called Total Revolution to fulfill the promises of the Freedom Movement for all Indians; his opposition to Indira Gandhi brought him a jail sentence during the Emergency that deteriorated his health irreparably; nevertheless he became the symbol of the Janata movement that defeated Indira Gandhi in the 1977 election.

Nargis (1929–1981): Famous film actress; born Fatima Rashid, Nargis became a national icon through her role as Radha in the classic film, 'Mother India'; her personal and professional relationship with the actor/director Raj Kapoor ended quite publically in the late 1950s, when she married another prominent actor Sunil Dutt.

Nehru, Jawaharlal (1889–1962): India's first Prime Minister, he was also a major leader of India's independence movement; studied at Cambridge and called to the Bar in 1912; engaged in socialist politics in England and joined the Fabian Society; Nehru's vision for India was strongly influenced by his beliefs in socialism and secularism and in his desire for an industrial path to modernization.

Patel, Vallabhai (1875–1950): An Indian Freedom Fighter and follower of Gandhi, who became the first Home Minister and Deputy Prime Minister in the post-independence government; he was also the Chair of the Committee on Minority Rights; Patel came from the conservative wing of the Congress Party.

Phoolan Devi (1962–2001): Elected to Parliament both in 1996 and in 1999, she championed the rights of women and depressed classes. Coming from a depressed class community, Phoolan Devi survived a brutal gang rape by powerful members of the Thakur community. She ran away and became a bandit. Known in India as the 'Bandit Queen,' she was jailed for 11 years for committing revenge murders against a group of Thakur men.

Rao, Nandamuri Taraka Rama NTR (1923–1996): Elected four times as Chief Minister of the state of Andhra Pradesh, NTR was a popular politician, who came from the film industry to form the Telegu Dessam Party (TDP) The TDP defended state's rights, Telegu language, and the programmes support- ing the poor and disadvantaged. He passed legislation to assure women equal rights to inherit land and put a ceiling on the price of rice for the poor.

Rushdie, Salman (1947–): Prominent novelist, born in Mumbai (Bombay), whose fiction often evokes the politics of India and Pakistan; his second novel, *Midnight's Children*, which won the Booker Prize in 1981 and the Booker of Bookers, dramatizes themes of nation-building and India's Emergency in 1975.

Shah Bano (1916–): Divorced by her husband in 1978, she appealed to the courts for maintenance; her case became the basis of political controversy between Muslim Personal Law and the secular courts.

Subramaniam, C. (1910–2000): A physicist and statistician, who was Minister of Food and Agriculture in 1965 when he set in motion India's Green Revolution; he was first elected to parliament in 1962 and served in several subsequent Congress governments.

Subramanyan, K. G. (1924–): Painter and sculptor, known for his contribu- tion to modern art in India; born in Kerala, he studied at Shantiniketan, in West Bengal with leading artists of the mid twentieth century; from 1966– 1980, he was professor of art at the University of Baroda; particularly in the 1970s he actively incorporated regional crafts into his work.

Swaminathan, Monkombu Sambasivan (1925–): A geneticist by training, Swaminathan scientific research facilitated dramatic increases in agricultural production in India, known as the Green Revolution.

Vajpayee, Atul Bihari (1924–): Prime Minister of India briefly in 1996 and again from 1998 to 2004; leader of the Bharatiya Janata Party and a long time member of Parliament for Lucknow; positioned himself as more moderate than the Pro-Hindutva wing of his party.

Glossary

Bahujan: Literally majority; term used by the Bahujan Samaj Party to underscore that lower caste interests represent a majority in Indian politics.

Bharatiya Janata Party (BJP): A Hindu-nationalist political party that also supports small business interests; it served as the ruling party briefly in 1996 and then from 1998 to 2004.

Bollywood: A genre of formulaic Hindi films characterized by song and dance sequences; as a more general term, it is used to mean India's Bombay (now Mumbai) film Industry, hence the name.

Caste: See *jati*.

Committee on the Status of Women in India: Appointed by the government and comprised of academics, politicians, and social workers, the committee's task was to examine in broad terms the status of women in India; its far-reaching report, *Towards Equality*, published in 1974, became influential in government policy-making in the 1980s.

Communalism: Sectarian violence, almost always referring to violence between Hindus and Muslims. Sometimes used more broadly to mean heightened identification with one's community.

Communist Party of India (CPI) and *Communist Party of India-Marxist (CPI (M))*: Most histories cite the founding of the CPI in 1921; a strong force in supporting left-leaning popular movements in India, the CPI strongly supported and was supported by the Communist Party of the Soviet Union. In 1964, the party split over division in tactics, strategies and political emphasis. The CPI (M) for Marxist supported peasant mobilization and severed ties with the USSR. The CPI (M) has achieved more electoral success, particularly in Kerala and West Bengal and there have been a number of alliances between the two communist parties toward the end of the twentieth century.

Cooperative movement: A government programme in the 1950s and 1960s intended to encourage farmers to poor resources, particularly in the area of rural credit. It was inspired by Mahatma Gandhi's philosophy of independent self-sufficient village communities. The programme, however, failed and by 1965, it was abandoned by the government.

Chennai: The contemporary name for the city known in British India as Madras. Borrowed from the name of a town on the south side of the original settlement that ultimately merged Madraspatnam and Chennapatnam together. Chennai became the official city name in 1996.

Dalit: Self-designation for groups of citizens, who have traditionally experienced discrimination come from underprivileged groups of castes, often called Scheduled Castes in Indian law.

Green Revolution: The period in the late 1960s and early 1970s during which there was a dramatic increase in agricultural output in India, particularly of rice and wheat, made possible by new technologies and research into special varieties of food grains.

Hindutva: Literally 'Hindu-ness'; a term used to refer to advocating Hindu nationalism; it is the politic philosophy that puts Hindu beliefs at the centre of state interests in India.

Indian National Congress (INC): A major political party in modern India; founded in 1885, it was the main organization of India's Freedom Movement; after independence it became the dominant political party; under Indira Gandhi's leadership the party split in 1969; the Congress Party lost power in 1977 in a backlash against the Emergency; in 1978 Indira Gandhi reorganized the party as the Congress (I) – I for Indira and won again in 1980; since then it has shared power and competed with other parties for majorities in parliament.

Janata Party: When Indira Gandhi called elections in 1977, bringing to an end the Emergency, the opposition – both right and left – joined together to form the Janata or People's Party; the Janata Party won in 1977, but was soon plagued by infighting due in large part to the vast ideological differences the Emergency had temporarily allied; after Janata's defeat in 1980, a number of parties took up the Janata mantle with variations on its name.

Jati: Literally, birth group; the word for endogamous marriage groups characterized by similar rituals, cultures, religious expression, and sometimes language; jatis are often what people refer to as castes; there are thousands of them and although their identification is fluid and changes from place to place there are often hierarchical notions of their relationship to one another; prevention of discrimination against certain jatis is a major issue of Indian legislation and of social reform.

Kolkata: The contemporary transliteration of the Bengali name for the city that the British called Calcutta and was originally the capital of British India; it became the capital of the state of West Bengal after independence and changed the spelling of its name in 1996.

Mandal Commission and controversy: A Commission under the leadership of Parliamentarian Bindeshwari Prasad Mandal in 1978 to examine ongoing discrimination against underprivileged groups; 'Mandal' and 'mandalization' has come to mean the advocacy of certain benefits for these groups.

Mukhti Bahini (Freedom Fighters): Bangladeshi militants, armed by India, who resisted the suppression of East Pakistan during the Pakistani Civil War that led to the establishment of Bangladesh.

Mumbai: The contemporary name for the city that was called Bombay during the period of colonial rule; Mumbai is from the local Marathi language and probably referred to some settlement in the area; the name change, which took place in 1995, was first in a series, announced by state governments, aiming to install names from local languages for their capital cities.

OBC (Other Backward Classes): Borrowed from language in the Indian Constitution to assure social equality across class, the term has come to mean a specific set of citizens (defined by caste and class), who were underprivileged and underrepresented; OBCs have gained 'reservations' in some areas to remedy economic disadvantage; OBCs were specifically addressed and identified in the Mandal Commission Report.

Panchsheel Agreement: Five-point agreement between India and China for mutual cooperation and peaceful coexistence; because its official title was 'Agreement Between the People's Republic of China and the Republic of India on Trade and Intercourse Between the Tibet Region of China and India,' it also suggested tacit approval on India's part of Chinese control over Tibet; it was signed in 1954 and has guided relations between China and India (on and off) since that time, despite the China War.

Plebiscite: A general vote on a specific question or referendum. A plebiscite in the autonomous state of Junagadh made it part of the Indian union, but despite calls for a plebiscite in Kashmir, it never materialized.

Privy purse: A term for maintenance stipends given to former rulers of regional states, upon accession to independent India.

Reservations: Indian Government policy that provides seats in government, government jobs, and positions in education institutions for categories of citizens who have experienced discrimination in the past.

Sahitya Akademi: An institution to promote literature established by the government in 1954.

Separate electorates: An election practice in 1937 and 1946, in which constituencies were designated for Muslims or women or Christians, and, candidates represented both a geographical and social community.

Standstill agreement: Initial arrangement between the Indian Government and the Princely States to smooth their succession into the Indian nation.

Total Revolution: The movement backed by Jaya Prakash Narayan and centered in Bihar in the 1970s to call for the fulfillment of promises for increased social equality that had been incorporated into the constitution.

Zamindar: A word borrowed from the Mughal land system referring to powerful intermediaries on the land who collected taxes for landlords or the empire. Under British administration, many came to be landowners, while the cultivators who worked the land were either tenants or labourers. At the time of independence land reform and the elimination of 'intermediaries' such as zamindars, was a high priority and one of the policies designated as key to economic development.

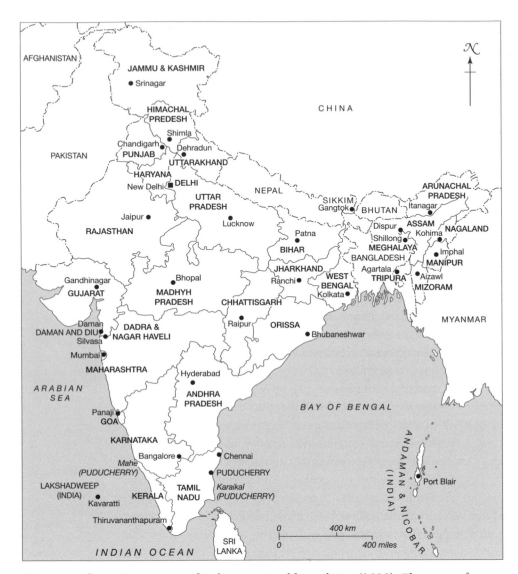

This map reflects Government of India recognized boundaries (2010). The states of Chhatisgarh, Jharkhand, and Uttarkhand were added in 2000. There has been a political movement for a new state of Telangana to reflect the region in the northern part of Andhra Pradesh.

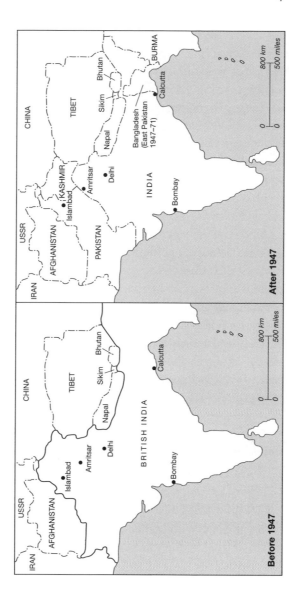

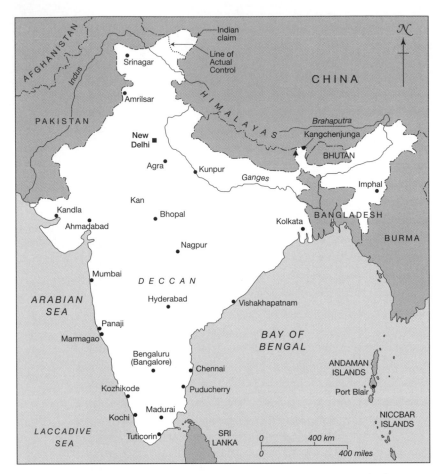

The United States CIA map of India has caused controversy in India because it shows the Kashmir border (just beyond Srinagar) at the ceasefire line with Pakistan, rather than the territory that India recognizes following the accession by the Maharaja of Kashmir in 1949. Also India's claim of the Andaman and Nicobar Islands is not identified on the CIA map. This version of the map is often used by international news services as well. https://www.cia.gov/library/publications/the-world-factbook/geos/in.html (2010).

Part 1

ANALYSIS

Introduction

When India achieved independence in 1947, who could imagine the dramatic changes that would take place in the following six decades? In a brief moment of history, India transformed from a British colonial possession to one of the fastest growing economies in the world. At the time of independence, the problems that confronted India of forming a government, dealing with a hostile neighbor, and supporting 360 million people, including refugees, seemed staggering. The literacy rate was 18 per cent in 1951 and nearly 83 per cent of the population lived in villages. In the following decades, it built democratic institutions, a stable economy, and a thriving nation-state. By 2001 the population had trebled and literacy rates increased to 65 per cent. Large numbers of people had left the countryside for cities, so that rural India, which accounted for 83 per cent of the population in 1951, comprised 72 per cent by 2001. Plus India became a global exporter not only of software, textiles, and steel, but also of **Bollywood** films and prize-winning literature, and had built connections with an influential diasporic community. The interim struggles, the detours and pitfalls, and the remarkable successes make the story of India's first sixty years a compressed narrative of astonishing development. All this comes from a culturally, linguistically, and religiously diverse nation that still contends with serious economic and social inequalities. Indians deal with these competing realities, through a vibrant political culture that thrives both inside and outside formal institutions.

Bollywood: A genre of formulaic Hindi films characterized by song and dance sequences; as a more general term, it is used to mean India's Bombay (now call Mumbai) film Industry, hence the name.

And most relevant to our understanding of the contemporary world, as the writer Sunil Khilnani has put it, the challenges we see in India mirror those being addressed every day in other societies around the world.

> The themes and conflicts that animate India's politics today have a surprisingly wide resonance – the assertion of community and group rights and the use of democracy to affirm collective identities; the difficulties of maintaining large-scale multi-cultural political unions; [and] the compulsion to make democracy work despite economic adversity.
>
> (Khilnani, 1999: 8–9)

There is an irony here too, however, because in the 1960s and 1970s India was the object of development not an example of it. Like many other so-called developing countries or Third World countries, India's progress was measured against the patterns established in the history of older democracies or Western powers. It is indeed a re-imagining of the world for India to suggest models of growth and change and development to other nations.

Any book about India must begin with a range of descriptors that demonstrate the vastness of the land and the diversity of its people. This book is no different and given its chronological task from 1947 to 2000, it is valuable to take a snapshot of this diversity as it appeared at the beginning of the twenty-first century. India in 2001 had 28 states and 7 union territories governed by a mix of national and regional political parties. Its citizens (1.028 billion, according to the 2001 Census) spoke 844 languages and dialects, 22 of which were recognized for legal use in India's Constitution. Among these were Hindi and its related language Urdu, which were spoken by more than 470 million people. English was the first or second language of about 90 million people as estimated by the English-language news media. India is religiously diverse as well and although the Census showed that about 80 per cent of the population was identified as Hindu, the category of Hindus has a wide range of meanings in different contexts. Also the Census shows 13 per cent of the population to be Muslim, giving India the second largest Muslim population in the world. In addition there are communities of Christians, Sikhs, Jains, Parsis, Buddhists, animist practitioners, and other religious groups as well.

Geographically, India is the seventh largest nation in the world, bordered on the north by the Himalayan Mountains, China, and Nepal and on the West by Pakistan. On both sides of the southern peninsula is the Indian Ocean and the nearest southeastern neighbor is Sri Lanka. On India's eastern border is Bangladesh and beyond the far eastern Indian States is Burma. The land varies from fertile agricultural land to desert and from tropical jungle to temperate mountain forests. As a result crops and foods also vary from region to region.

This begins to suggest the complexity of the nation, which sometimes easily and sometimes uneasily integrates the various regions and cultures. In fact, the story of national integration is one of the common narrative threads that characterize this period in Indian history. Historical narratives are strongly influenced by the moment in which they are produced. Writing this moment in Indian history has different inflections depending on when we end the story. For example, the year 2004 projected an optimistic narrative – the economy was growing rapidly, a national election – India's 14th – brought a secular coalition to power, and intellectual, artistic and cultural arenas celebrated new achievements. In the course of this book, however, we will see that this date as a belated ending of the twentieth century was surely not inevitable. If we sliced our history at other moments, we might see communal conflict (that is tension between Hindus and Muslims) as a dominant force in Indian history or political uncertainty that threatened democracy, for example, when Prime Minister Indira Gandhi instituted the Emergency.

So the lesson of this very compressed lightening speed of development is that within just a few decades tens of narratives can be produced, telling the dynamic history of contemporary India. Just as news travels faster today than at any time in the past, so too do the patterns and mechanisms of historical change.

I come to this project as an historian of the twentieth century. Interested in oral histories of peasant movements in the 1930s, I found myself collecting those histories against a backdrop of contemporary politics. In every case, what was going on at the time, influenced people's telling about the past. And so, through the methodology of oral history, as I heard it, post-independence history became part of the history of the colonial period, not simply the other way around. Therefore, the histories I have written of the post-independence period, for example of elections, take these issues into account. Some of the continuities – perhaps legacies of peasant movements and the Freedom Movement – become clear in this volume. For example, in India, movement politics and social activism have taken place along side parliamentary and institutional politics.

However writing the history of the sixty some years from independence to the end of the twentieth century presents special challenges. As events unfold, the meanings of this recent past change radically and quickly. In addition, while on the one hand there are nearly an overwhelming number of sources of recent history, some of the most useful ones to historians are also the least accessible. For example, government documents remain sealed for forty years and most private papers remain private. Also the actors in this history may continue to be agents of change, leaving each story, to some extent, unfinished. The sense of ongoing transformation, then, infuses each chapter.

The documents provided with this text not only elaborate on the events they describe but also suggest some of the possibilities of sources available for this period. They give a reader the opportunity to analyze different kinds of sources of modern history from court documents to personal narratives to sculpture. The format of a written text such as this, alas, does not allow me to include video and film images. But there are so many that would provide valuable evidence for analysis that they are mentioned in the text. Also the documents and references include a number of analytical sources that have been produced by significant participants in the history they describe. It is especially true of recent history that the words are available of key participants. But it is also true that their interpretations of even their own pasts change over time.

Therefore, a critical part of the task in integrating sources and selecting relevant documents has been seeing the relationships between changes in sources and changes in the phenomena they describe. Most studies of recent periods come from the disciplines of political science, anthropology, or sociology and they are organized thematically, without particular attention to chronology and dates. Therefore, the format of the Seminar Series is particularly valuable for contextualizing these contemporary themes in a broad time line.

The chapters of this book progress thematically and chronologically, focusing on both changes and continuities over time. Since at the core of history are the stories, in some ways each chapter is a collection of interrelated stories of the events and people of the time. As stories unfold, sometimes we have to move back in time or incorporate critical definitions. So the discussion of conflict over a mosque in 1992 requires the stories from ancient times and of medieval emperors.

But this too is a feature of contemporary history. The history of recent events are also for many people this history of recent memory. And when people tell the past they move not chronologically but rather from important theme to important theme. So, this is a hybrid exercise that blends the necessary chronology with the stories of movements, politics, art, and development. What has been critical at every step of the way is to provide rich and vivid examples – specific films, stories, life histories, planned cities, election contests, court cases, etc. These are meant to get beyond the larger narrative and provide texture and palpable reality to the history described.

As with any such project, each revision raises new questions about what is included and what has been excluded. But such is the ongoing process of all history-making, especially, histories of such a contemporary moment.

1

Implementing a secular state

Long years ago we made a tryst with destiny, and now the time comes when we shall redeem our pledge, not wholly or in full measure, but very substantially. At the stroke of the midnight hour, when the world sleeps, India will awake to life and freedom [**Doc. 1, pp. 134–5**].

With these now famous words, India's first Prime Minister, Jawaharlal Nehru, began his speech celebrating India's moment of independence. Delivered just before midnight on 14–15 August 1947, the speech actually served as the preamble to a motion he introduced to the Constituent Assembly, asking his fellow legislators to take a pledge of dedication to 'the service of India' (CA, 14 August 1947) [**Doc. 1, pp. 134–5**]. The Constituent Assembly was a governing council, elected just a year before in 1946 and at this time functioned both as a provisional parliament and as a deliberative body to write India's Constitution.

As Nehru intoned that 'a moment comes, which comes but rarely in history, when we step out from the old and into the new,' he stood in the Council Hall, the central chamber of a grand round building designed by Herbert Baker in 1921 to house a colonial legislature for India. This legislature was created by reforms implemented in the Government of India Act of 1919 that signalled the beginning of power sharing between Indians and the British. The building, indeed, signified the old and the new, as Indian representatives, wearing the nationalist uniform – a long white cotton shirt and pants (kurta pajama) or a formal wrapped cloth (dhoti) for men and a sari for women – carried out the business of the Assembly. The scene was formal, with the air of a normal legislative day, a few aides walking through the aisles.

The text of the speech set out three critical elements that shaped Nehru's vision of the world. First, he showed remorse for Partition, the fact that at the moment of independence British India was divided into two states – India and Pakistan. In fact, when he said that the pledge of freedom was not redeemed in 'full measure,' he referred not only to the fact of Partition, but also to the horrific violence that surrounded it. Second, he was eager to put Partition behind and move on to the task of nation building, creating a just and equitable society. As he put it, the goal of society was to end 'poverty and ignorance and disease and inequality of opportunity.' And finally, he already saw India as a major world power engaged in the events of foreign policy and part of the mission to ensure 'world peace and the welfare of mankind.'

This chapter, therefore, examines various elements of the promises of independence that embodied that moment. A political optimism was reflected in the dynamic velocity with which democratic institutions were created and developed, e.g., the Constitution, elections, and land reform. And it was also reflected in how India faced challenges to the new nation, such as resettlement of refugees and war with Pakistan.

There was a powerful duality that characterized the first few years of independence – freedom and also violence, deliberations about fundamental rights and also mobilization for war, celebration and mourning. Two contrasting images of 1947 signify the complexity of that moment. On the one hand, the Constituent Assembly engaged in intensive and exhilarating debates about good government that led to India's democratic Constitution. On the other hand, the Partition of India and birth of Pakistan yielded tragic and convulsive violence, which accompanied the transfer of populations to and from Pakistan and determined the indeterminable status of Kashmir.

While it took a long time for historians to be able to discuss Partition, i.e., to be able to step back and analyze it, there is now a growing rich body of scholarship about it. For the Constituent Assembly, however, Partition was implicit and explicit in much of its discussion. And historians have treated the Constituent Assembly differently – it has received little attention, assumed to be part of the continuity with the late colonial period. Therefore, although this chapter focuses on both Partition and the Constituent Assembly, it deals with them differently.

The story of Partition presented here has to acknowledge the nuances in the evolving scholarly debates on the subject, as an equal partner to the events of Partition itself. This is certainly one of the few subjects of post-independence history that provides such an opportunity to see the disagreements and variations among so many historians.

CONCURRENCES – PARTITION AND THE CONSTITUENT ASSEMBLY

There are many dates we could use as a starting point to talk about the decision for India's independence on 15 August 1947. It was the culmination of India's grassroots-organized freedom movement and the goal of nationalist leaders, most famously Mohandas K. Gandhi. And surely it was inevitable, long before 1947. While that story is not part of this text, it is critical to bear in mind that India's independence was hard-fought. While Nehru gave his statesman's speech to the Constituent Assembly, all over India there were celebrations and mass-gatherings to acknowledge this long awaited moment, and many of the ceremonies on Independence Day commemorated the martyrs of that struggle as well. For example, on this occasion in Patna, the capital of the state of Bihar and a central site of politics of the Freedom Movement, the Governor laid the foundation stone for a monument to seven student protestors killed by police during the Quit India uprising of 1942.

In this way Independence Day was a commemoration, a celebration, and an acknowledgement of a grave and consequential political compromise in the form of the creation of two states – India and Pakistan. It is impossible to separate the history of independence from the history of Partition, which resonates in both India and Pakistan as the manifestation of communal conflict, i.e., a permanent marker of the potential animosity between Hindus and Muslims. Partition symbolizes the momentary triumph of the argument put forth by Mohammad Ali Jinnah that a government in a Hindu-majority nation could not protect the rights of a Muslim minority.

Like so many other stories, the history of Partition has many precursors in the politics of Hindu and Muslim and secular nationalism in India. The Muslim League as an organization that articulated the rights of Muslims was founded in 1906. But the demand for a separate Muslim state did not gain substantial traction until after 1942 and the full contours of the two separate nations were not clear until just before independence itself. To untangle some of this story, let us begin with most narrow construction of the events that immediately led up to independence and the form it would take.

Why 14/15 August 1947?

The date of Indian independence – or the transfer of power, as British histories record it – was selected by the British. Many dates had more resonance to Indian nationalism. In fact, in 1930, the **Indian National Congress** declared 26 January Independence Day, and continued to hold rallies and meetings to honour that day for years afterward. In 1950 the government officially declared 26 January Republic Day, a commemorative national holiday. Other days 2 August, the beginning of the 'Quit India' movement or 13 April, which marked a massacre of peaceful Indian protestors by British led troops, would have signified important moments in Indian nationalism.

Rather, the British set the date and timetable by government decree. On 3 June 1947, the prime minister of Great Britain, Clement Attlee, announced

Indian National Congress (INC): A major political party in modern India; founded in 1885, it was the main organization of India's freedom movement; after independence it became the dominant political party; under Indira Gandhi's leadership the party split in 1969; the Congress Party lost power in 1977 in a backlash against the Emergency; in 1978 Indira Gandhi reorganized the party as the Congress (I) – I for Indira and won again in 1980; since then it has shared power and competed with other parties for majorities in parliament.

in the British Parliament that Britain had agreed with nationalists in India to independence. The plan for the 'transfer of power', stated that areas with a majority Muslim population would comprise a new nation of Pakistan and the remaining portion would become the independent state of India. The details were to be thrashed out by committees.

British commitment to the idea of Pakistan as a Muslim homeland represented a victory by Mohammad Ali Jinnah, head of the Muslim League, who argued that Muslim majority areas deserved a separate state in order to guarantee minority rights. His conviction was confirmed by the elections of 1946, in which Indians voted for representatives to government and the Muslim League won major victories in Muslim majority areas. Meanwhile the Indian National Congress won decisive victories nearly everywhere else.

At the same time the British sent a Cabinet level mission to India under Sir Stafford Cripps to discuss the transfer of power. On the table were several configurations of the new independent state; Jinnah supported a two-nation theory for a Muslim and Hindu homeland. However the proposals suggested different versions of power sharing including a federal system with a co-ordinating Central Government but much stronger separate states, which would negotiate policy. These issues remained unresolved when Mohammad Ali Jinnah declared a day of Direct Action for 16 August 1946 to push for a separate state for Muslims.

Direct Action Day unfolded amidst great tension between the Muslim League supporters and those of the Indian National Congress and riots ensued in Calcutta, killing thousands of people. The violence continued in Bihar and west to what was then called the United Provinces (today Uttar Pradesh). This background of violence coloured all the continuing negotiations and plans for independence. 'Partition violence', a concept prominently associated with the story of India's (and Pakistan's) independence, therefore, began before the actual Partition took place and influenced the nature of the Constitution building.

On 9 December 1946, the Constituent Assembly began the process of debating and drafting an Indian Constitution – the structure of government, the rights of citizens, the substance of a new democracy. Most of the delegates, however, were members of the Indian National Congress, including some Muslims. The Muslim League boycotted the Assembly on procedural grounds, calling for all Muslim delegates to be members of the League, which it saw as representing Indian Muslim interests.

Therefore, by stark contrast to the deliberate meetings of the Constituent Assembly, political conflict continued all around it – at high levels of government about the size and shape of the state and among people on both sides of a soon-to-be border. The last Viceroy of India, Lord Mountbatten, arrived in March 1947 to hammer out a final agreement. Then on 3 June 1947 Viceroy

Mountbatten announced the independence of India in the form of two established states, India in the Centre and a bifurcated Pakistan to the east and west, where large Muslim populations lived. The two provinces of British India most immediately affected were Punjab in the west and Bengal in the east, each of which were Partitioned into Indian and Pakistani portions [see map, p. xxv].

Just as the wisdom or necessity of creating two nations remains an issue of historical debate, so too is the inevitability of dividing the provinces. Who established the contours of independence? How did it happen so suddenly and starkly? Scholars continue to contest the issue of who is most responsible for Partition. For example, Mushirul Hasan vividly describes a few leaders in seclusion negotiating territory that tragically affects the lives of millions of people (Hasan, 1994). Ravikant and Tarun K. Saint describe Partition coming 'perhaps on account of sheer exhaustion, after prolonged negotiations towards the transfer of power (Saint and Saint, 2001: xii). Even in Pakistan historiography, while the creation of the state is a celebrated achievement, the 'actual Partition of the subcontinent often has about it an air of betrayal' (Gilmartin, 1998: 1079). The fact that Pakistan was a bifurcated state, with each wing on the 'other side' of a hostile neighbour was one sign of this betrayal.

Clearly the British were eager to divest themselves of empire, perhaps at any cost. Most historians of South Asia see the rapid series of events instigated by Britain's precipitous decision to move ahead with independence on an accelerated schedule as a key factor contributing to Partition violence (Metcalf and Metcalf, 2002: 217–219). As Ayesha Jalal points out, the accelerating violence on the ground often took the form of battles over property, rather than clear ideological or religious conflict (Jalal, 1998).

Most recent historical studies focus on the failure to reach a compromise due to haste in the final months of empire. For example, as Ayesha Jalal and Sugata Bose point out in *Modern South Asia*, conversations about an independent and united Bengal (still viable in May of 1947) came to an abrupt end with the 3 June agreement (Bose and Jalal, 1997). Mohammad Ali Jinnah wanted to assure the rights of Muslim minorities, but feared the clearly increasing power of the Indian National Congress, which projected itself as the inheritor of Indian independence.

As for many of the painful events of the time, the haste of independence has been powerfully evoked in fiction. In his novel, *Looking Through Glass*, Mukul Kesavan, an historian by training, described the meetings between Jinnah, Congress leaders, and Mountbatten in the hill station of Shimla. The narrator of the book has magically fallen back in time from our moment to the moment of independence. He is working as a waiter in Shimla to escape the summer heat and the relentless politics of Delhi. One day, however, he recognizes with some excitement the leaders of the Muslim League at one of his tables. He listens to them evaluate the prospects for negotiating a power-sharing agreement with the British. The fictional Jinnah says, 'Nehru believes he has History on his side . . . [that] the Congress will inherit an undivided country. You remember . . . how he rode to the Lahore Congress on a white charger? That horse was History' (Kesavan, 1995). The truth to this fiction, however, was that events – history – were indeed speeding out of the control of the Indian politicians.

Ultimately, even Nehru could not rein in the horse. Mountbatten pushed up the date of independence, forcing Jinnah to agree to a Pakistan that included two culturally defined provinces that themselves were divided; i.e., the Muslim majority districts of the Punjab went to Pakistan while the eastern section went to India and the Muslim majority districts of Bengal went to Pakistan while the western section went to India. However, Nehru failed to get the India 'in full measure' he hoped to achieve.

In addition, there was no clear, plausible voice to mount an Indian objection. As the historian Peter Robb points out, the Constituent Assembly, comprised as it was of members from British provinces, did not adequately represent all of India and therefore could not, in any authoritative way, challenge British proposals about regions outside its representation or about national boundaries. The fact that princely states, such as, Kashmir – separate kingdoms never fully incorporated into British Indian governance – did not participate in the Constituent Assembly also kept open the Constitutional question of how many countries would inherit the physical area of colonial India (Robb, 2002: 203). By the time the Constituent Assembly next convened – on 14 July – committees in the Provinces of Bengal and Punjab had already determined to divide these regions, as part of the overall decision to divide the nation. As a result, the 3 June agreement was a reminder to the members of the Constituent Assembly, which had begun to think of themselves as a sovereign body, that momentous political decisions still happened outside their deliberating process, and members expressed their outrage that the Constituent Assembly as a body was not consulted [**Doc. 2, pp. 135–6**].

Excluded from the negotiations over the timing, manner, and shape of independence, the Constituent Assembly focused on the immediate task of creating a Constitution for India and in the process, it established procedures and rules, and a specific political culture based on them. Of course, Partition played a central role in the language and principles reflected in the final document. For example, a committee formed by the Constituent Assembly was assigned to examine minority issues beginning in January of 1947. That committee's report, submitted in September, following independence and much catastrophic violence, proposed policies and legal principles to assure minority rights, but also stem future violence [**Doc. 3, pp. 136–7**].

In practical terms, the culmination of the work of the Constituent Assembly was the Constitution, which had been completed by November of 1949. It was signed by all the states and came into force on 26 January 1950, a day already remembered as a symbol of India's independence movement. (On this day in 1930, the Indian National Congress had initially declared India's independence from Britain.) Then the Constituent Assembly dissolved, its task complete, and the members of the Assembly reconstituted themselves as a Provisional Parliament, serving as government until elections took place. While the history of the Constituent Assembly had a logical ending of sorts (though its legacy in Parliament and the Constitution continued), the story of Partition had a much more difficult and tragic trajectory.

THE PARTITION: THE PROBLEM OF HISTORIOGRAPHY

While the Partition of India, even as articulated in the Constituent Assembly, referred to the division of land that established the nation of Pakistan, the concept of 'Partition' written with a capital 'P' has come to mean the violent upheaval that preceded and accompanied that political process. Estimates suggest that 15 million people moved across borders and as many as 1.3 million were killed in concomitant violence.

The actual boundary lines of Partition were not revealed until near the moment of independence. In Punjab, where there were districts with Hindu majorities and districts with Muslim majorities, the exact location of the border provoked tension, especially because there was a third religious community, the Sikhs, who saw themselves caught between Muslim-dominated and Hindu-dominated politics. India vowed to be a secular state proclaiming its support for a Muslim minority, but the prospect of a Muslim homeland – the perceived need for a Muslim homeland – undercut that claim [**Doc. 3, pp. 136–7**]. Furthermore, in the agitation for Pakistan, violence had already become a fact of communal – Hindu and Muslim – lives. For example, riots took place in 1946 in the eastern province of Bengal, in response to Jinnah's call for 'direct action' for Pakistan. As a result, thousands of people died even before the Partition of the subcontinent was announced.

The details of Partition violence were so brutal and powerfully felt that historians were unable to write about it for many years. Rather the personal narratives of Partition most vividly emerged in fiction. Sadaat Hasan Manto's story, 'Toba Tek Singh', characterized the senselessness of dividing lands and villages. When told that his village was now in Pakistan, the title character, an inmate in a mental institution, asked, 'How could the village move?' In the end Toba Tek Singh, while being moved from an institution in Pakistan to one in India, died literally on the border. Kushwant Singh's *Train to Pakistan* untangled the process through which former neighbors – Hindus, Sikhs,

Muslims – came to distrust one another. An enduring image in the book that set in motion further violence was the sight of 'ghost trains' filled with corpses being sent back across the border.

Not until 50 years after the events did historical accounts of violence become possible. An early example, in this case of oral histories, appeared in Urvashi Butalia's, *The Other Side of Silence*, first published in 1998. Butalia described the process of telling the histories of Partition as almost cathartic for many of the people she met, who needed, wanted someone to hear and retell their narratives. Butalia and some other people, including Swarna Aiyar, had published essays earlier about Partition, but these were rare exceptions (Butalia, 1993 and 1998 and Aiyar, 1995).

The inability of historians, and also sociologists and anthropologists, to articulate the human horror of Partition rests in the limitations of the tools of social science. The literary critic, M. Asaduddin understands that predicament.

> History cannot tell us the whole truth. It conceals more than it reveals. Every generation negotiates this tension between closure and disclosure in its own way. As regards India, the spate of books that have appeared on the theme of Partition in recent years demonstrate that the culture of remembrance is at its peak, and that story-telling has come to be validated as one of the ways in which individuals try to grapple with the past in an age when the canons of historiography and political thought fail to put the past in order.
>
> (Asaduddin, 2001: 21)

It is impossible given the limited statistical sources to provide a very complete analysis of the extent of violence of the period. However, David Gilmartin, in an essay about the problems of historiography on Partition, suggests some patterns that emerged and one of the most powerful of them demonstrates how the violence, especially in Punjab, represented a convulsive purification of territory. Forcing out the other community, the violence enforced a segregation of populations. In his words, 'purificatory violence in a sense symbolically sealed the relationship between territory and a new vision of moral community that was promised by the Partition decision' (Gilmartin, 1998: 1086).

Most historians, however, have focused on the politics of Partition rather than the experience of violence. This contextualized the violence: it was significant that 'the new governments on both sides of the border were able with surprising speed to contain the violence,' despite the fact that they had barely 'established themselves in office' (Metcalf and Metcalf, 2002: 93). Still historians disagree on how this happened. Bipan Chandra *et al.* attribute it to 'decisive political and administrative measures' on the part of the new government' (Chandra *et al.*, 1999). For example, in Delhi, the army was deployed immediately to stop looting. This had both the effect of calming tension, but also of showing that the government was in control and would not tolerate violence. Furthermore, Nehru refused to be drawn into communal language and ideologically supported minority rights.

This is especially important because of the real fear, prevalent at the time, that the communal polarization characterized by Partition and its concomitant rioting would engender continuing communal rifts in Indian politics. In fact, historians have argued or simply assumed that subsequent communal violence in India, particularly in the 1990s, was set in motion or substantially exacerbated by Partition (Van der Veer, 1996). Since approximately 40 million Muslims remained in India, their security and safety was an immediate and present concern. Other historians point out that Congress successfully channelled Hindu **communalism** into the activities of nation building and in the process took some of the momentum away from what might have been retribution for the tragic experiences described by Hindus, who fled Pakistan (Banerjee, 1990: 39).

Communalism: Sectarian violence, almost always referring to violence between Hindus and Muslims. Sometimes used more broadly to mean heightened identification with one's community.

Then, Gandhi – the unqualified advocate of non-violence – was assassinated in January 1948 by a Hindu extremist, lending a symbolic interruption to the cycle of violence and retribution between communities. Because of the complex nature of Gandhi's politics, his assassination perhaps advanced, at least for a time, the communal peace he had articulated, although not always accomplished, throughout his life. Because Gandhi's politics had often invoked Hindu symbols and seemed to represent a 'Hinduized' ideal society, it drew criticism from some secular and Muslim politicians. Yet, he always vocally advocated Hindu–Muslim unity. He had fasted to stop rioting in Bengal in 1946 and vowed to make a trip to Pakistan to ease tensions in 1948. His death crystallized the moral indefensibility of communal violence, especially since his assassin – Nathuram Godse – had been a member of radical Hindu organizations, the Rashtriya Swayamsevak Sangh (RSS) and the Hindu Mahasabha. Nehru is reported to have said, once the assassin was revealed, 'Thank God it was not a Muslim,' because of the prospect such a turn of events might have had.

PARTITION AND THE CONSTITUTION

Within the Constituent Assembly, issues raised by Partition and Partition violence, certainly influenced the Constitution in terms of Fundamental Rights and the process of holding elections. To underscore the new nation's commitment to minority rights, both Article 15 and Article 29 under Fundamental Rights protect minorities. Article 15, in fact prohibits 'discrimination on the grounds of religion, race, caste, sex or place of birth' and Article 29 applies specifically to educational institutions. In fact, the Constituent Assembly wrote some of this language in August of 1947, just following Partition [**Doc. 4, p. 137**].

Second, the Constituent Assembly eliminated the system of separate electorates, which had determined elections based on community in 1937 and 1946. Rather the Constituent Assembly established universal suffrage, in which voters directly elected their representatives to the lower house of Parliament, called the Lok Sabha. The Constitution defined India as a parliamentary democracy with an upper house – the Rajya Sabha – elected from the states along with the more powerful lower house – the Lok Sabha. Article 326 (Elections) of the Constitution guaranteed equal voting rights for all citizens.

This contrasted with the system introduced by the British for the 1937 and 1946 elections in which electors selected candidates based on communities. In those elections there were separate constituencies for Muslims as well as for other groups – women, landlords, Sikhs, etc. These separate constituencies were eliminated in the Constitution in July of 1947. One member in fact, suggested that separate electorates had precipitated a 'separate sthan' – that is Pakistan (CA, 17 July 1947). Blamed for Partition, the practice of separate electorates could not be maintained either for Muslims or for other groups they had served. Politically, therefore, the Partition echoed in the deliberations over India's Government and continued to influence government policy in the next decades.

While the political influence of Partition was addressed at the time (and continues to be re-evaluated today), the social toll was suppressed for several decades. In the early years of independence the language for addressing this social upheaval produced by Partition was 'rehabilitation and repatriation.' In fact, the Indian Government had a Ministry devoted to rehabilitation of refugees. The famous Urdu short story, 'Lajwanti' written by Rajinder Singh Bedi in the mid-1960s describes some of the painful issues of 'rehabilitation,' especially for women. Lajwanti is a woman caught on the wrong side of the border at Partition. After great difficulty she is reunited with her family, but remains always an outsider; she is viewed with suspicion over the possibility of rape or whatever might have happened to her in the violence and confusion (Ramakrishnan, 2000: 515–29).

To resettle refugees arriving from Pakistan, the Indian Minister of Rehabilitation, K. C. Neogy, established camps and organized programs toward the goal of employment and education. Similarly, there were transit camps for Muslim families waiting to travel to Pakistan. As an extension of the social service they had performed during the Freedom Movement, women members of the Indian National Congress, now a political party, were appointed to the ministry to aid in the settlement of women refugees.

One of them, Manmohini Zutshi, described the programmes that the ministry established. In Delhi 'the Women's Section ran a home for displaced widows and their children . . . [where they] were taught how to tailor and how to make dhurries [carpets]. The small children lived with their mothers, but older children were sent to school' (Forbes, 1994: 127). The ministry paid for their schooling at existing residential schools and established additional schools when necessary. In addition, the Loan Section provided shopkeepers and students with funds to re-establish themselves.

Another Freedom Fighter turned rehabilitation worker, Sucheta Kripalani, commented on the difficulties of the task of providing services for refugees. While she explained that 3.5 million rupees was spent to create a settlement at Faridabad, there was no employment nearby for the residents.

In stone quarrying about 300 to 400 people are working. This venture is heavily subsidized by the government. It is not economic and self-supporting. I am told 800 to 1000 people everyday come from Faridabad to Delhi to do what? – a wonderful kind of work. They come to work as unskilled labourers, as coolies and the expenditure is borne by the government to give them even this employment is disproportionate.

Furthermore, she pointed out that government programmes to allot land (reclaimed from Muslim families that left for Pakistan) functioned slowly and inadequately (Kripalani, 1995). In other words, even with great attention given to the problems of refugees, it was not enough.

ONE HUNDRED MILLION VOTES

The election of 1952 took place amidst continued efforts at rehabilitation. Nevertheless 105,944,495 people voted, which comprised 45 per cent of the electorate (Singh and Bose, 1986). As the first election based on universal suffrage, it was technically and administratively monumental. The *Report on the First General Elections in India*, published by the Election Commission in 1955 acknowledges the controversies surrounding universal suffrage – the magnitude of the potential Indian electorate and the question of political sophistication of illiterate voters. It then argues that the success of the election proved the inaccuracy of these criticisms (Sen, 1955).

One major challenge was enrolling adults eligible to vote. The process took several years; in fact a forward-thinking Election Commission began creating election rolls based on the 1941 Census as early as 1947. The Commission demarcated constituencies and canvassed in districts throughout the country in order to create, revise, and publish electoral rolls by 1951.

Ultimately, over 170 million voters were enrolled, 45 per cent of whom were women. A shortcoming in the process proved to be notifying and recording women voters. Due to inadequate counting and difficulty establishing the names of women voters who had identified themselves only through their husbands' or sons' names, 2.8 million women were struck from voting roles just before the election (Sen, 1955). This became a main issue for attention in preparation for the second general election of 1957 and as a result, the number of women voters enrolled increased dramatically.

Furthermore, the 1952 and 1957 elections were unique in the way they provided representation for disadvantaged groups. From the time of limited franchise elections under British auspices, special seats had been reserved for 'scheduled castes and tribes'. The term 'Schedule' refers to a list created by the British administration to record the names of **castes** and communities that had been subjected to discrimination in Indian society.

Caste: See *jati*.

CASTE

The subject of caste is an important category in understanding Indian history and especially Indian historiography. Castes are social communities, not unlike what sociologists mean when they talk about ethnic groups, with internal social identification, specific customs and religious practices, and usually endogamous marriage traditions. In addition, however, many specialists perceive caste collectively as 'a system of elaborately stratified social hierarchy' (Bayly, 1999: 1). This accounts for the complex relationships between castes and discrimination that takes place on the basis of caste. In everyday life caste is a social marker of connection to people – within one's own caste – and distinctions – sometimes hierarchical – with others outside one's own caste. Of course, there are other markers of social relations, including class, regional identity, language, etc., and these coexist with caste identity. In post-1947 India, the government, on the one hand, advocated a casteless society. On the other hand, it instituted legislation designed to rectify past discrimination, which has had the effect of reinforcing caste categories.

The ways in which scholars of India approach caste influences many other historiographical questions, therefore it is worth an overview of some of the major arguments about caste and Indian society. While some scholars had once considered caste an ancient and immutable Indian principle, recent scholarship demonstrates the dynamic and changing nature of castes. In fact, the changes became so pronounced during the colonial period, some scholars considered it nearly a British invention. It is the resilience of caste identity in India that seems most exceptional. In fact, some scholars even suggest that caste is something fairly unique, a key characteristic that defines Indian society.

For example, while it is predominantly a Hindu custom, many Muslims and Christians whose ancestors converted generations ago still identify themselves with caste groups. Furthermore, the meaning of 'caste' in the contemporary Indian state combines several different categories of groups. The English word 'caste,' really of Portuguese origin, can be used to mean either *varna*, i.e., four categories of society described in Hindu texts or **jati**, i.e., numerous social groups that signify different communities in local villages. While ancient Hindu texts describe the four *varnas* as Brahmans (traditionally priests), Kshatriyas (traditionally warriors), Vaishyas (agriculturalists or traders) and Shudras (labourers), the concept of *jati* has more resonance in every day life. *Jati* means birth and is variously described as one of perhaps a thousand different groups, each identifying a common history, sense of origin, marriage practices, and social customs. While *jatis* often seem to fit into categories of *varna*, where they fit may be contested, and some *jatis* remain outside the *varna* system completely.

As Burton Stein argues, the spread of agrarian society in the early medieval period (from about 500 to 1200), created a more intricately hierarchical sense to caste. Particularly, many forest-dwelling communities became incorporated into peasant villages as additional *jatis*, some of whom – particularly those who resisted the spread of settled agriculture 'were forced into dependency upon landed households.' Many of these new settlers came to be considered 'outcastes' or outside of caste culture. They were 'untouchable,' in that they were excluded – or initially may have excluded themselves – from communal life (Stein, 1998: 114).

Susan Bayly, in the most comprehensive study of modern caste society, argues 'that Caste has been for many centuries a real and active part of Indian life, and not just a self-serving Orientalist fiction.' Nevertheless, she shows that until well into the colonial period 'much of the subcontinent was still populated by people for whom the formal distinctions of caste were of only limited importance' (Bayly, 1999: 3). The colonial period, especially toward the end of the nineteenth century, imposed new changes on caste. The colonial Census concretized categories that had once been vaguer. Orientalist scholarship, and nationalist reformers who resisted caste distinctions or embraced them, gave greater credibility to rigid notions of caste categories. In practice, British officers and civil servants reinforced them. An example from Susan Bayly illustrates the point. While Indian ideas about purity and cleanliness relegated jobs as sweepers and latrine cleaners to castes such as Mahar, Chamar or Bhangis, considered 'Untouchables' and labelled that way in British Censuses, the British reproduced those patterns in their own homes and institutions. While

paying lip-service to ideals of pragmatic 'modernity,' [they] too hired people from the same communities to serve as sweepers in their homes,

Jati: Literally, birth group; the word for endogamous marriage groups characterized by similar rituals, cultures, religious expression, and sometimes language; *jatis* are often what people refer to as castes; there are thousands of them and although their identification is fluid and changes from place to place there are often hierarchical notions of their relationship to one another; prevention of discrimination against certain jatis is a major issue of Indian legislation and of social reform.

and in railway stations, 'the cleaning of bathrooms was . . . the province of the smartly uniformed 'sweeper', still generally a man of . . . 'untouchable' origin in khaki shorts.

(Bayly, 1999: 228)

Therefore, while caste changed over time and the concept of untouchability also changed and evolved, by the time of Indian independence, there were established and widely held ideas about caste and caste-hierarchy. And although there remained ambiguity among some people about what untouchability meant, in the independent Indian state there was a large population who experienced discrimination based on caste status.

THE CONSTITUTION AND UNTOUCHABILITY

In fact, through social mobilization in the twentieth century, people from communities that were called 'Untouchables,' gained a number of political rights. The 'Untouchable' leader B. R. Ambedkar – a jurist and author of India's Constitution – had been advancing the case for special representation for 'Untouchables' two decades before the 1952 elections took place. Despite disputes with Gandhi over how such representation should be defined, Ambedkar succeeded in retaining special constituencies for 'Untouchable' communities in the Indian Constitution. Using the schedules, i.e., lists, created by the British for provincial elections in 1937 and 1946, the Constitution established **reservations** in government for 'Scheduled Castes' and for 'Scheduled Tribes,' the latter were communities with separate religious and social affiliations, who lived in forest areas.

Reservations: Indian government policy that provides seats in government, government jobs, and positions in education institutions for categories of citizens who have experienced discrimination in the past.

Labels are significant. Gandhi labelled 'Untouchables' 'Harijans,' meaning children of God. He meant this as a sympathetic appellation, though some of his critics found it condescending. Many of Ambedkar's followers joined him in converting to Buddhism in the 1950s and they came to be called New Buddhists. In fact, there continue to be Buddhist influences in contemporary political movements associated with Ambedkar. Once the Schedule was introduced for implementing legal reform, 'Untouchables' came to be called Scheduled Castes. None of these terms are adequate, though each illustrates a particular history and politics. More recently, organized groups from among Scheduled Castes call themselves **Dalits** meaning 'oppressed or broken.' Dalit is, therefore, a self-designation used politically by members of a variety of *jatis* to find common ground and in order to rally together for greater rights.

Dalit: Self-designation for groups of citizens, who have traditionally experienced discrimination and come from underprivileged groups of castes, often called Scheduled Castes in Indian law.

In 1952 and 1957, the delimitation of constituencies in India established dual member constituencies (one winner from the Scheduled community and one from the general population) for 83 parliamentary seats out of the total 493. An additional 11 seats were reserved exclusively for Scheduled Castes or Tribes. As a result, in the first and second parliaments about 19 per cent of the Members of Parliament were members of Scheduled Castes and Tribes. In fact in 1957 one Scheduled Tribe candidate defeated a sitting MP in a General seat as well. Two member constituencies were double the size, often including twice as many voters and a much greater geographic area. Therefore, they were 'unpopular with the candidates and the adminis-tration alike' (Sen, 1958: 60). Finally, by 1961, the Parliament eliminated dual member constituencies, establishing instead separate reserved seats for Scheduled Castes or Scheduled Tribes in areas based on their population density. Although the mechanism had changed, members of Scheduled Castes and Tribes still maintained control over 19 per cent of seats in Parliament.

Still, the concept of reserved seats remained controversial. R. P. Bhalla, an administrative officer in the Election Commission, wrote in 1972 that 'the system of reservation should be ended as soon as possible.' He cited the difficulty of delimitation of reserved constituencies and the potential disen-franchising of Scheduled Caste voters in General constituencies as some of the reasons. Bhalla supported a proposal in the 1960s to rotate Scheduled Caste and Tribe Constituencies, but that never came to pass (Bhalla, 1973: 72–74).

Later experience has reinforced the value of reservations and extended them in local government to other disenfranchised groups. However, espe-cially with the passage of time and success achieved through reservations, the degree of disability experienced by individual members of Scheduled Castes has become quite uneven. Continued efforts toward social and economic equality for Dalits demonstrate limitations of the reservations policy. This, however, is part of the continuing story of reservations that will follow in later chapters of this book.

ZAMINDARI ABOLITION AND LAND REFORM

Even before national elections were complete, land reform was immediately on the agenda of several of the states in newly independent India. Peasant movements had played a major role in rural politics in the 1930s. Most were organized by tenant cultivators who demanded direct control over their land and the abolition of *begari*, a kind of forced labor imposed by landlords. The Kisan Sabha, a major peasant organization that articulated these interests, lent support to the Indian National Congress at crucial moments before indepen-dence. Therefore, the Congress Party in independent India recognized the

Zamindar: A word borrowed from the Mughal land system referring to powerful intermediaries on the land who collected taxes for landlords or the empire. Under British administration, many came to be land owners, while the cultivators who worked the land were either tenants or labourers. At the time of independence land reform and the elimination of 'intermediaries' such as zamindars, was a high priority and one of the policies designated as key to economic development.

political necessity to address peasants' demands. In north India, a main issue was 'Abolition of **Zamindari**,' i.e., the elimination of intermediaries, such as landlords, between peasant cultivators and the state. A logical way to accomplish this was to give peasants, who were tenants on the land, ownership of the land they cultivated. However, the power and financial influence of landlords in politics made the implementation of land reform an ongoing challenge.

Bihar took the initiative, passing the Zamindari Abolition Act in 1949, which sought to guarantee the right of land ownership to cultivators (Act XVIII of 1949). On the one hand that Act was written in vague terms, which minimized its effect; it gave land rights to *raiyats* (peasants) over landlords and compensation to landlords in exchange. But the Act did not define *raiyats*, so that some very large tenant cultivators found their position enhanced, which was not in the spirit of the legislation. Also, landlords found ways to place holdings in the names of relatives and close associates.

On the other hand, because the Act did articulate the rights of peasants to own their own land, landlords immediately resisted it in the courts. Therefore the Act presented the first challenge to the new Constitution. In fact, the first amendment to the Constitution reinforced the legitimacy of land reform legislation by exempting land reform from challenges based on Constitutional protections of 'Fundamental Rights.' Similarly the fourth amendment buttressed the right of states to impose land ceilings and assured the legitimacy of such laws, but also regulated the process

The Indian President, Rajendra Prasad, who was himself a Bihari land owner, encouraged the Bihar legislature to include more comprehensive land reform in the legislation, rather than solely direct it as zamindari abolition. As a result the Act was repealed and replaced by the Bihar Land Reform Act of 1950.

Like Bihar, West Bengal, Tamil Nadu, and other states began implementing land ceilings, with various degrees of enthusiasm and resistance, and redistributing land in excess of the ceilings. Each state followed a plan that took into consideration the prevailing tenancy patterns – zamindari in the north, raiyatwari (peasant proprietors) in the west, and janmam rights (land grants) in the south. While the initial series of land reform legislation proved only minimally successful in redistributing land, the immediate attention to land reform showed the importance of this issue to the new state. This was a legacy of the Freedom Movement, which had indeed relied on peasants as a demonstration of its mass nature.

Subsequent movements for land reform, perhaps most notably Operation Barga in West Bengal beginning in 1978, showed both the continued need and commitment to the process and the limitations revealed in the first efforts expended in the 1950s.

CONCLUSION

As India 'awoke to life and freedom' on 15 August 1947 some processes were already in motion. The conflict over Partition and the violence it evoked perhaps paused for a night, but remained palpable for citizens waking up that day. The Constitution was also in progress in the meetings of the Constituent Assembly that had been taking place for more than 8 months. But other changes were new and abrupt. The specific boundaries established that day created a firm geographic reality, beyond what had been imagined and with territory there were institutions to divide and laws to make. This first chapter introduces some of the issues that arose in the immediate wake of India's independence. Documents associated with this chapter on independence, Partition, rehabilitation, elections, reservations, and land reform reinforce these early moments of the Indian state.

However, many of these themes continue throughout the twentieth century and therefore, throughout this book. We will return to land reform, reservations, and the legacies of Partition in other chapters. Some of the key actors in creating both Pakistan and India did not survive much beyond this moment. By the end of 1948, both Jinnah and Gandhi were dead – one of illness and the other of an assassin's bullet. But neither had the chance to see or continue to shape the states they had fostered.

Most significantly, this chapter focuses on the ways in which the moment of India's independence was a real break in history. Historians dwell these days on the ambiguities of the past. How much can we know, anyway? And with what we do know, are there any certainties? On the subject of India's independence, and even of the suitability of a book that begins with 1947, this chapter demonstrates real changes and political and social agendas that begin with Indian independence.

Of course there were real continuities as well that span the British colonial and Indian independent period. India's Constitution incorporated what was useful from earlier British Indian law. In fact, in 1952 most states simply reused the election manuals that had been used in the 1946 elections. And of course, land reform in independent India evolved specifically from the peasant movements of the 1930s, a social movement come to fruition under a new regime.

This chapter acknowledges those histories, but also shows that these continuities emerged in a different light once India made its 'tryst with destiny.' The tensions that precipitated the Pakistan Movement, the question of assuring minority rights within a pluralist state, were surely left over business from the pre-independence period, but they were set in a new context after Partition. And the Constituent Assembly's deliberation in producing the Constitution reflected the realities of this change. The new Constitution emphasized Indian's rights as free citizens and as indebted as the Constitution might have been to existing law, it forged new paths borrowing from other useful texts, including the American Constitution.

This is illustrated in the words of the preamble:

> WE THE PEOPLE OF INDIA, having solemnly resolved to constitute India into a Sovereign Democratic Republic and to secure to all its citizens:
> JUSTICE, social, economic and political;
> LIBERTY of thought, expression, belief, faith and worship;
> EQUALITY of status and of opportunity;
> and to promote among them all
> FRATERNITY assuring the dignity of the individual.

Implementing these goals set in motion a flurry of activity to build the institutions and structures of a new state that we will see in future chapters. The obligation of the state to its citizens was to guarantee these human rights. Here too the realities of Partition violence manifested in the language of the Constitution as a fierce adherence to human rights in a multi-religious, diverse society.

But the first concern of the state was defining its territory. While Partition created boundaries in Punjab and Bengal, much was still left to define. Also, the fact of Partition showed the arbitrariness of borders and lines of sovereignty. If the natural contours of India had ever been assumed, this was no longer the case. Immediate challenges, such as war with Pakistan, negotiation with regional rulers, legal wrangling over territory, and the consolidation of states, shaped the actual geographic boundaries of both India and Pakistan. The next chapter takes up the delicate negotiations, intrigue, and military actions required to integrate regional territories into the Indian state.

2

Consolidating the nation

I n the first five years of independence, India had absorbed eight million refugees, completed its Constitution, and held an election of 178 million voters. These were remarkable feats in themselves. But at the same time, India had fought its first war with Pakistan over Kashmir, had integrated 600 other semi-autonomous princely states into its union, and had initiated its First Five Year Plan for economic development.

The process of nation-building accelerated as the decade progressed, particularly in terms of creating Central Government programs and institutions. The Second Five Year Plan, which began in 1957, proved more extensive than the first and emphasized large-scale industrial growth. In addition, Goa, the Portuguese colony on India's west coast acceded to the union, thus fulfilling India's goal of territorial consolidation. In foreign policy India joined the Commonwealth of Nations – a group of former British colonies that continued to work cooperatively – and, at Nehru's instigation, co-founded the Non-Aligned Movement – another strategic grouping of nations, which sought to gain independent influence in a bipolar, Cold War world. Relations with China had dramatic swings from the peace and trade agreement of 1954, to border tensions throughout the 1950s and India welcoming the Dalai Lama in 1959. The high-stakes relationship with China manifested in 1962 with a Chinese invasion that perpetrated a humiliating military defeat over India's Army.

This chapter focuses on these internal and external challenges to national integration from 1947 to 1964, a period shaped by Nehru's leadership. It will use four examples,

1. the integration of princely states, particularly the contrasting examples of Hyderabad and Kashmir,
2. India's China and Tibet policies, leading up to the war with China,
3. the incorporation of the Portuguese colony of Goa, and
4. regional assertion, in this case, the Communists in Kerala.

KASHMIR AND HYDERABAD

The status of Kashmir remained throughout the twentieth century one of the most divisive problems in South Asia, producing ongoing tension between India and Pakistan. From the perspective of Indian post-independence politics, in addition to relations with Pakistan, several other issues coalesced to perpetuate Kashmir as a crisis – the general process of integrating princely states, Indian ideology of secularism, and India's China policy.

Even before independence, Indian leaders began negotiating with some 562 states, governed by hereditary rulers, with whom the British had established relations of some degree of autonomy, known as 'paramountcy.' From January 1947, the British sent conflicting signals about the future status of these states, sometimes suggesting that they could opt for independence when the British withdrew. However, following the announcement of Partition on 14 June, Lord Mountbatten pursued a policy (based on negotiations with Jawaharlal Nehru) designed to 'prevent the further Balkanization' of India. He called for the princely states to accede to India or Pakistan, depending on their geographic location. Before 15 August, most states had agreed to accession.

As historian Barbara Ramusack writes in *The Indian Princes and Their States*, 'most princes acceded for a variety of reasons including patriotism, the advice of their ministers, the pressure of popular political leaders in their states, and a sense of abandonment' by the British (Ramusack, 2004: 273). From the perspective of the princes, accession followed more than 20 years of direct negotiations with the British about the meaning of their treaty relationships. Princes resented the concept of 'paramountcy' because, while it suggested a kind of autonomy, the British used it to encroach increasingly on the internal affairs of their states. In response to continued pressure from princes for a forum to discuss common concerns, the British inaugurated the Chamber of Princes in 1921, a consultative, advisory body comprised of 120 princes representing 225 states. The Chamber of Princes had limited success either in finding areas of agreement among themselves or in negotiating with the British.

Standstill Agreement: Initial arrangement between the Indian government and the Princely States to smooth their succession into the Indian nation.

Privy purse: A term for maintenance stipends given to former rulers of regional states, upon accession to independent India.

After independence Vallabhai Patel, India's Home Minister, who served as chief negotiator for the government, sought to regularize the government's relationship with the princely states and integrate them into the new Indian nation. He offered each something called a **Standstill Agreement**, which granted the princes control over their budgets and properties, and also maintenance stipends, called **privy purses**, but they had to accede to the Indian Government's three main powers – defence, foreign affairs, and communication. While the concept of a Standstill Agreement appeared to confirm the *status quo* of partial autonomy that had been established between princes and the British, in reality it became a step toward integration.

Mysore state, for example, established its first Congress Party Government on 24 October 1947 following a period of marches by Congress supporters calling for the end of the Maharaja's rule. These were ironic or symbolic in that the Maharaja had already agreed in principle to accession. However, in the intervening time, Congress protestors were arrested or driven out beyond the Mysore boundaries. After brief negotiations in October the agreement was made and the Maharaja of Mysore, like so many of his fellow princes, was supported by the government in the form of a privy purse – in his case of 2,600,000 rupees a year. This stipend replaced the stipend the princes had been given by the British Government before independence.

Other states, however, resisted accession. Three of these – Junagadh, Hyderabad, and Kashmir – initially signed Standstill Agreements and all three ultimately joined India through different processes and with different degrees of willingness. Junagadh, a state on the western coast of India with a Muslim ruler and majority Hindu population, initially sought accession to Pakistan. After some initial conflict, however, it ultimately joined India, through a negotiation process that included a **plebiscite** – a general vote of the population.

Plebiscite: A general vote on a specific question or referendum. A plebiscite in the autonomous state of Junagadh made it part of the Indian union, but despite calls for a plebiscite in Kashmir, it never materialized.

Hyderabad and Kashmir proved most contentious and most serious given their size and geography. Hyderabad, a landlocked state completely surrounded by India, covered 82,000 square miles and had a population of about 17 million people. Kashmir on the other hand bordered both India and Pakistan. Although its area was about the same size as Hyderabad, it had only 4 million inhabitants. The story of these two states took very different turns.

Hyderabad's Muslim ruler, the Nizam, held an ancestral title that dated back to the Mughal Empire, which then controlled most of South Asia. In 1713, the then Governor of Hyderabad, Asaf Jah, attained *de facto* independence from the Mughal Emperor. By the twentieth century, Hyderabad continued as a principality with a ruling Muslim elite and a population that was about 87 per cent Hindu. When Winston Churchill visited the state during his tour in the British Army at the turn of the century, he commented on the bold sense of independence apparent there (Churchill, 1896). It was also diverse, comprising three regions – Telegu-speaking Telangana, Marathi speaking Marathwada and Kannada speaking Karnataka – but Telangana was the largest.

In 1947 the Nizam hoped to gain complete sovereignty over this diverse and populous state. He hired a British lawyer, Sir Walter Monckton, to negotiate on his behalf; meanwhile he intended to build up his military. On 29 November 1947, Hyderabad concluded a Standstill Agreement with the Indian Government, seeing this as a way to buy time, while he continued to seek independence. Mountbatten (Governor General at the time) reported that it was with 'very great regret' to India, that the Nizam did not sign an 'instrument of accession' (H. E. H. The Nizam, 1948: 10) [**Doc. 5, p. 138**].

However, perhaps due to its 'great regret,' India immediately began to undermine Hyderabad's hope for independence. Within Hyderabad, the Nizam had to contend with internal problems as well. The state Congress organization, with support from outside members of the Indian National Congress, was mobilizing for accession. In addition, concerned Muslim elite had organized against the perceived threat of a Hindu majority, and communists, whose allegiance to Congress vacillated but whose support among some peasants remained strong, consolidated their local base. The peasant movements in British India that led to Zamindari abolition, also started in the 1930s. In Telangana too, peasants mobilized against intermediaries on the land. Particularly from 1939 to 1945, villages established organizations called Sanghams that agitated against landlord excesses, such as *vetti*, a compulsory tax. The Nizam's government openly supported the landlords and banned the communists who defended, and at times organized, the peasant Sanghams.

A militant communal organization – the Ittihad ul Muslimin – further antagonized an already tense situation by enforcing the rule of the establishment. Using its paramilitary wing called the Razakars, the Ittihad ul Muslimin employed force against peasants in the countryside. In Telangana, village men and women formed squads to fight against Razakars as well as landlords. Taken together these armed peasant movements, which incorporated popular resistance to the Nizam, and resistance against Razakars, came to be known as the Telangana Struggle. A key characteristic was the participation of women in armed resistance [**Doc. 6, pp. 138–41**].

While the Telangana Struggle was not intended as a movement to bring Hyderabad under Indian control, it did indirectly precipitate integration. Because it revealed real fissures in the Hyderabadi society, it provided an opening for the Indian Government to take action against the Nizam. Citing the breakdown of law and order in Hyderabad as a cross-border threat, the Indian Government demanded the Nizam take action. As a form of pressure, the Indian Government exercised its considerable control over the flow of commerce in and out of Hyderabad State. Partly, this was designed to stop the flow of arms from Karachi; in Pakistan, however, the Nizam claimed that medical and other basic supplies had been cut off as well (Talbot, 1949: 325). In a complaint filed before the United Nations, the State of Hyderabad claimed that India was encroaching on its sovereignty, encouraging internal dissent, and inflicting a damaging economic blockage [**Doc. 5, p. 138**].

Finally, in September 1948, the Indian Army marched into Hyderabad and the Nizam surrendered in three days. Nehru granted the Nizam the same rights given to rulers in other princely states, including retaining a title – Rajpramukh – keeping most of his immense wealth, and gaining a privy purse of five million rupees.

The significance of this process of incorporating Hyderabad lends itself to wide interpretation, both at the time and among historians. As Bipan Chandra *et al.* describe it, the Indian Government 'decided to be generous and not punish the Nizam' (Chandra *et al.*, 1999: 76). However, Ayesha Jalal points out that this was an example of the heavy-handed tactics Nehru used in the aftermath of independence (Jalal, 1995: 46). A contemporary observer, Frank Moraes, then editor of the *Times of India*, similarly said,

> Nehru's treatment of the princes subsequent to divesting them of political power is an illustration of his strength as a strategist and weakness as a tactician. To allow the princes to exercise special political powers, privileges and prerogatives after independence would have been anomalous.

But having integrated them, Moraes argued, Nehru went too far in aggregating and disaggregating their states by reorganizing their administration. This simply antagonized them (Moraes, 1960: 150).

However, the resolution of the Hyderabad issue, did not address the concerns of Telangana peasants; the Indian Government did not step forward to meet their demands, although the process of gradual land reform did bring some change in the countryside. In fact, the agrarian issues in the region continued to be a source of political conflict. The government, however, instituted some reforms. Beginning in 1950 as a series of reform acts passed in other states, the government sought to distribute agricultural land to tenant cultivators, providing them with the rights of ownership. Most legislation proved limited in effectiveness due to poor wording and ineffective implementation. By 1967, however, elimination of unfair taxes, imposition of effective land ceilings, and protection against fragmentation of holdings provided a basis for a more equitable land tenure system [**Doc. 7, pp. 141–3**]. Although uneven in implementation, these reforms provided a basis for legal expectations that land and livelihood were rights of citizenship. Ongoing agrarian political movements sought to demand the redemption of those rights, although government reports recorded these as property crimes and a law and order problem [**Doc. 7, pp. 141–3**]. Another consequence of these ongoing movements was securing Telangana, as a region with separate identity within the state's legal boundaries.

If Hyderabad was a difficult case, Kashmir proved even more contentious. In demographic terms it was the inverse of Hyderabad; here a Hindu ruler governed a state more than 70 per cent Muslim. Another difference was that Kashmir bordered both Pakistan and India, providing a logical case for accession to either. Furthermore, Kashmir remained a strategic issue for both nations on the border not only of each other, but also, of China and Central Asia, which at the time of independence was controlled by the Soviet Union.

At the time of independence, Maharaja Hari Singh sent telegrams to both India and Pakistan seeking Standstill Agreements [**Doc. 8, p. 143**]. Given the position of the state, its telegraph and rail connections remained with Pakistan after independence and it depended on Pakistan for supplies. In an effort to force accession, Pakistan took advantage of its control over commerce (presaging the tactic India used in Hyderabad a year later) blockading the region. At the same time, Pathans, an ethnic group from the North West Frontier Province of Pakistan, began moving into Kashmir to liberate the people from the Maharaja. Many of the Pathans were equipped with weapons from Pakistan and had the implicit consent if not direction of Pakistan's Army. They also found some support among Muslim peasants in Kashmir.

The political situation within Kashmir, however, was complicated. There was an ongoing democracy movement led by a politician named Sheikh Abdullah, whose organization came to be called the National Conference in 1939. The National Conference had resisted the authority of the Maharaja, but it was also sympathetic to the Indian National Congress, which had a branch in the state. In fact, Sheikh Abdullah was in jail at the time of independence, because he launched a Quit Kashmir movement against the Maharaja in 1946.

As the Pathan irregular army marched toward the Kashmiri capital of Srinagar, the Maharaja first appealed to Pakistan to stop them and then sought military aid from India. But India, both for strategic reasons and in accordance with Mountbatten's legal advice, refused to defend the kingdom, unless the Maharaja signed an accession agreement [**Doc. 9, pp. 143–4**]. Once he did, India immediately began flying soldiers into Srinagar. Militarily, India pushed back the Pathan/Pakistani forces out of Srinagar and out of the heart of Kashmir – the Kashmir valley.

This case too went to the United Nations. India initially registered a complaint under Article 35 of the UN Charter calling for UN assistance in settling the dispute. Some Indian commentators at the time thought this was a tactical mistake, because it implied equal culpability with Pakistan and perhaps equal claim to Kashmir. Indeed, the UN expanded the complaint to include Pakistani accusations that India had committed genocide against Muslims. Ultimately, the UN established a committee to look into the issue, which, after much negotiation with both countries, finally set a ceasefire line in early 1949.

The historiography of this early clash over Kashmir is especially controversial because of its implications for ongoing disputes between India and Pakistan. Writing in 1950 in the *Political Science Quarterly*, Taraknath Das states boldly 'it became evident that Pakistan was the real invader and the raiders [pathans] were mere subsidiary forces' (Das, 1950: 268). Philips Talbot, at about the same time, wrote about the implications the conflict might have on the possibility of holding a plebiscite in Kashmir. According to Talbot, the ongoing conflict made the mechanics of large-scale voting impossible (Talbot, 1949: 332).

While India had set the precedent for using a plebiscite to determine accession in the case Junagadh, when Pakistan called for a similar scenario in Kashmir, India resisted. The government claimed that a fair vote could not take place until there was a more stable situation on the ground, meaning that refugees could return and foreigners had left. This raised a number of questions. Who would determine when all non-residents, i.e., Pathans and other Indian or Pakistani nationals had withdrawn and therefore would not try to participate in the vote? Similarly, how would refugees who had fled be able to make their interests known? Finally, should a single referendum determine the position of the whole state or should the vote be carried out on a regional basis, opening the door for some future Partition? These questions took on even greater relevance as time passed, given the increased violence and displacement of populations in the region.

While at the time of independence, there was a strong grassroots claim for accession to India, the years of ongoing violence, seemingly to assure that claim, undermined it. Ayesha Jalal, in *Democracy and Authoritarianism in South Asia*, blames the leaders of Pakistan and India in the 1940s and 1950s for permitting communalism (in South Asia meaning conflict between Hindus and Muslims) to thrive and as a result the interests of the Kashmiris themselves were neglected (Jalal, 1995). As fiction often evokes these images in powerful detail, Salman Rushdie's novel *Shalimar the Clown* focuses on ordinary Kashmiris caught in the conflict between states and non-state militant activists (Rushdie, 2005).

Kashmir was a potent symbol for both states. In India it represented the nation's commitment to secularism. As the only Muslim majority region to remain within its boundaries, it portrayed India's multicultural diversity and exemplified the secular ideology explicitly articulated by its Prime Minister. Nehru himself came from a Kashmiri family, which had a sense of a Kashmiri culture that included Hindus and Muslims together. For Pakistan, Kashmir embodied the essence of its nationalism. Here was a region where Muslims literally were living under a Hindu king, who made momentous decisions, such as accession, without consulting the people. It underscored the need for a Muslim homeland and characterized Pakistan's sense of its geographic boundaries. Furthermore, in one tradition, the name Pa-k-istan was an acronym for Punjab, Kashmir, Sindh, and Baluchistan – the regions intended to comprise the state.

The Kashmir dispute had implications beyond India and Pakistan as well – underscoring its strategic significance. China too claimed a portion of Kashmir as its territory. Therefore, Kashmir entered the story of conflict between India and China.

THE CHINA WAR (1962)

Conflict with China was not inevitable; even before independence, the Indian National Congress had supported China – against Western imperialists and also against Japan. Immediately after independence, India embraced China and was one of the first to recognize the new People's Republic in 1950. In fact, on 24 April 1954 India and China signed a significant treaty of mutual cooperation, known as **Panchsheel**, or Five Principles [**Doc. 10, p. 144**]. When, in accordance with the first principle, the two nations proclaimed mutual respect for each other's territorial integrity and sovereignty, they did not specify official borders and boundaries. While there was some dispute over the border created by Sir Arthur McMahon, who had drawn the British boundary in the northeast, these issues were set aside during the negotiations for the Panchsheel Agreement. Nor did India question China's occupation of Tibet, which had begun some years earlier and India gave up any claims to outposts the British had established in Tibet. The war with China thus came as somewhat of a surprise to most observers.

Panchsheel Agreement: Five-point agreement between India and China for mutual cooperation and peaceful coexistence; because its official title was 'Agreement Between the People's Republic of China and the Republic of India on Trade and Intercourse Between the Tibet Region of China and India,' it also suggested tacit approval on India's part of Chinese control over Tibet; it was signed in 1954 and has guided relations between China and India (on and off) since that time, despite the China War.

Of course there had been tension on and off over the contours of the border. In 1956 Chinese engineers began building a road across the Aksai plain, which traditional British maps, noting the McMahon line as boundary, placed in India's territory. The road linked Xinjiang Province in China to Tibet. Not until 1957 did China publish a map of the road and India still had not dispatched official observers until 1958. By then the *de facto* occupation of land claimed by India had been accomplished and Nehru sent a series of very strong letters to Chou En-lai protesting the incursion. Recently released CIA papers on the subject show close American scrutiny of these events at the time, reflecting American concerns about the outcome of an escalating dispute. The CIA analysis of the situation suggests China misled Indian diplomats, who sometimes wilfully and sometimes naively ignored warning signs (United States Government. CIA Report, 1963).

Aksai lies in the Indian region of Ladakh, a part of Kashmir, compounding the complicated implications of a military build up in a region disputed with Pakistan. Furthermore, whatever concerns Nehru had about this area in the northwest were equalled by attention to a military build up of Chinese troops on the eastern border. Indian soldiers faced Chinese soldiers along the border of the North-East Frontier Agency, particularly on a ridge of the Himalayas called Thagla since about 1959 and there had been occasional incursions one way or another across the ridge.

On 8 September 1962, Chinese soldiers attacked an outpost on the Thagla Ridge and then waged a full-scale invasion on 15 October. In the first few encounters, India lost 513 soldiers (including officers) and China captured 50,000 square miles of Indian territory. It took weeks for Indian reinforcements to reach the remote passes in which the fighting took place. India appealed to the United States and Britain for assistance, but on 10 November the Chinese withdrew from all of the territory they had taken in the east.

What remained was Chinese occupation of the Aksai region of Kashmir, leaving open speculation that the eastern conflict was a distraction from the more important Chinese expansion along the Tibetan border in the west. However, Chinese claims to the eastern territory, which later became the Indian state of Arunachal Pradesh, resurfaced periodically.

Historical accounts of the war portray India as unprepared, though different sources suggest the reason for this lack of preparedness. Some blame Nehru's industrial policy that failed to modernize the military. Also both Nehru and the Defence Minister Krishna Menon seemed to miscalculate China's strategic goals (Cohen, 2001: 131; Frankel, 1978: 76). Some also describe Prime Minister Nehru as naive in the face of Chinese expansionist ambitions, blinded by a desire to keep open friendly relations (Khilnani, 1999: 40). Others suggested that Nehru arrogantly refused to negotiate boundaries with China. Along these lines, Neville Maxwell, a political analyst, went farthest in arguing that India provoked China through the 'Forward Policy' that pushed Indian border patrols closer and closer to the McMahon line – the border that India recognized as the legitimate one (Maxwell, 1970).

However, K. Subrahmanyam, a politician and political thinker, who joined the Ministry of Defence after the China War, reflected on Nehru's performance in less harsh terms. He argued that Nehru had a subtle understanding of China, but chose not to provoke the Chinese directly, because he was looking at a longer-term strategy. On military preparedness, Nehru advocated a strong and gradual build up, which simply had not been complete by the time of the unexpected war. Subrahmanyam dismissed the 'Forward Policy' argument directly and in detail (Subrahmanyam, 1976: 102–130).

The China War spread a wider fear among Indian citizens and encouraged reflection far from the area of conflict. A contemporary issue of the American *Saturday Evening Post* magazine portrayed women college students at Lady Sri Ram College in Delhi engaging in rifle drills (Sharrod, 1963: 65). The debate over the China War and its causes and influences on Indian foreign policy continued long after the events. An article in the Indian newsmagazine *Frontline* in 2003 directly addressed the continuing influence of the China War on Kashmir policy. A. G. Noorani demonstrated the importance of Aksai Chin to China's control over Tibet and reviewed the historical treaties that presented conflicting versions of the actual boundary. (Noorani, 2003)

A related issue then was China's Tibet policy, which came to concern India as a sizeable Tibetan refugee population steadily crossed the border from 1959 onward. Nehru never condemned China's occupation of Tibet, although some Indian politicians thought he should. Nevertheless, in 1959

Nehru did grant asylum to the Dalai Lama, when he fled Chinese rule to India's border [**Doc. 11, pp. 144–5**]. Nehru's speech in Parliament about the rescue of the Dalai Lama met with some opposition from colleagues concerned about the implications this would have on the prevailing 'Hindi Chini Bhai Bhai' (India China Brothers) policy. (At that time Chinese and Indian relations had been moving toward increased trade and friendship.) After this event, the *People's Daily*, China's official newspaper, did begin to refer to India as an imperialist power.

Noorani's article in *Frontline* claims that China's Tibet policy did influence its claims about its border with India. This may also explain why, despite military superiority, China chose not to advance into India; perhaps China was indeed simply consolidating its control in Tibet. Reporting on his interview with Nehru during the China War, the American reporter for *The Saturday Evening Post*, Robert Sharrod, reflected on the sudden change in atmosphere between late October and November 1962. When they first met, Nehru was determined to defend the nation by fighting the Chinese on the border and he clearly feared further advances into the Indian plain. The nation had mobilized for war – civilians were training to use rifles and women donated gold for the war effort. The relief after 10 November, Sharrod explained, was palpable. Nehru's attitude toward China had returned to normalcy (Sharrod, 1963: 67).

China's acquisition of Aksai Chin changed the map of Kashmir in a small way, but that shift opened up the possibility of dividing Kashmir further. Both this reality and India's perceived weakness encouraged Pakistan to wage war on India again in 1965, although not in the Kashmir region itself. The war focused on the Rann of Kutch (on the west coast of India), which had a border with Sindh Province in Pakistan; it extended to military clashes in Kashmir and Punjab as well. An open question in 1965 was whether China would also join the conflict; however, it did not. Ultimately, the United Nations resolved key border issues attached to the war in a treaty signed at Tashkent.

UN intervention in South Asia, mainly by brokering diplomatic agreements, signalled an attempt by the organization to smooth the process of decolonization. One last example, of a post independence conflict – the forced accession of Goa – shows India's complex position in the world community as a fledgling and embattled democracy on the one hand, and regional superpower, on the other. Here too the UN played a role.

GOA: THE LAST EUROPEAN COLONY?

Unlike Hyderabad and the other princely states, it took until 1960 for India to integrate Goa and finally it did so, using the army. What surprised Nehru and Parliament was the international condemnation for what seemed to them a logical step.

If India's arguments for Kashmir and Hyderabad's accession had to do with prevailing continuities in those states with the Indian society that predated independence, the logic for the integration of Goa was more convoluted, especially given the striking discontinuities. Goa had been a Portuguese colony for 400 years and maintained a Portuguese administration. The vast differences between political and institutional structures in Goa and those in the rest of India demonstrated the overwhelming influence that European colonialism imposed. Therefore, the integration of Goa served as a lesson in how very different colonial influences shaped the Indian subcontinent.

Beginning in 1947, the government of India set out to negotiate the accession of Goa. India initially perceived Goa, unlike the princely states, as a European colony which, like the provinces, should become absorbed into the Indian state. The anti-colonial logic made sense in a global context. After World War II, when many European powers were divesting of their imperial holdings, Portugal declared its colonies 'overseas provinces' in an effort to maintain control over them. Furthermore, especially following a high profile public meeting by the socialist leader Ram Mohan Lohia in 1946, it seemed that a growing movement against the Portuguese dictator was gaining greater popularity. However, the Portuguese Government did not negotiate and in 1961 the Indian Army marched in to take possession of Goa, easily subduing Portuguese resistance. In two days – 18 and 19 December 1961 – Indian soldiers marched into the territory from several sides, in an operation called 'Vijay' or victory. Many Goans greeted them with nationalist slogans and with Indian flags, indicating that the invasion was seen – at least at that moment – as liberation.

Nehru was in fact surprised by the international protest that followed. A vote in the United Nations called for an immediate ceasefire. What complicated matters was a political and cultural system in Goa that defied easy integration. While the Indian Government immediately set up an administrative system for Goa, it was based on practices of governing that had been functioning and developing in India over more than a decade, with origins in British law. These new principles of government immediately produced conflict.

Language became an issue and perhaps a metaphor for the larger issue. The Indian legal system imposed on Goa was based on laws written in English and translated, as needed, into Indian languages. Indian civil servants and most jurists functioned in an English milieu. Since Goans were not trained to implement the new government, Indian officials from other states came to facilitate the legal integration. But communication was a serious obstacle because not only were these government officers seen as outsiders, but they primarily relied on English as a medium of communication, which exacerbated the alienation. Goan judges not only did not know the new laws, but they could not read them. Arun Sinha, a historian of Goa, described the disorientation of liberation. 'Prices soared, incomes dipped, jobs were lost, rules changed and in the absence of qualified Goans, Indians from other states came to occupy key posts in government' (Sinha, 2002: 37).

Furthermore, there were conflicts within Goa among pro-Portuguese groups and pro-Indian nationalists, but also along lines that did not necessarily coincide with pro-Portuguese resistance, there was tension between Christian and Hindu Goans. The neighbouring states of Karnataka and Maharasthra both placed claims on Goa, based on the linguistic divisions within the territory.

The solution for Nehru was to maintain Goa's independence – defining it as a separate entity under the principle of 'unique identity.' To do so, the Central Government made Goa, along with Damon and Diu – nearby islands that were also acquired from Portugal – Union Territories that would be administered and supported financially from New Delhi.

For many Christian, Portuguese-speaking Goans, this unique identity specifically validated the argument that their culture, shaped by Portuguese legacy, was central to Goan identity. For some Hindus who resented Christian privilege under the Portuguese, the language of 'unique identity' polarized society. In addition, in Goa, as we have seen in other regions, there was a class and caste dimension to political alliances. Labourers, agricultural workers, and lower caste Hindus, many of whom had joined in pro-India politics before liberation, had high expectations for a post-Portuguese society. Courted by regional politicians in neighbouring states, they equated liberation both with economic and social advancement, on the one hand, and with integration into one of those states, on the other.

Arun Sinha argues that Nehru erred strategically in Goa's case. First of all he instituted too many changes too quickly. Especially frustrating was the dramatic increase in the use of the English language, both in schools and government. Second, he missed opportunities to celebrate and promote Goa's older history before the Portuguese. Relying on a colonial definition for Goa's 'unique identity' that was imbued with Portuguese cultural referents, just as India was disposing of many British colonial trappings, proved counterproductive (Sinha, 2002). In addition, Nehru's emphasis on industrial development and infrastructure – building roads and bridges – while benefiting Goa's economy, did not bring agricultural changes as quickly as many peasant cultivators, who had supported Indian integration, expected.

The Central Government postponed a decision on the most contentious issue – that of Goa's merger with one of the neighbouring states – by initiating development programmes financed by the Centre and setting a date for Assembly elections. In other words, the conditions were put in place for establishing a separate state government. The exercise of forming a democratically elected government in Goa demonstrates a successful Indian strategy that assumed democratic participation and instilled nationalism and political integration. Indeed when the first Assembly elections took place on 20 December 1963 more than 65 per cent of voters (240,000) turned out.

Three parties contended for seats. The Maharashtrawadi Gomantak Party (MGP) supported the view that Goa belonged to the state of Maharashtra based on the regional culture and traditions of Hindus in both the states as well as their claim that Marathi, the language of Maharashtra, was the original mother tongue of all the Goans. Of course this defied contemporary practice; all Goans did not speak Marathi. The other key party, the United Goans Party (UGP), emphasized such contemporary realities. The UGP leaders comprised Christians as well as upper caste Hindus; their platform defended Goa's separate existence. Finally, there was a presence of the Congress Party in Goa. However, it waffled on the issue of merger with neighbouring states, focusing instead on a plank that called for development first and decisions about merger later.

Congress badly miscalculated and lost miserably, not winning a single seat in the 30-member Assembly. Rather, the MGP won 14 seats and the UGP 12. With three independents supporting the MGP, it gained a majority. A critical preoccupation of the first Assembly, which met from 1963 to 1966, was the question of language. The first Chief Minister known as Bhausaheb – Dayanand Bandodkar – envisioned Goa as part of Maharasthra and advocated Marathi language, much to the frustration of the opposition. UGP members by and large did not understand Marathi, but rather spoke both Portuguese and Konkani. The Central Government position, laid out for all union territories, called for official transactions to take place in Hindi or English.

Bandodkar, who had run on a platform of merger with Maharasthra mellowed his position in the years after the election. Some argue he was persuaded by Nehru to maintain a separate Goa (Sinha, 2002: 58). Others suggested that once in power Bandodkar saw the potential for his own administration to continue – either in the interest of regional development or as an ambitious politician. Either way, in practice, Bandodkar postponed merger; the Assembly continued to meet and began to deliberate in Konkani and, most impressively, it set a date in 1967 for a plebiscite to finally decide the question of merger.

While plebiscites obviously had a mixed history in India, in Goa the plebiscite was successful in the sense that 80 per cent of eligible voters participated. The results were somewhat surprising to the ruling MGP. While the MGP had won the election on the merger plank, the vote for merger failed with only 43 per cent of Goans supporting it.

Therefore, Goa maintained its separate Legislative Assembly and state government. In the long run its integration into India was less a matter of imposed laws or language, but rather the economic boom of the growing tourist industry, brought to Goa by the lure of its beaches. The historic process that made Goa an Indian state, therefore followed a number of narrative trajectories, not just the Portuguese versus the Indian competition for control, but also the overlapping interpretations of events by Goan Christians, rural Goans, advocates of merger with Maharashtra, and Portuguese-speaking elites.

THE COMMUNIST PARTY IN KERALA AND REGIONAL ASSERTION

The act of consolidating contiguous principalities into the Indian state – such as Goa or Hyderabad – also served as a proxy for another one of India's main concerns: preventing secessionist movements in regions of the already existing nation. Separatist movements formed, for example, early on in Tamil-speaking areas, now the state of Tamil Nadu, and in the late 1950s (after severe food shortages) in the northeast state of Mizoram. Such movements were suppressed militarily, accommodated politically, and dissipated through economic development. Tamil Nadu became a distinct Tamil-speaking state when Madras was divided and the Mizo movement resulted in the Mizoram Accord in 1985, which brought increased stability to that state. But the issues of separatism remained a concern of the Indian Government over the decades.

Linked to this concern was also regional autonomy, which manifested in part in the political assertion of regional parties. Political scientists, in fact, have debated whether opposition-party governments in various states represented a challenge to the Centre or a useful safety valve (Brass, 1974, Hardgrave, 1993) and, of course, the answer can be both depending on the context. A number of parties developed which advocated specific regional concerns – the Akali Dal in Punjab or later the Telegu Dessam Party in Andhra Pradesh. But perhaps the most interesting case is the history of the Communist Party which, although a national player, developed strongholds in two states – on opposite sides of the country – Kerala in the southwest and Bengal in the east.

From independence to the end of the twentieth century, the Communist Party formed the government in Kerala, winning majorities in the Legislative Assembly nine times, alternating victories with other parties – primarily the Indian National Congress. In West Bengal it served as a coalition partner or sole government for seven terms (twice in the 1960s and then beginning in 1977, winning continually). Nevertheless the history of the Communist

Party in post-independence India demonstrated the importance of the Left in both regional and national politics, shaping political discourse to address a peasant and worker constituency.

In addition, its success showed that a communist party could function within a democratic state. And the implications of that participation ultimately fuelled an internal conflict within the Party about the relative importance of mass mobilisation versus electoral integration. As a result the Party split in 1964, giving birth to the **Communist Party of India** (Marxist) – CPM, which went on to achieve great electoral success.

Perhaps precipitating this conflict was the victory of the as yet undivided Communist Party of India in Kerala in the first Legislative Assembly elections there in 1957, under the leadership of E. M. S. Namboodiripad, a celebrated freedom fighter. The anomaly that Indian communists succeeded in a multi-party electoral system and remained strong in regional pockets inspired not only the attention of historians and political scientists but also the literary imagination of Arundhati Roy. Her Booker Prize winning novel, *The God of Small Things*, which is set in Kerala, describes the attraction communism held for a character of that 1950s generation, Chacko Kochamma, whose political sympathies antagonized his landowning father but gained him communist sympathies in college. The narrator calls this 'the euphoria of 1957, when the communists won the State Assembly elections and Nehru invited them to form a government. Chacko's hero, Comrade E. M. S. Namboodiripad, the flamboyant Brahmin high priest of Marxism in Kerala, became Chief Minister in the first ever democratically elected communist government in the world. Suddenly the communists found themselves in the extraordinary – critics said absurd – position of having to govern a people and foment revolution simultaneously (Roy, 1997: 67). Put in historical terms, Namboodiripad dealt with the political contradictions by developing a theoretical model for what he called in a published pamphlet of the same name, the *Peaceful Transition to Communism*. But it was precisely this sense of accommodation to the state that sparked dissension in the national party.

The novel itself focuses on the intimacies and antagonisms fostered by the close contact between classes and castes thrown together by the necessities and traditions of small-town life. It turns on the tragic consequences to one particular Christian family, which comes from the landed classes, when one of its members crosses caste and class lines. In this context an ironic narrator muses about the reasons the Communist Party was so successful in Kerala.

There were several competing theories. One was that it had to do with the large population of Christians in the state. . . . Structurally – this somewhat rudimentary theory went – Marxism was a simple substitute for Christianity. Replace God with Marx, Satan with the bourgeoisie, Heaven

Communist Party of India (CPI) and Communist Party of India-Marxist (CPI (M)): Most histories cite the founding of the CPI in 1921; a strong force in supporting left-leaning popular movements in India, the CPI strongly supported and was supported by the Communist Party of the Soviet Union. In 1964, the party split over division in tactics, strategies and political emphasis. The CPI (M) for Marxist supported peasant mobilization and severed ties with the USSR. The CPI (M) has achieved more electoral success, particularly in Kerala and West Bengal and there have been a number of alliances between the two communist parties toward the end of the twentieth century.

with a classless society, the Church with the Party, and the form and purpose of the journey remained similar. . . . The trouble with this theory was that in Kerala the Syrian Christians were, by and large, the wealthy estate-owning (pickle factory-running) feudal lords, for whom communism represented a fate worse than death. A second theory claimed that it had to do with the comparatively high level of literacy in the state. Perhaps. Except that the high literacy level was largely *because* of the communist movement. The real secret was that communism crept into Kerala insidiously. . . . The Marxists worked from *within* the communal divides, never challenging them, never appearing not to. They offered a cocktail revolution. A heady mix of Eastern Marxism and orthodox Hinduism, spiked with a shot of democracy.

(Roy, 1997: 66)

This critique indeed coincided with the challenges from the Left wing within the Communist Party of India before the 1964 split.

The split in the party is often described as Right v. Left and as historian, Ross Mallick suggests, the Left attracted more pro-Chinese members and advocated more immediate mass revolution, while the Right was characterized by intellectuals, many of whom were trained in Europe and leaned toward the Soviets (Mallick, 1994: 30–45). Therefore, when the China War broke out, many on the Left argued that a fellow communist state could not possibly be an aggressor. In this configuration Namboodiripad was a Centrist, like his colleague in West Bengal, Jyoti Basu; both saw the need for a popular base, not only to build a revolution, but also to win elections. As Namboodiripad articulated it, mass revolution and the mobilization of the proletariat was still the ultimate goal of the Party, but in the mean time, there were immediate needs to be met. The 1957 government did not adequately meet those needs and ultimately fell.

The Central Government of India perhaps helped shape the contours of the party split, when it arrested some 60 leaders of the Communist Party of India in West Bengal following the China War on the grounds that they harboured Chinese sympathies (Mallick, 1994: 38). Fatefully, the government arrested the Centrists along with the Left-wing camp. This set the stage for common ground between the two and leaders like E. M. S. Namboodiripad and Jyoti Basu, after much negotiation, joined the new Communist Party of India Marxist, known as the CPI (M) or CPM. Indeed the CPM under Namboodiripad's leadership in Kerala returned to power in 1969.

In both Kerala and West Bengal the Communist Party showed its ongoing participation in Constitutionalism and multi-party democracy. The integration of communists into the structure of government showed another kind of consolidation of the Indian nation as in Hyderabad, Goa, and Kashmir.

But also as the history of Kashmir showed – national integration once achieved is not necessarily ongoing. The next decades showed continued conflict over Kashmir and new secessionist movements, such as the one in Punjab. The CPM, in fact, played key roles in influencing parliamentary politics. By the late 1970s and early 1980s, Right-wing parties, most of which evolved from Pro-Hindu politics, as well as secular communists, challenged the Congress Party, which continued to win a majority of elections at the Centre. This story re-emerges in Chapter 4.

CONCLUSION

For Nehru's visions of India as a player in world politics, the success of integrating princely states and Portuguese Goa was as important as defining foreign policy. Furthermore, the consolidation of contiguous states served as a bulwark against regional tensions within India's established borders. The ability to integrate Hyderabad and Goa set useful examples for Tamil Nadu and Kerala – and perhaps vice versa.

While Kashmir remained the most contentious issue in both India's domestic and foreign policy, the ultimate integration of Hyderabad, Goa, Junagadh, and the support of the princes in what became the Indian state of Rajasthan, symbolized India's commitment to cultural diversity. Nevertheless, Nehru clearly did not have a template to apply to each set of negotiations. Plebiscites, military intervention, economic coercion, encouragement of popular mobilization, and diplomacy all played a role.

A critical feature that united these cases was the involvement of the fledgling United Nations. Hyderabad sought redress in the UN, as did Portugal. This underscored the blurred line between domestic crises and international ones. Nowhere was that debate more potent than over the border conflict with China. What became crystallized in the China War and in China's surprising unilateral withdrawal was also a domestic debate about where India stood in Asia, what was its relationship with China, and how did it define its international borders.

Just as India was engaged in these political and geopolitical debates about its national identity, it was also defining itself in terms of art and culture. In fact, with the serious blow of defeat against China, the task of building up cultural institutions took on even greater importance. The next chapter examines some of those cultural institutions and expressions in the 1950s and 1960s.

3

Modernism, government and the arts

> 1959: The city of Chandigarh is planned to human scale. It puts us in touch with the infinite cosmos and nature. It provides us with places and buildings for all human activities by which the citizens can live a full and harmonious life. Here the radiance of nature and heart are within our reach.
>
> Le Corbusier

With this 'edict' the architect, Le Corbusier introduced the city of Chandigarh, the planned capital of Punjab that came to represent India's commitment to modernity [**Doc. 12, pp. 145–6**]. Although Nehru's vision for Chandigarh was to create a monument to Indian nationalism, the fact that Nehru reached out to the best architects in the world, demonstrated both his nationalist and internationalist perspective.

This chapter focuses on the relationship of the arts to Indian independence, especially structures and institutions that promoted them in the 1950s and 1960s. The creation and re-creation of museums, arts institutions, and colleges of art all intersected with the project of nation-building. The government of independent India consciously promoted art, architecture, and literature to demonstrate India's cultural sophistication in a rapidly changing modern world. Interestingly, artists, filmmakers and writers joined in on the modernizing project. Within those creative communities too, trends in the 1950s and 1960s were for modernist, and often nationalist, expression.

'The issue of being modern involves establishing a sense of identity which incorporates technological and social change while maintaining connections to the past', writes the art historian Vidya Dehejia (Dehejia, 1997: 411). Therefore, the practice of negotiating the modern was not at odds, but in fact complementary, to the simultaneous practice of negotiating Indian-ness. And these concerns were shared across a number of genres.

This chapter examines the interconnection of modernism, nationalism, and the role of government in the arts. It focuses on a series of examples: the planning of Chandigarh, the founding of the National Museum in Delhi, the establishment of the Museum of Modern Art, and other movements in modern art, the development of the **Sahitya Akademi** with the objective to promote literature, and finally, the burgeoning film industry. Politics and art were inextricably linked. Artists struggled with ways to probe meanings of Partition, Constitution-building, war, and national consolidation. In addition, the institutions associated with art were similarly influenced by the changing political events.

Sahitya Akademi: An institution to promote literature established by the government in 1954.

CHANDIGARH AND MODERNISM

Chandigarh, the new capital of Punjab, was built to be a monument to modernity and, what better architectural form than modernism to produce such a monument? The city was a product of Partition; the old capital of Punjab – Lahore – lay in Pakistan and so the new Indian state required a capital. The fact that Punjab not only lost its historical capital but also experienced the tragedy of Partition violence more profoundly than nearly any other state encouraged the decision to build a grand capital, an ideal opportunity for Nehru to showcase a modern vision for India. Toward that end, the government pursued the most prominent modernist architects of the day, those with a vision that would be new to India, departing from both British imperial architecture and indigenous forms that might be identifiable as either Hindu or Mughal.

Le Corbusier, an already well-known Swiss architect living in France, ultimately agreed to the project after some persuasion. He began by revisiting a design proposed by an American-based team, the Polish-born architect Mathew Nowicki and Albert Mayer. While Nowicki and Mayer's plan was organic, built around the rivers of the city, Le Corbusier chose a grid pattern with straight roads and a central large walking plaza for the capital complex [**Doc. 13, p. 146**].

This appealed to Nehru, whose goal was to make architects in India and abroad 'sit up and think'. Le Corbusier achieved this not only by the buildings themselves, but also through his philosophy, which he laid out in a written contract [**Doc. 14, pp. 146–7**]. Beyond the government buildings, Le Corbusier created housing sectors, parks, and markets along specific lines, including separate sectors for different income groups.

The capital complex itself exemplified key elements of Le Corbusier's design and mandate. Its buildings were grand in scope, capturing Nehru's ambition of a monument to the new nation, and it was set apart from the mundane action of daily life. As architectural historian Charles Jencks points out, Le Corbusier sought to find unifying symbols of authority and power that defied the divisions attached to the recent Partition. An obvious choice in the heat of the Punjab plain was the sun and so much of the architecture of the city celebrated or tamed the sun (Jencks, 2000). For example, a large arcade shades the entire building of the High Court, and a monument nearby, the Tower of Shadows, provides an intentional study of the movement of the sun. Most of the structures were made of concrete, using bright coloured downspouts, doors and windows as striking contrasts to the grey. The design presented new architectural features to India, including the sculpted roofs and variegated shapes that created unusual spaces, some of which were designed for ceremonial occasions. For example, the plaza served as the scene of the swearing-in ceremony for the members of the state Legislative Assembly.

Nevertheless, many critics note that because the capital complex is separate from everyday life, the people of Chandigarh do not casually or by happenstance walk through the plaza, which gives the appearance of a separation between government and citizens (Lang, 2002: 63). However, an observer might note, as critic Vikramaditya Prakash does, that citizens adapt spaces to their own uses. 'There was always someone from Kansal, the village just north, bathing a buffalo, washing clothes, playing cricket . . . Even the security men have strung up lines to dry their laundry.' The judges and legislators, he reports, did not bother to walk through the plaza, entering and leaving from the car park below, leaving the space to this makeshift village (Prakash, 2002: 146–47).

In contrast to the regulated constraints of the Le Corbusier's 'Edict' and his 'Statute of Land Use,' that carefully governs additions, changes, and growth in official Chandigarh, there is another site nearby that was built from the leftovers of the first. The Rock Garden, constructed over eighteen years beginning in 1958 (about the same time as Le Corbusier) by Nek Chand Saini, an engineer for the Punjabi Transportation Corporation, is a whimsical place full of art. Nek Chand Saini collected stones, scraps of tile, porcelain, and industrial waste, such as old pipes and metal pieces and used them to make human figures and other designs in a wooded wasteland between the capital complex and the Sukhna Lake. The Rock Garden depicts real and fanciful creatures in various chambers often hidden around a corner or perched above a wanderer's head. The colours and patterns change from space to space – a palace wall here, an amphitheatre there and bird soldiers lined up in a row.

To Chandigarh, the Rock Garden has become an equally celebrated distinction. As its tourist brochures promise visitors, it mimics a 'make believe kingdom' next to the grand modern real one. In 1976, the Rock Garden was set aside as a preserved urban site, 'free from the interference of architects and town planners', notes the government website. (http://citco.nic.in). The coexistence of the romantic garden and the modernist Le Corbusier structure have come to signify the integration of various elements of Indian design – folk art, rural culture, urban industry, and modernity [**Doc. 15, p. 147**].

A critical change in Chandigarh followed the creation of a new state of Haryana, in keeping with Nehru's programme to divide states on linguistic grounds and a movement in Punjab for a separation between Hindi- and Punjabi-speaking regions. Established in 1966 Haryana also has Chandigarh – barely finished in its first stage – as its capital. Chandigarh now holds three administrations: that of Punjab, Haryana, and of the Union territory of Chandigarh City itself.

LE CORBUSIER'S INFLUENCE ON INDIAN ARCHITECTURE

Le Corbusier's influence transformed a generation of architects. In addition to his work in Chandigarh, Le Corbusier also designed buildings in Ahmedabad and Orissa. He also brought with him colleagues – his cousin Pierre Jeanneret, Maxwell Fry, and Jane Drew, who collaborated on these projects. Jeanneret worked in India the longest, from 1951 to 1965, and was involved in site planning for Punjab University.

This infusion of modernist design energized many Indian architects, who were attracted to Le Corbusier's futurist vision and some copied elements of his buildings directly. For one thing, Le Corbusier hired Indian architects to work on his projects: B. V. Doshi had worked with him in Paris before becoming site director on the Chandigarh project (1954–57). Young architects involved in Chandigarh went on to design their own projects, building on his influence. Also, the Chandigarh College of Architecture, established in 1961, with Le Corbusier's tacit support, used the city's buildings as part of its curriculum and employed faculty interested in local research and study. Other prominent schools of architecture – the J. J. School of Art in Bombay and the National Institute of Design in Ahmedabad – began to focus intently on basic design, following elements of modernism that coincided with, and perhaps were generated from, the Chandigarh project.

In fact a small group of major designers, who had variously interpreted modernism, produced some of the most influential architecture of the period. Among them were Habib Rahman (who built the new West Bengal Secretariat and a number of public works buildings in Delhi in the 1950s and 1960s) and Achyut Kanvide (who worked in Ahmedabad and Lucknow and was known for introducing new technologies to Indian building processes).

Their work, visible in major cities throughout the country, was 'there to be seen and discussed and to be emulated or not' (Lang, 2002: 72). The necessity for so many public buildings in such a short time permitted innovation, but also generated some rote imitation. Examples of this can be seen in government buildings and annexes to buildings throughout the country. Even the buildings of the Tibetan administration in exile in Dharamsala portray the institutional forms that grew out of Indian-modernist-government design.

In terms of city planning, Chandigarh's design also manifested clearly, for example, in Gandhinagar, which became the capital of Gujarat and was begun in 1960. Gujarat needed a new capital city with buildings to house its legislature, courts, and other government institutions when the old province of Bombay was divided into the new states of Gujarat and Maharashtra. Maharashtra kept the traditional capital of Bombay (now called **Mumbai**), while Gujarat gained a new government complex. Unlike Chandigarh which was carved out anew, Gandhinagar was built adjacent to a very old city – Ahmedabad. The architect, Hargovind Mewa, followed a similar grid pattern for sectors and developed a capital complex on a large scale along the lines of the Chandigarh.

Mumbai: The contemporary name for the city that was called Bombay during the period of colonial rule; Mumbai is from the local Marathi language and probably referred to some settlement in the area; the name change, which took place in 1995, was first in a series, announced by state governments, aiming to install names from local languages for their capital cities.

While architecture and city planning displayed the new India outwardly and on a grand scale, government support for the arts provided other avenues for creativity and public expression. The aim of the government was to preserve existing art forms and to encourage the production of new ones. Of course in many of these instances the mission of architects and planners coincided with those of artists and preservationists.

FOUNDING MUSEUMS, PROMOTING THE ARTS

The Government Museum and Art Gallery in Chandigarh, also designed by Le Corbusier, brought the monumental qualities of the capital complex to a much more populist enterprise. The Chandigarh Museum (one of only two run by India's Central Government) collected the objects of the past in order to construct an image of the new nation's present. In many ways, this was a compatible but alternative view to Nek Chand's Rock Garden, which collected modern refuse to create a fantasy world of the past.

The aim of museums in independent India was to render India's rich cultural past into a modern idiom. They also served to contextualize the British period. Nehru considered the development of national museums – both existing ones and new institutions – as a critical demonstration of India's position in the world of advanced nations, advancing both his ideology of modernity and his desire to link India to a grand historic past. The

Government Museum in Chandigarh, the National Museum in Delhi, and the National Gallery of Modern Art (all established between 1948 and 1954) articulated these goals, as new institutions created by the Indian state. However, the Madras Museum, which celebrated its 100th anniversary in 1954, used the moment of independence as an opportunity for transition and reorganization along similar lines. This section will look more closely at museums as sites for nationalist expression.

True to Le Corbusier's style and Nehru's ambition for something impressive, the Chandigarh museum used the movement of the sun to illuminate different portions of the massive, concrete structure throughout the day. Also, like Chandigarh itself, the museum was a product of Partition. Literally, it was the receptacle of an extensive collection of art and antiquities housed in the Lahore museum of an undivided Punjab. When that collection was officially divided in 1949, 40 per cent went to India. Among its treasures were ancient Gandhara sculpture from the western regions of Pakistan that dated to the period before 500 CE and Mughal and Rajasthani painting from the twelfth to the sixteenth centuries. The heart of the collection were art objects that connected India's history to regions now part of Pakistan and to centuries of Muslim (Mughal) and regional Hindu kingdoms.

The nationalist significance of the collection prompted special galleries to be built just for this material and Chandigarh, as the showcase city, was the logical site. After nearly two decades of shifting locations from Amritsar to Shimla to Patiala, the collection finally arrived at its permanent home in Chandigarh in 1968. As one of only two art galleries supported by the Central Indian Government, the Chandigarh Museum also developed collections of modern art and decorative arts and crafts. Along with the National Museum of Modern Art in Delhi, its mission was to represent India's arts across a broad spectrum.

The National Gallery of Modern Art opened in 1954 in Jaipur House, one of the many residences of princes that had been built in the capital before independence. (As the princely states acceded to India, their former rulers also gave up much of their property. Charged taxes by the state, they found that divesting themselves of property lent their names to new institutions and relieved them of a tax burden at the same time.) The idea for a Gallery of Modern Art emerged from a conference in Calcutta in 1949. Its mission, 'to preserve and acquire works of modern art from 1850 onward', demonstrates the recognition of artistic continuities before and after independence. Furthermore, the National Gallery of Modern Art from its inception considered that it had a major role in encouraging 'higher studies and research in the field of art history, art criticism, art appreciation, museology and the interrelations on visual and performing arts' [**Doc. 16, pp. 147–8**].

Among its original acquisitions was contemporary art, an investment in the future. For example, it displayed sculpture and paintings by K. G. Subramanyan, an already known artist who taught at the Baroda University where he trained a number of younger artists. Subramanyan came out of the nationalist tradition and studied at Shantiniketan, the university established by Rabindranath Tagore near Calcutta (now, Kolkata). Rabindranath Tagore, who won the Nobel Prize for Literature in 1913, was also an accomplished painter, and established Shantiniketan to promote education in the arts. Befitting Shantiniketan's emphasis on blurring the lines between craft and art, Subramanyan incorporated a variety of images, themes, and perspectives into his work, which was often set in naturalist setting. As an art educator, Subramanyan has written books about contemporary art and he became a significant figure in advancing Baroda as a centre of new artistic production. In 2004 the documentary filmmaker, Bikram Singh, produced 'A Rabbit's Leap in the Moonlight', using cinematography to portray Subramanyan's views on art and modernity.

The National Gallery of Modern Art saw its mission as representing the history of Indian modern art as well and made concerted efforts to acquire works of major figures in the Indian art world. One of India's most prominent modernist painters, Amrita Sher-Gill, was an obvious example. A Hungarian born and European trained painter, Sher-Gill settled in India after 1934, first in her family's ancestral home in what is now Uttar Pradesh and then in the city of Lahore before Partition. Her work reflected her travels in Indian villages and keen observations, especially of women's lives, but always challenging artistic traditions and calling upon fellow artists to do the same. As one of India's best known painters of the twentieth century the body of her work was an important centrepiece for the National Gallery of Modern Art, which holds the largest collection of her work, 103 paintings. Sher-Gill died in 1941 before she could witness some of the inventive art movements that flourished in the next two decades.

MODERN ART

Chennai: The contemporary name for the city known in British India as Madras. Borrowed from the name of a town on the south side of the original settlement that ultimately merged Madraspatnam and Chennapatnam together. Chennai became the official city name in 1996.

The art scene from the 1940s to 1960s proved to be another vital arena that experienced a transformation in the immediate post-independence period. In fact, 1947 represented a transition in modern Indian art that was only partly related to independence. In that year artists including M. F. Husain and S. N. Souza formed the Progressive Artists Group in Bombay, the most prominent of similar organizations that had been gathering in Calcutta and Madras (now **Chennai**). Heavily influenced by some of the same modernist ideas that were reflected in architecture, these artists rejected the existing movements of nationalist art, reflected in the Bengal school. Many of the prominent artists before independence – from Abanindranath Tagore to Jamini Roy – had come from Shantiniketan. The Progressive Artists Group sought a more radical approach, calling for greater contact with international modernism. The most outspoken of the group was Souza, who dismissed the Bengal school altogether (though many art historians consider unfairly) as derivative of an older British style.

By the 1950s most members of the group had actually gone abroad to experience and participate in an international arena. Souza (who left India in 1949 when some of his work was accused of obscenity) and Avinash Chandra, a Delhi-trained painter, were among popular artists in London in the late 1950s and early 1960s. Their work was collected by the Tate Gallery and the Victoria and Albert Museums. And although Husain did not – at that point – move abroad, the recognition that he received in France, England, and Latin America enhanced his prestige in India as well.

Most critics claim that sales of art and support of artists was slow to develop in major Indian cities. Roy Craven, who had a Fulbright Scholarship to study contemporary Indian art in 1964, noted at the time that most exhibitions in Mumbai consisted of one-artist shows in rented gallery space (Craven, 1965: 227). However, with increasing recognition from abroad and steady government purchases for public buildings and Air India, a market in art gradually emerged. Commercial galleries opened and expanded, beginning in 1959 with the appropriately named Gallery 59, established by the painter Bal Chhabda, in the Bhulabhai Institute in Mumbai. Several more galleries, particularly in Mumbai and Delhi, opened in rapid succession.

Perhaps responding to the call of the Progressive Artists, most art in the 1950s and early 1960s was essentially experimental and the art scene was not financially viable. Those artists who travelled to Europe found that after a brief moment of attention, they did not achieve commercial success or institutional recognition.

Souza's frustration and alienation in Europe seemed to manifest in his paintings of the time – haunted lonely figures in melancholy tones. Tyeb Mehta in the 1950s produced bold figures symbolically reflecting the times. Often in his paintings human figures morphed into animals of different traits. Or similarly, a painting in 1955 of 'a giant bull all trussed up and lying helplessly on the ground' suggests that even great personal power or will was being restrained in the world he saw around him (Khanna and Kurtha, 1998: 30) [Doc. 17, p. 148].

Art historian Vidya Dehejia describes this moment as part of a universal struggle between modernity and traditional forms. 'Defining and grappling with modern identity is an important part of being an artist, and is relevant whether a person is living in the subcontinent or elsewhere' (Dehejia, 1997:

411). For artists from Husain to Souza and Mehta, the process of being modern and Indian was reflected in the forms, style and elements of their work and indeed changed over time.

The experimentalism of the 1950s gave way to greater realism as the 1960s progressed. Art historians Bajraj Khanna and Aziz Kurtha attribute the change to the politics of the decade – the 1962 war with China and the 1965 war with Pakistan – while Shiv Kumar suggests a disillusionment with Western art movements. Or in Dehejia's terms, the struggle for Indian modernity took on new shapes that invested more heavily in traditional Indian art forms. For example, one can see suggestions of the *Hamza Nama* (a medieval illuminated manuscript) on later works by Mehta (Khanna and Kurtha, 1998: 31), or in a series of important paintings in the mid-1960s, K. C. S. Panikar used words, language and Hindu symbols as a way to claim an Indian idiom. Panikar, in describing his art, suggested that Western art had ceased 'to be a vital source for the Indian *avant-garde*'. Rather he claimed he was 'guided by what he called "man's racial and national sense of seeing and shaping"' (Kumar, 1999: 19). Panikar's students went on to form the Cholamandal Artists Village, which supported this vision to look in Indian art forms for inspiration to 'fuse the apparent contradictions' between modern art as it evolved in the West and 'life in India today' (Tuli, 1998: 215).

Following similar instincts Meera Mukherjee not only appropriated the artistic design she saw in tribal art in Bengal, but actually learned wax rope techniques to create modern bronze sculpture inspired by Bastar tribal work. Her sculpture, 'Spirit of Daily Work', in the National Gallery of Modern Art illustrates this blending of forms. It characterizes her use of powerful female forms engaged in everyday situations and in this case the woman carrying a sieve looks at the viewer in a defiant stance [**Doc. 18, p. 148**]. The recognition Mukherjee achieved also paved the way for tribal artists, such as the Gond artist, Jangarh Singh Shyam, to be recognized by the art establishment.

A parallel development was occurring in handicrafts and village industries, i.e., government support, increased marketing, and changing designs. The government established the Central Cottage Industries Emporium in 1948 to promote small-scale industries and crafts and it became a premier buyer of local crafts as well as a high profile shop that welcomed international dignitaries as well as tourists and urban customers. Meanwhile, women politicians and volunteers working in refugee camps saw handicrafts as a means to mobilize women in the camps in ways that validated their cultural traditions, provided meaningful work and gained them a small income. The Refugee Handicrafts Sale Room later merged into the Cottage Industries Emporium. Similarly the All India Handicrafts Board advised the government of problems in handicraft industries and means to promote their development, preservation, and sale. Among its tasks was to collect examples of traditional arts for reference by artisans. A key player in the promotion of handicrafts, Pupul Jayakar, chaired the All India Handicrafts Board in the 1960s and promoted crafts as small-scale industry, both for export and domestic consumption. Jayakar brought Indian textiles and crafts to international attention in a series of Festivals of India in France, the United States, and Japan. She developed, with international support and consultation, the National Institute of Design (1961) that encouraged interdisciplinary attention to design that integrated traditional crafts and modernist trends. Finally, as an interesting twist on museums of art addressed above and the museums of history described below, she was instrumental in the establishment of the National Handicraft and Handlooms Museum, using crafts collected over decades and creating an arena of living artistic production with craft demonstrations on a daily basis.

NATIONAL MUSEUMS

The National Museum in New Delhi, inaugurated in 1949 to portray India's past, was not the first museum of history and archaeology in India. Antecedents existed in Calcutta, Bombay, and Madras. However, the impulse to create, project, and display the heritage of the new nation shaped the character of all these museums in the post-independence period. Writing in 2002, an official retrospective of the National Museum described its birth as requiring the end of colonial rule. While there had been attempts before independence to create a museum in Delhi, the process was fraught with controversy. In the Museum's words the 'time was never "opportune" [to implement plans for a museum] until a National Government with proper respect of its country's great heritage of artistry and craftsmanship could cut the knot of bureaucratic indifference and push ahead for the fulfilment of a long cherished dream' (Mathur 2002: 7). In this way the Museum portrays its own origins as a nationalist project. But before looking at the National Museum in detail, it is important to demonstrate the influence of older museums in India. India, in fact, held some of the oldest museums in the world and these too were reinvigorated by independence.

The Indian Museum in Calcutta was established in 1814 (one of the nine oldest in the world) and the Madras Government Museum was established in 1851. Built according to colonial interests, these older museums contained botanical, artistic, archaeological, and anthropological materials, not only from India, but other parts of the empire. Following independence, the question of ownership of certain objects came into play, reflecting the realities of a post-colonial era.

For example, the Madras Museum originally housed a series of friezes from a nineteenth-century excavation of an ancient Buddhist site (first to third centuries) near Amaravati in what is now Andhra Pradesh. The journey of Amaravati slabs shows the role of colonialism in museum building. A British colonel uncovered the stupa (a central feature of a Buddhist religious site) in 1796 and after excavations in 1845 and 1880 many of the carved limestone slabs were removed to the museum in Madras. Ultimately, officials transferred some twenty stones depicting Buddhist imagery and the life of the Buddha to the British Museum in London. Other objects from the Amaravati excavation remain in Madras. But a few from the British Museum are now displayed in the National Museum in Delhi and whether they were 'loaned' or 'returned' has been a matter of perspective. Discussions about who has the right to the Amaravati artifacts have periodically reopened among the parties. Both the British Museum and the Madras Museum include the story of Amaravati excavations as part of their histories.

The museum's role in the modern Indian state as a repository of Indian pasts and a showcase of objects from other cultures was broadened when Nehru inaugurated the National Art Gallery of Madras in 1951 on the same site. The Government Museum of Madras, therefore, became part of a modernizing mission of constructing museums for the state and also of integrating South India into the national project. The museum served to link artists from Bengal (celebrated in great detail in the *Museum Handbook*) to modernist artists in Madras. Among the works acquired for an anniversary exhibition were paintings by Jamini Roy and K. C. S. Panikar, illustrating the very different traditions that had developed in modern art across the country. This was especially important in 1951, when questions about regional identity and the integrity of the nation were fresh topics of debate.

If the Madras Museum was reinvigorated by independence, the National Museum in New Delhi was created by it. The core collection for the National Museum came from an exhibition held at Burlington House in London in 1947–48 and organized by the Royal Academy. It comprised 5000 years of Indian art borrowed from museums across undivided India as well as from private collections. After the London showing, the Indian Government displayed the collection at Rashtrapati Bhavan (the house of the Indian president) in Delhi and ultimately acquired it for permanent display (*A Guide to the National Museum*, 1977). The collection remained in Rashtrapati Bhavan until its own building was opened in 1960. At the time of the new building's inauguration, Humayun Kabir, Minister of Scientific Research and Cultural Affairs, said that he had once remarked to a friend, 'Delhi, though capital of the Indian Republic, could at best be described as a populous village, for it lacked the essential marks of a city so long as it was without a National Library, a National Museum, and a National Theatre' (Mathur, 2002: 9) [**Doc. 19, pp. 148–9**]. His comment emphasized the theme of the decade – modernism and nationalism expressed in cities and through the arts.

The National Museum, however, also staked claim to history-making. Through its exhibition of ancient Mohenjo Dara and Harappan artefacts (about 2600 BCE), it reaffirmed modern India's connection to the first civilizations of South Asia, even though their ruins fell within the political boundaries of Pakistan [Doc. 20, p. 150]. Interestingly, the national project was further advanced through internationalism. The museums saw part of their educational mission as bringing international art and history to India. As Robert Anderson, former Director of the British Museum, observed, this is an unusual impulse; most world museums served a national rather than international function (Anderson, 2005). But in this case, building on older diverse collections, Indian museums demonstrated the nation's integration into the modern world. The Indian Museum in Calcutta, for example, maintained a large collection of Tibetan thangkas and Southeast Asian art and artefacts. In addition, the Prince of Wales Museum of Bombay (now Chhatrapati Shivaji Museum in Mumbai), which possessed a collection of Chinese jade, donated by the Indian industrialist family, the Tatas, has planned a new global gallery to display international exhibitions.

NATIONALIST LITERATURES IN A MULTI-LINGUAL NATION

Like the museum project, the government's establishment of centres for art and culture – the Sahitya Akademi, the Sri Ram Centre for the Arts, the Lalit Kala Akademi – were intended to encourage cultural expression, further the aim of national integration, and promote the education of arts to the next generation. The Sahitya Akademi, dedicated to promoting literature, is an especially interesting example because its founding in 1954 accompanied a high stakes debate over national language [Doc. 21, p. 150].

According to the Constitution, Hindi became India's official language at the time of independence. However, a majority of Indians did not speak Hindi and so the Constitution assured that regional languages could be established as the standard in the states and that any citizen for purposes of redress could use their own language as listed in The Eighth Schedule of the Constitution (Article 344 and 351) [Doc. 22, p. 151], In addition, English – for a period of 15 years – would be retained for inter-state and Central Government communication.

The Official Language Commission [Doc. 23, pp. 151–3], established under Constitutional authority to review the situation, stated the problem succinctly: how does the government achieve 'the enfranchisement of the regional languages in appropriate fields and the forging of a common medium of expression for all relevant purposes . . . of pan-Indian intercourse'? The

Report's answer was that Hindi would in the future become the 'obvious linguistic medium' because at the time it was the language spoken by the single largest linguistic group. The Commission argued for the phasing out of English, since 'only about 1 per cent of the population has presently anything like an adequate linguistic ability in English' (*Report of the Language Commission*, 1956: 12).

Not surprisingly the most passionate passages of the Commission's report came from dissenters who feared 'Hindi imperialism'. In political terms, Suniti Kumar Chatterji wrote in his dissent to the *Official Language Report* that Linguism (i.e., Hindi chauvinism) would ultimately develop among Hindi speakers, if it were privileged as the national language. Rather, he called for the maintenance of the *status quo* – English as the medium of inter-state communication – with the voluntary promotion of Hindi in non-Hindi speaking states.

The *Official Language Report* reflected rather than anticipated on-the-ground politics in India. The states of India, which were established at the time of independence, had initially followed the geographic boundaries of older British Provinces, but almost immediately protests from language groups called for recognition of their own regions as states as well. The example of Goa in the previous chapter illustrated this point and Goa was caught in the longstanding battle in Maharashtra about its linguistic identity. One of the most vocal language movements emerged among Telegu speakers in Madras State. The capital of Madras lay in a region of the state dominated by the Tamil language, but the northeast part of the state was largely Telegu-speaking. In addition there were Kanada and Malayalam speaking areas. In 1953 after protests and the victory of pro-Telegu parties, the government carved out an Andhra State from the northern districts.

So just as the Official Languages Commission was deliberating language policy another group, the States Reorganization Commission, was contemplating a structure for the nation based on linguistic states. In 1956, as both commissions concluded, Parliament passed the States Reorganization Act, based on that commission's recommendations to divide states along linguistic lines. For example, the Andhra State created in 1953 gained a number of additional districts carved out of the Telegu-speaking regions of Hyderabad state, to be called Andhra Pradesh. Interestingly, despite linguistic commonalities, the regions of Andhra Pradesh continued to have different cultural identities, periodically manifesting in calls for separate states within Andhra. In particular, Telangana called for separate status on into the twenty-first century.

If the making of states seemed a partial political solution, the Official Languages Commission also saw the need to advance unity in a multi-lingual society. Suniti Kumar Chatterji, therefore proposed that the key to national integration was learning one another's languages. Just as he supported teaching Hindi in schools where Hindi was not the local language, he recommended that 'making one of the Modern Indian Languages (other than Hindi or Urdu) a compulsory subject of study for Hindi-speaking areas will be a very helpful gesture of voluntary reciprocity which will largely conduce to inter-lingual understanding'. This recommendation, which came to be called the three-language policy, was implemented in some Indian schools (Chatterji, 1956: 281).

As a consequence, government publishing and promotion of literature in regional languages underscored the balance Nehru wanted to strike between establishing 'a national literature' on the one hand and promoting multi-culturalism on other. This was a difficult task, as literary critic, Aijaz Ahmad, states unequivocally, 'At some level, of course, every book written by an Indian, inside the country or abroad, is part of a thing called "Indian literature."' 'But,' he goes on to write, 'the institution that could produce a coherent and unified knowledge of the various language-literature clusters in India' com-paratively, systematically, or holistically does not exist (Ahmad, 1992: 246). However, in the 1950s the government did make an effort to create one – the Sahitya Akademi – and its continuing efforts have indeed promoted a wide range of Indian literatures.

The founding of the Sahitya Akademi was part of an artistic solution to the political as well as intellectual challenges of a multi-lingual nation. Inaugurated by the government in 1954, the Sahitya Akademi held as its mission to be India's National Academy of Letters, a 'central institution for literary dialogue, publication, and promotion in the country' (Sahitya Akademi, 2008). It promotes literary excellence through book awards in 22 languages, including English, and engages in translation projects from one language to another. By 1956 it became a society autonomous with the government and its broad mandate plus limited resources mean that it has neither the authority nor the ability to be comprehensive.

Other efforts to promote literatures as a force to bridge, rather than divide, language groups emerged in universities. Beginning in the 1950s and 1960s universities developed and expanded their departments of languages and literatures. As a result there was a dramatic increase in translations by the end of the century, as these students began working in universities themselves.

E. V. Ramakrishnan, a scholar and writer in English and Malayalam, com-mented in an edited collection of short stories that he published for the Sahitya Akademi, that he found important commonalities in the literature he collected for the book. True to the mission of the Akademi, his aim, collect-ing stories from a variety of languages, translated into English and spanning the twentieth century, was to present a provisional history of modern Indian literatures across regions – and to identify some common themes.

For example, he found that writers in the 1950s and 1960s shared a profound sense of dislocation, which he identified not as the dislocation of colonialism, but rather a consequence of two frustrations with independent India. First, there was frustration with the increasing consolidation of the Indian state as a source of power. Then toward the end of the 1960s there was a more individualized dislocation, reflecting the migration of elites for education and opportunity from villages to towns and from provincial towns to metropolitan centres in India and abroad. Individuals, who anticipated that independence would bring greater inclusion in the governing of the country, now saw the state as a separate and bureaucratic institution, and those who left the communities they knew for larger environments wrote about a profound alienation. Illustrating this expression of alienation in the volume are stories from G. A. Kulkarni (Marathi), M. Mukundan (Malayalam), and Nirmal Verma, and Krishna Baldev Vaid (Hindi).

If Ramakrishnan's impressions do suggest a trend, it reveals a slightly different pattern than the one apparent in modern art. Modernism in the short story may have manifested in more intimate forms or in different timeframes. What art historians call the realism of the 1960s, Ramakrishnan identifies in the fiction of the 1980s. At this juncture, he argues a new generation of radical writers (such as Mahasweta Devi and Baburao Bagul) forcefully interrogated social categories of caste, family, and gender, using what he calls neo-realist style that moved back and forth between the 'inner and outer' worlds of the characters (Ramakrishnan, 2000: 215, 217).

Similar concerns emerged in Indian film, both popular film and more obviously in the genre known as art film. However, unlike painting or literature, which was part of the purview of the Ministry of Education and Culture, film was part of the Ministry of Information and Broadcasting, where it received greater government scrutiny and censorship. However, if the promotion of literary translation seemed to fit the goal for linguistic unity, film advanced that aim even more vigorously. Regional language films flourished, encouraging Tamil, Telegu, and Bengali cinema traditions, but at the same time the Hindi films of Bollywood generated a common idiom and provided a popular incentive to understand Hindi – one the government could never have imposed.

FILM

India's film industry, which by 1978 became the largest in the world, had already earned acclaim in the 1950s. By 1958 a number of Indian films received official recognition at Cannes, the Oscars, and the well-known Karlovary festival in Czechoslovakia. In 1952, India held its own international festival featuring entries from Japan, eastern Europe and the Soviet Union, an event that filmmaker Shyam Benegal claims had 'far-reaching influence' on the direction of Indian films (Damodaran and Unnithan-Kumar, 2000: 319). Then in 1960, the Indian Government established the Film Finance Corporation and the National Film School, to demonstrate (if belatedly) its material commitment to film.

Unlike its promotion of art, literature and architecture, the government of independent India had an ambivalent relationship with film. The government understood the power of movies in the popular imagination and sought ways to associate with it – especially in the international arena – but also ways to control it and benefit from it – through censorship and taxation.

The 1940s, 1950s, and 1960s were heralded as a 'Golden Age of Indian Cinema'. The period was known for the rising popularity of great male and female leads, such as Nargis and Raj Kapoor. Raj Kapoor, who was also a filmmaker, along with Mehboob Khan and Bimal Roy, produced some of the most creative cinema of the day. But there was also some diversity in the kinds of productions. Often a distinction is drawn between commercially successful formula films – romances, melodramas and comedies – produced in Bombay, and art films – with political themes – produced in Bengal. Regional language cinema in Tamil or Kannada also had an established tradition and, in fact, there were as many south Indian cinema halls, playing films in these regional languages, as there were cinema halls across the Hindi-speaking north. Still, despite the differences, perhaps more interesting was the fluidity among the different industries. Often the same actors, directors, and financiers crossed over from one arena or even one language to another (Chakravarty, 1993: 44, Ahmed, 1992: 292).

Hindi films brought exciting, and often convoluted, plots to a big screen, which still might not seem big enough for extravagant dance numbers or dramatic fight scenes it contained. When critics and film historians write about the Hindi films of Bombay, they inevitably comment that they were largely formulaic: dependent on the appeal of one or two big stars usually engaged in a romantic plot. But the formula drew huge crowds not only in India but abroad as well. Hindi films were known for incorporated singing and dancing to highlight the romance and provide relief to the dominant mode of melodrama. A common narrative in films involved the chance meeting of a hero and heroine, who then must overcome obstacles – usually provided by the movie's villain – ultimately to be united in the end. Into this basic story were interjected lengthy and increasingly complicated song and dance sequences.

Centred in Bombay, and hence later taking on the moniker 'Bollywood', the Hindi film industry prospered on the success of this formula. The best filmmakers demonstrated their distinction even within this mode. Raj

Kapoor, for example, blended the patterns established for popular films with his own sense of realism in post-independence India. He produced and directed a series of films ('Awara', 'Shree 420') that featured the underdog hero, a poor villager who overcomes adversity and makes it as a success in the end. Films that explored such social issues, were in fact termed, 'the social'.

One 'social', 'Shree 420', featured Raju, an honest, educated village boy (played by Raj Kapoor), who comes to Bombay in search of a job. Unable to make a living he finds himself on the street and is then drawn into the corrupt and criminal world of Seth Dharmanand, who has a scheme to exploit the poor by promising them cheap houses. The drama of the film is Raju's dilemma between Vidya (a school teacher, with whom he has fallen in love) and Seth. Kapoor manages to portray the story in a light-hearted Chaplinesque manner. But the moral outcome – Raju's break with Seth (with Vidya's intervention) – defeats the source of exploitation (Shree 420, 1955).

'Shree 420', named for Section 420 of the Indian penal code, under which defrauders and dacoits (bandits) are prosecuted, was written by K. A. Abbas, a leftist writer, who began his career in Calcutta in the Indian People's Theatre Association. Raj Kapoor collaborated with Abbas on several of his screenplays based on a common attraction to proletarian themes.

In the spirit of the era, their films met immediate international success in Arab countries, the Soviet Union, and China. Soon Raj Kapoor and his co-star Nargis, were international hits. Just as the subject matter attracted audiences in socialist and developing countries, equally critical to their films' appeal was the chemistry between Kapoor and Nargis who carried on a long-term affair. Audiences looked forward, in part, to the on- and off-screen romance of the two actors.

Nargis also played the lead in the most overtly nationalist film of the decade – 'Mother India', in which she embodies India through the character of Radha. Radha, a peasant woman raising four sons on her own, faces tragedy and adversity, but ultimately becomes the matriarch of her village through her perseverance. She fights against nature, bad luck, and the manipulations of the local moneylender, who both cheats her and tries to extort her into being his mistress. The nationalist themes are underscored visually; for example, during a scene, as Radha sings to villagers about Mother Earth, following devastating floods that killed two of her sons, 'a map of pre-Partition India forms on the screen' (Roy, 1998: 159). In the end, Radha is forced to kill one of her remaining two sons who has become a bandit and threatens the welfare of the village. The personal drama of the story, which reaches epic proportions, also plays out against the backdrop of the story of the coming of modernity. The film begins with tractors, power lines, and construction machinery and ends with the opening of a life-saving dam ('Mother India', 1957).

Both 'Shree 420' and 'Mother India' demonstrated that in the hands of the most creative directors – Raj Kapoor and Mehboob Khan – the formula of Hindi cinema could indeed dramatise fundamental questions facing Indian society in the 1950s. But the ritual patterns of the Bollywood formula seemed constrictive to other filmmakers. An alternative cinema reflecting different styles had developed particularly in Bengal, following the path-breaking film, 'Pather Panchali' (Song of the Road) (1955) by Satyajit Ray.

Ray, who, like the artist Jamini Roy, had been trained at Shantiniketan, came out of the Bengal tradition of art and literature. Not surprisingly, 'Pather Panchali' took an acclaimed literary work by Bibhutibhushan Banerjee and translated it to the screen. The story takes place in an early twentieth century village where a family struggles with the daily challenges of rural life. The three-dimensional characters – particularly, the daughter, Durga, and son, Apu – present a children's view of the world. The film ends when Durga dies tragically from illness, following the monsoon rains (which, of course, are also the source of life, permitting crops to grow in the fields). The small family then slowly leaves the village to try to start over in the city of Benares.

As director, Shyam Benegal, puts it, 'Pather Panchali' 'was neither experimental in nature, nor did the form seem untraditional'. Rather it used 'a language and idiom that transcended regional and national borders and made' the story of Apu's family 'universal'. In fact, it was nominated for an Oscar for best foreign film in 1956. Its critical success inspired other independent filmmakers, such as Mrinal Sen and Ritwik Ghatak, who used individual style to produce films that challenged the Hindi film pattern. By and large this new cinema remained associated with Bengali films for most of the 1960s.

As Benegal sees the history of Indian cinema, not until the 1970s, with the film 'Garam Hawa' by M. S. Sathyu, did this form of realism find commercial success in Bombay. 'Garam Hawa' powerfully portrayed the human challenges of Partition – a subject so painful that it was only rarely addressed in most art and literature for decades. It succeeded financially where Raj Kapoor's 'Boot Polish' (1954), about street children who make a living shining shoes, and Bimal Roy's 'Do Bigha Zamin' (1953), about a peasant family's struggle for control over its land, did not.

Meanwhile, the international acclaim, nationalist sentiments, and, of course, mass appeal of Indian films, attracted government attention. As a result, the government established the Film Finance Corporation in 1960, which helped support innovation in film production. On the other hand, the state levied increasing taxes on film, which generated ill-will in the industry. In addition, filmmakers had to contend with the capricious rulings and increased vigilance of government censors [**Doc. 24, p. 153**]. For example, in 1953, the Central Board of Film Censors announced a move to examine all stories and scripts before they reached the set.

Frustrated by heavy taxation and censorship, the film industry established its own organizations such as the Film Federation of India, founded in 1951 to negotiate with the government, and the Indian Motion Picture Producers Association, to find private sources to finance projects. Filmmakers also relied on long-term contracts with stars, who often served as the main draw.

As an ambassador of Indian culture, Bollywood was welcome especially in cinemas in the Arab world and Eastern Europe. The Soviet adoration of Indian actors manifested in a brisk trade in posters and frequent invitations for Russian travel. Raj Kapoor, a Soviet favourite, in part because of the socialist themes in some of his dramas, capitalized on his popularity designing films with the Soviet market in mind. In fact, 'Mera Naam Joker' (1970), which was a powerful story about the hardships of life as a circus clown, featured a prominent Russian trapeze artist and actress, Kseniya Ryabinkina. The setting – a visiting Russian circus in India – placed Ryabinkina and Kapoor in starring roles, highlighting the struggle to communicate, across linguistic and cultural barriers. Another Indian film, 'Disco Dancer' (1983), starring Mithun Chakraborty, took Soviet cinemas by storm, bringing a Western style dance to a Soviet audience, which, in the Cold War, did not have access to the original Western version.

CONCLUSION

Art served as a means for expression of the challenges and frustrations facing a new Indian nation in the 1950s, but it also, as so much else, engaged in the nation-building project. This chapter does not propose a unitary purpose of vision in art, literature, film, or architecture, but rather that the period from the late 1940s to the 1970s reflected experimentation in artistic forms – some popular, others more narrow in audience. The needs of the nation underwrote some kinds of art – architecture, translation projects, etc., but cultural expression was also a popular sport generated from the ground up by writers, filmmakers, and painters. This chapter has moved back and forth between institutional and artistic imperatives because neither existed in a vacuum. Nor did they remain apart from the politics of age.

By the twenty-first century, Bollywood cinema attained status as an international phenomenon, even its music transcending the genre and appearing in stage and film productions in other countries and cultures in surprising ways. The American film 'The Inside Man' (2006), which has no Indian cultural references in its characters or plot, begins with Bollywood music, and the British production, 'Slumdog Millionaire' (2008), relied on Indian influence for award-winning success.

Indian literature has transcended the nation as well, both at the forefront of an academic study of what is called post-colonial literature and in prize winning circles. The Indian-born writer, Anita Desai won the Sahitya Akademi award for literary excellence in 1978 for her novel, *Fire on the Mountain*, and was shortlisted, at least three times for the Booker Prize in England for later work. Other Indian novelists – living at home or abroad – who reflected on the conditions of the state and the consequences of imperialism – Salman Rushdie, Amitav Ghosh, and Rohinton Mistry – have produced images of the Indian nation that find resonance both inside and outside India. Therefore, even as Indian artistic production has expressed national and nationalist themes, it has influenced larger movements of cultural production in the world.

In the early period of independence, as artists, architects, writers and film-makers came to terms with modernity, modernism played a central role in representing independent India. Nationalist expression, regional integration, urbanism, and internationalism all manifested in the arts and in government promotion (or influence upon) the arts. Set against the cultural products of artists and writers were the monumental and institutional achievements of architects and museum planners, who gave shape and structure to independent India's representation of national culture. The changing nature of national identity became expressed in political movements described in the next chapter.

4

Green and other revolutions

When Indira Gandhi became prime minister on 24 January 1966, no one imagined how India would be transformed under her stewardship. In twelve years, India moved from being dependent on the international community for food to becoming a food exporter. In addition, in contrast to the non-definitive military conflicts of the 1960s, it soundly defeated Pakistan in a war that created the new nation of Bangladesh. Meanwhile, India experienced widespread political mobilization by peasants and other disadvantaged groups – both non-violent and violent – over unfulfilled promises of development and the need for social and political change. Following this and in a shocking departure from democracy, Indira Gandhi imposed an 'Emergency' in 1975, suspending civil liberties, arresting opponents, and postponing elections. In doing so, Indira Gandhi was exercising a provision in the Constitution that provided 'Emergency powers' under the extraordinary circumstances of a threat to the nation. This chapter is not about the Emergency – that comes in Chapter 5 – however, the political movements and monumental events described in this chapter are linked historically to the Emergency and so it appears, tangentially, in these pages as well.

Specifically this chapter traces the rapid economic and political change from 1965 to 1975, in terms of the fissures and frustrations it exposed in Indian society. It is not surprising that such names as the **Green Revolution**, the **Total Revolution**, and the Naxalbari Rebellion attached to this time. Nor is it surprising, that political opponents call this period, 'Indira Raj', underscoring the prime minister's increasingly autocratic power as ultimately demonstrated in the Emergency.

Therefore, this chapter is about sweeping political and economic changes and some of their unintended consequences. But there is a lesson about history here too. This period – and this chapter – illustrates three important characteristics of post-independent Indian history. First of all, national politics

Green Revolution: The period in the late 1960s and early 1970s during which there was a dramatic increase in agricultural output in India, particularly of rice and wheat, made possible by new technologies and research into special varieties of food grains.

Total Revolution: The Movement backed by Jaya Prakash Narayan and centred in Bihar in the 1970s to call for the fulfillment of promises for increased social equality that had been incorporated into the Constitution.

as practiced by leaders and elites is always in dialogue (if not literally, then figuratively) with Indian citizens. Perhaps it is a legacy of the Freedom Movement that movement politics, grassroots organizing, and public protest are never far from the surface. Indian people articulate their political aspirations in all sorts of ways to get the attention of those in power. The dialogue is not always successful and the consequences are not always intended, but one can hear the voices of politics in every arena. Second, young and old intellectuals in India engage in politics at all levels – as activists, as student protestors, as members of government, as those lobbying government, and as those explaining the issues of the day. Therefore, the sources of history – newspapers, manifestoes, posters and wall paintings – are often the products of history-makers themselves.

However, there are two caveats to the shape of the discussion set out in this chapter. First, it is important to recognize that even in these dramatic times, everyday life continued. Women and men in villages woke up to go to the fields and plant paddy. Little girls in crisp white skirts gathered their books tied with a strap and went to school. The annual Madras music season featured thousands of performances with increased demand in the early 1970s, and theatres filled with spectators watched Amitabh Bachchan, the great cinematic hero, in films such as 'Dewar' in 1975.

Second, despite Indira Gandhi's overwhelming power, the prime minister is not the dominant character in this chapter. A series of other, particularly economic and social forces, shaped events in this period as well. For example, the so-called Green Revolution in high-yielding grains that transformed Indian agriculture began in the term of Indira Gandhi's predecessor, Prime Minister Lal Bahadur Shastri. The peasant rebellion in the Naxalbari district of Bengal, which has come to symbolize armed agrarian resistance in general, originated as a regional phenomenon, not directly related to Mrs. Ghandi administration. But the collective consequences of all these events ultimately did connect to the Indian Government as a whole.

This chapter, therefore, which begins with the Green Revolution, traces other dramatic – similarly revolutionary – transformations, such as the Naxalite Rebellion, the Bangladesh War, the Anti-Price Rise Movement, Jaya Prakash Narayan's Total Revolution, and the call by the Committee on the Status of Women for radical measures to assure women's equality. As Nandita Gandhi said in relation to the Anti-Price Rise Movement, 'there is a "culture" of politics that has evolved, and been developed by women and men in different ways as a result of their historical experiences, and their expectations of the political system' (N. Gandhi, 1996: 14). This chapter provides much evidence for the diversity of that political culture as it was projected in the 1960s and 1970s.

THE GREEN REVOLUTION

The Green Revolution was in many ways neither 'green', at least in the current use of that term, nor was it a 'revolution' in the political sense and it was not a solely Indian phenomenon. Rather it was a globally supported movement to increase crop yields through chemically and technologically enhanced agriculture. In the 1960s Indian economic development, as elaborated in the First and Second Five year plans initiated by Jawaharlal Nehru, emphasized centralized planning, industrial growth and improvement of infrastructure. Through models developed by P. C. Mahalanobis (who was by training a physicist and statistician) the Indian economy pursued a policy of import substitution that concentrated government resources on the heavy industries. By the mid-1960s, it became apparent that these development models increased, rather than alleviated, social and economic inequality; bureaucratic, entrepreneurial, and professional classes faired far better than urban workers or anyone in the countryside.

Two immediate effects were significant. First of all, while legislation for zamindari abolition (i.e., reform of the land system) had been introduced, the actual reallocation of land was slow to take place, where it happened at all. Landlords used loopholes to retain property or gave it to loyal tenant cultivators and relatives. In addition, peasant cultivators who gained land often found access to seeds, water, and markets still out of their control. As a result, opposition political parties began calling for more intervention by the government [**Doc. 25, p. 154**].

Second, and perhaps related to the first, India continued to have food shortfalls, due to inefficient production as well as droughts and floods; India, therefore, imported grain in large quantities. An innovative example of a trade deal from this period arose between India and the United States, under the PL480 programme, a law that permitted developing countries to purchase grain with their own currency. One consequence of PL480 trade with India was the development and advancement of the field of South Asian studies in the United States. The U. S. Government made the rupees available to major research centres to build their library collections and support research abroad in India.

From India's point of view, however, relying on food aid created a complicated relationship with America and undermined its well-cultivated policy of non-alignment. Domestically, it also revealed a blatant contradiction between aggressive industrial growth on the one hand, and gradual agrarian reform on the other, increasing the economic distinctions between wealthy urban and poor rural communities. In the words of the journalist Gurcharan Das, this policy produced 'capitalism for the rich and socialism for the poor'. But, he claimed, neither was working (Das, 2002: 130).

In 1965, after Nehru's death, he was succeeded by Lal Bahadur Shastri, and a number of pressing domestic and international issues faced the new prime minister. Shastri turned his immediate attention to the confrontation with Pakistan over the Rann of Kutch invasion (on India's west coast) and so did not focus on agricultural issues immediately, but the World Bank pressured him to implement agricultural reforms in order to boost food production. Therefore, he delegated agricultural decisions to C. Subramaniam, the Minister of Food and Agriculture, who began to implement dramatic changes in agricultural policy.

Subramaniam shared the view advanced by experts from America and the World Bank that massive investment in modern technology provided the key to increased agricultural output. Therefore, he proposed a restructuring of agricultural policy. He abandoned farm cooperatives, a policy inspired by Gandhian philosophy that under the purview of the Community Development Ministry had met with striking failure. Gandhi had believed India's future lay in the establishment of self-sufficient village communities; he had created several of these in his lifetime. Inspired by these, the Community Development Ministry established cooperative societies, largely for the purpose of providing rural credit. While the government targeted 64 per cent participation in cooperative schemes by 1967, in fact participation rates proved as low as 36 per cent and did not improve over time (Bansil, 1975: 261). However, there were some successes in the **cooperative movement**, particularly in the sugar industry. In addition, several states including Punjab, Tamil Nadu, and Andhra Pradesh saw dynamic increases in agricultural loans; however, the number of defaults on loans was staggering.

Instead of increasing support to the cooperative movement, Subramaniam implemented a three-pronged plan that included:

1. new policies, which stressed scientific techniques and privileged regions with assured rainfall or existing irrigation systems;
2. incentives to farmers including fixed prices for agricultural products, and
3. adoption of new high-yield seed varieties, fertilizers, and pesticides.

Eagerly, the United States and the World Bank financed these radical changes in hopes of showing India as a model of agricultural development and food independence in the Third World.

To combat political resistance in Parliament, Subramaniam sought rapid and dramatic results. He embraced the most aggressive policies of agricultural engineering. He reportedly chartered several Boeing 707s and imported 16,000 metric tons of seed of a remarkable dwarf wheat plant created by an American scientist in Mexico. The variety, called 'Lerma Rojo', took off in Punjab, and the production of wheat there tripled from 1951 to 1966 and even more

Cooperative movement: A government programme in the 1950s and 1960s intended to encourage farmers to poor resources, particularly in the area of rural credit. It was inspired by Mahatma Gandhi's philosophy of independent self-sufficient village communities. The programme, however, failed and by 1965, it was abandoned by the government

dramatically nearly doubled again between 1966 and 1968, from 2,494,000 to 4,520,000 tons [**Doc. 26, p. 154**]. However, before these benefits could be fully realized, there was another crisis.

Even as India embarked on what came to be known as the Green Revolution, the monsoon failed in 1965 and its new prime minister, Indira Gandhi, was compelled to seek additional food aid from the United States. Indira Gandhi became prime minister when Lal Bahadur Shastri died in office. She had served as Minister of Broadcasting and as President of the Congress Party previously, but she had little experience in public office. Rather as the daughter of Jawaharlal Nehru she had apprenticed with a great politician.

In the event of the food crisis, her negotiations with Lyndon Johnson in Washington in March 1966 led to a massive injection of assistance in the form of grain and loans. In exchange, Johnson expected further measures in India to reform the economy and increase food production and Mrs. Gandhi did, in fact, devalue the rupee. However, the discomfort of the encounter furthered her commitment to show India's independence and non-alignment. Therefore, she chose to follow her state visit to Washington with a state visit to the Soviet Union – and this at the peak of the Cold War. She also issued sharp attacks on United States intervention in Viet Nam.

As American dissatisfaction registered (Johnson not only protested, but restricted and trickled out the promised aid), Mrs. Gandhi plunged further into high-yield agricultural policies. C. Subramaniam, who continued to serve as Agriculture Minister, increased support to agricultural institutes and grain research. Particularly, he challenged and supported M. S. Swaminathan at the Indian Agricultural Research Institute in New Delhi to carry out cutting-edge research on wheat and rice varieties. India also invested in rice varieties created in the Philippines and Taiwan. For example, the Taiwanese rice, introduced in Tamil Nadu, was also highly responsive to fertilizer and gave extraordinary yields of 5000 to 6000 pounds per acre – three times that of local varieties.

Overall, the Green Revolution remarkably increased total grain production in India by a factor of 25 per cent by 1971 and by 1975 India reached its goal of food self-sufficiency. Of course, that language of self-sufficiency, so important politically and materially in the 1970s, seems outmoded in today's global economy. In fact in 1979 and 1987 India did import grain in order to deal with droughts. However, the achievement of the Green Revolution was the terms on which agricultural trade now took place and that by the mid-1980s, during the height of the famine in Ethiopia, India provided food aid, as it has in many other crises since then.

Environmental consequences of the Green Revolution took decades to emerge; for example, the depletion of soil, lowering of the water table, and health damage to farmers from heavy chemical fertilizers and pesticides gradually revealed themselves. By the beginning of the twenty-first century,

Punjab, once a key beneficiary of Subramaniam's policies because it already had irrigation systems and received good rainfall, suffered from water shortages because too much water was being pumped out of the ground, and, in addition, dependence on pesticides and mono-cropping made fields vulnerable to new blights. Each new disease or resistant insect required another pesticide and more chemical intervention.

Other consequences of the Green Revolution appeared right away. Agriculture so dependent on special seeds, fertilizers, and pesticides required access to capital. As a result even the benefits of the Green Revolution replicated, and in some cases exacerbated, social and economic inequalities. Peasants in regions not favoured by Green Revolution policy organized resistance. A major peasant rebellion in 1967 in the Naxalbari district of Bengal called attention to a simmering crisis in the countryside, prompted by inadequate land distribution.

THE NAXALBARI REBELLION

Lal inqalab se	The red revolution
Ho gaya, jahan ilaka	has arrived in this whole region
Upar neeche lal	Above and below is red.
Dekh lal aftab,	See the red sunrise
Utho gareeb inqalab	Awaken O poor to revolution.

These words from a revolutionary peasant song expressed the ideological spirit of peasant agitations that had recurred periodically in various parts of India since the 1930s. In most of those examples, the idea of revolution was symbolic and protests were largely non-violent. However, like the Sanghams in the Telangana movement in the state of Hyderabad in the 1950s, another armed struggle emerged in the Naxalbari region of West Bengal in 1967.

The Naxalbari rebellion, named after the district where it took place, reached its peak between March and August of 1967. Initially peasants, many of whom came from the tribal communities of West Bengal, formed village committees to take back land they believed was theirs. They occupied fields, burnt land records and began to arm themselves. According to Prakash Singh, a police officer turned writer, the following event characterizes the early movement:

March 3, 1967: Three sharecroppers, Lapa Kishan, Sangu Kishan and Ratia Kishan, supported by 150 CPI (M) (Communist Party of India-Marxist) [party workers], armed with lathis (wooden staffs) bows and arrows and carrying party flags, lifted the entire stock of paddy (rice) from the [landlord's storehouse] .

(Singh, 1995: 3)

The CPI (M) referred to in Singh's note is a political party that in the1967 election emerged as a major political force in the government of West Bengal. The kind of clash he described continued to take place with increasing violence through to the end of May. Then using massive force and wide-scale arrests, the government suppressed the rebellion by the end of July. Most significant about the Naxalbari rebellion was the high degree of organization. Since the 1950s, peasants of Naxalbari had been locally organized; however, their agitation had become absorbed into the communist movement, so that by 1967, the local CPI (M), cadres (i.e., party workers), of neighbouring towns, Siliguri and Darjeeling, formed a critical part of the resistance.

The causes of unrest were longstanding, having to do with the excesses of power exerted by rural intermediaries, who behaved as landlords, collecting rent and controlling production. They represented the oppressive agrarian system that encouraged peasant indebtedness and landlessness. However, several circumstances in 1967 provided the immediate catalyst for rebellion. Ironically, one of them was the election of a left-wing government in West Bengal, which was obviously caught in the middle by the agitation.

The victory of the United Front in state elections in West Bengal raised hopes for implementation of long-awaited land reform because a key participant in the governing coalition was the CPI (M). The CPI (M) as a political party, resulted from a split of the Communist Party of India in 1964 based on divisions over tactics, strategies and emphases. Those who remained loyal to Soviet-style communism and received support from the USSR kept the name CPI and those who advocated peasant mobilization and perhaps greater sympathy toward Mao became the CPI (M). In fact, in the West Bengal United Front government of 1967, the Minister for Land and Land Revenue, Harekrishna Konar, was a veteran CPI (M) peasant leader. His first stated goal was to enforce existing land ceilings and redistribute land to poor peasants and landless laborers.

However, two factors encouraged rebellion. First of all, Naxalbari, which lies in the far northern part of West Bengal contained a large population of Scheduled Tribe communities – Santhals, Oraons, and Rajbanshis (often called tribals) – who practice different religious and cultural traditions from the largely Hindu and Muslim Bengalis. Tribals felt doubly disenfranchised because their land had increasingly been controlled by non-tribals, such as Hindu Bengalis and other north Indian tea planters. Many of the leaders of the rebellion emerged from these local tribal communities.

Second, the United Front government exacerbated local tensions in part by raising expectations. Even Konar found implementing land reform through legal means frustrating. In the years since land ceilings had been imposed, landlords had found creative means to circumvent them, for example establishing *benami* tenures, i.e., giving away land to loyal peasants and relatives. Also, as soon as Konar announced plans to enforce the law, landlords began evicting peasants to undermine the on-the-ground reality of their claims to the land. So local CPI (M) cadres, who in the past were supporters of rebels, were now tainted by their party's participation in the United Front government. Therefore, to people in Naxalbari, the failures of the United Front revealed the limitations of even an expectedly sympathetic government.

However, the United Front was not perceived as wholly sympathetic. One of the CPI (M)'s first acts upon taking leadership was to distance itself – or at least its legislators in the Assembly – from the peasant movement in Naxalbari. Two prominent leaders, Charu Mazumdar, whose theoretical positions formed a critical basis for the movement, and Kanu Sanyal expressed deep frustration with this rejection by the party. Both had been loyal members of the CPI (M) until this time, and Jangal Santhal, a tribal peasant leader, had actually stood for election to the West Bengal Legislative Assembly on a CPI (M) ticket. However, Santhal and Sanyal were both arrested before the election under the Preventive Detention Act, and Santhal stood for election and was defeated from jail (S. Banerjee, 1985: 84).

Therefore it was in the context of this frustration – not certain where most CPI (M) loyalties lay – that one of the first violent clashes took place on 23 May. Armed tribals killed a policeman, named Sonam Wangdi, who had come to arrest some peasant leaders. The police, with state sanction from the Chief Minister, Ajoy Mukherjee, responded without restraint. According to academic reports, more than 1500 police were dispatched to the region (Franda, 1971). In one police firing nine people were killed. Students, along with some CPI (M) leaders, protested the government action in Calcutta (now Kolkata) demonstrating that divisions were developing within the party.

It was symbolically significant that wall paintings – a popular form of political expression in West Bengal – which some months before promoted CPI (M) candidates, now protested against the same government that the CPI (M) had joined. Between June and August 1967 the peasant committees waged open war, seizing guns and using homemade weapons in violent clashes to take over land and force out landlords. Accounts differ on how the rebellion ended; however, most sources estimate that 1300 people were arrested, including Jangal Santhal, and most of the leadership. The Central Government in Delhi, represented by Home Minister, Y. B. Chavan, provided support and resources to West Bengal to quell the rebellion. It appears that by August the movement had lost its force.

The most lasting consequence of the Naxalbari rebellion was the organized armed insurrection it spawned in a number of rural areas in Andhra Pradesh and later in Tamil Nadu, Punjab, Bihar, and Kerala, under the name 'Naxalites'. While most of the original Naxalbari leaders were arrested in 1967 or in

Kanu Sanyal's case, 1969, Charu Mazumdar remained underground until 1972, and their inheritance continued among diverse and often rival organizations. In fact, the divisions among Naxalite groups manifested in the various names of their organizations – the People's War Group (PWG), Maoist Coordination Committee (MCC), as well as the CPI (M-L), meaning Marxist-Leninist. This splintering of the movement has led to largely local activism among Naxalites and perhaps has diffused the possibility for a unified assault on Indian Government institutions.

However, significant rebellions continued. For example, in the districts of Bihar in the 1980s there were well-organized attacks against landlords in response to highly publicized landlord atrocities and, in Andhra Pradesh from 1980 onwards, the PWG assassinated a member of Parliament and three state-level officials and in 2003 made an attempt to assassinate the chief minister. In some pockets, Naxalite groups maintained semi-autonomous control over villages or even districts in defiance of usual government structures; by contrast in other areas CPI (M-L) candidates ran for public office as part of the electoral system.

The next challenge to face West Bengal, however, was of international implications: in 1971 West Bengal began to absorb a dramatic influx of refugees from East Pakistan, who were fleeing the Pakistani civil war. This crisis triggered India's direct intervention in the creation of the nation of Bangladesh.

INDIA AND THE REVOLT IN EAST PAKISTAN

The Pakistani civil war most immediately presented India with a refugee crisis, but also represented instability on two divergent and strategically important borders. Watching the visible disintegration of India's neighbour and rival, Indira Gandhi entered the war first indirectly, then directly, and achieved India's first decisive military victory. The Bangladesh war in 1971 transformed Indira Gandhi's leadership by consolidating her recent electoral victory and the split she had forced in the Congress Party. Second, it left India undisputedly the most powerful nation in South Asia. To understand this, it is important to examine some of the details of both the war and Indian politics preceding it, because several historical currents came together at this moment in 1971.

Indira Gandhi became prime minister in 1966 at the sufferance of a powerful group of Congress Party leaders called 'the Syndicate'. Faced with the sudden death of Lal Bahadur Shastri and possible instability, the Syndicate chose Indira Gandhi for the post, hoping that they might govern from behind the scenes. However, once in power Mrs. Gandhi immediately tackled a number of pressing domestic problems, as her agricultural policy, cited above, demonstrates. In the 1967 elections, the Congress performed poorly, not only in parliamentary elections but in the state elections as well. The victory of the United Front in West Bengal represented one of six states to form non-Congress governments. Mrs. Gandhi blamed the situation on infighting within the party and saw Congress leaders undermining her control.

She pressed on with a number of controversial policies that appealed to the Left (and particularly the left-wing of the Party), including land reform, increased taxes on wealth, and nationalization of major banks. In addition, she made several personnel decisions that thwarted the Syndicate – relieving Morarji Desai, one of its members, of the finance portfolio and supporting V. V. Giri in the election for President of India over the official Congress nominee. The Congress leadership, which was dominated by the party's conservative wing (and also by the Syndicate to which she was showing her independence), expelled her for 'indiscipline' on 12 November 1969.

However, secure that she had sufficient numbers of loyal followers, Indira Gandhi responded by splitting the party and calling for a confidence vote in Parliament. Although a majority of Congress MPs stayed with her, it was not enough to form a government of its own. She turned, therefore, to the Communist Party and regional parties to build a majority and as a result she remained prime minister. She continued to consolidate her support both in Parliament and among the people. Under the slogan 'garibi hatao' (eliminate poverty), she campaigned throughout the country and emphasized the ideological basis of the party split. This also showed her appreciation for the support of the Communists. Then she called early elections for 1–13 March 1971. The elections confirmed her control over the party: her faction won a larger majority in Parliament in 1971 than the undivided Congress had achieved in 1967.

It was following this decisive victory that Indira Gandhi tackled the political situation rendered by internal conflict in Pakistan. For three months the situation in East Pakistan had been deteriorating, as a Constitutional crisis became a military and humanitarian one. Indira Gandhi used careful diplomacy and strategic military force to advance the interests of both India and the Bangladeshis. This may have been the height of her political prowess.

PAKISTAN'S INTERNAL CONFLICT

Pakistan – East and West – held elections in December 1970, during which cleavages between the eastern and western wings of the nation manifested themselves so severely, they precipitated the secession of East Pakistan. Since

Pakistan's creation in 1947, there remained a number of political imbalances between the East and the West. The military personnel largely came from West Pakistan and its government, which twice had ended in martial law, had always had a West Pakistani leader. Linguistically and culturally, East Pakistan saw itself as distinct, for example, celebrating its Bengali identity through language, rather than adopting the Urdu spoken in West Pakistan. In the 1950s language riots in Dacca (in the East) forced the Pakistan Government to recognize Bengali along with Urdu as co-equal national languages. The Awami League (originally the Awami Muslim League, founded in 1949) advanced the interests of ethnic Bengalis within the Pakistani state.

In 1966, the Awami League leader, Sheikh Mujibur Rahman, announced a Six Point Plan for greater autonomy in East Pakistan. It argued for a more equal distribution of resources for healthcare, schools, and other government services. From the point of view of the national government in the capital of Islamabad – which also was located in the West – Bengali autonomy threatened the integrity of the nation. East Pakistan was larger than any single province in the West and the government was concerned that linguistic autonomy for East Bengal might encourage some of the western linguistic minorities in Baluchistan or Sindh to make similar demands.

Meanwhile, Pakistan prepared for its first direct election to a National Assembly in December 1970. General Yahya Khan, Martial Law Administrator and President of Pakistan, endorsed a Constitution that granted East Pakistan 162 out of 300 seats in the Assembly. This reflected the distribution of population across East and West and served as a gesture toward some of East Pakistan's demands.

The election, however, proved more politically conclusive than expected. Running on the separatist Six Point Plan that outlined Bengali autonomy, the Awami League won 160 of 162 seats in East Pakistan. This gave it an absolute majority, not only in the East, but also in the National legislature. Zulfikar Ali Bhutto's Pakistan Peoples Party, the main contender in the West, did not fair as well; it won only 81 seats, the rest going to small minority parties. Therefore, technically, Sheikh Mujibur Rahman (popularly called Sheikh Mujib) would have become prime minister of the entire nation. However, neither Bhutto nor Yahya Khan found this acceptable and Yahya Khan postponed the inauguration of the National Assembly.

From January to March 1971, negotiations continued in order to resolve what had now become a Constitutional crisis. The Awami League called for non-cooperation in East Pakistan, holding out for the Six Point Plan and regional autonomy. The convulsive response in East Pakistan to non-cooperation reflected longstanding frustrations and there were clashes in the streets. It was on the excuse of quelling this violence that Yahya Khan sent in the army to East Pakistan. But the army too exerted undue force. Students at Dacca

University, intellectuals, and prominent Awami League leaders were rounded up, jailed, or killed, and on 25 March Sheikh Mujib was arrested, though not before he declared Bangladesh an independent nation.

The West Pakistan army then attacked East Pakistan with full force, compelling hundreds of thousands of refugees to flee to India. Especially destructive was a systematic process in the army that intentionally targeted teachers, lawyers, and, in general, the intelligentsia of Bangladesh. Refugee camps too became targets of the Pakistani military. Meanwhile, India began arming Bangladeshi militants called the Mukti Bahini (Freedom Fighters) and became further drawn into the conflict.

The situation in Bangladesh became a test of Indira Gandhi's will. Having just secured her own electoral victory, Mrs. Gandhi became a public and international advocate of the Bangladeshi people. At great cost – from $3 to $4 million a day, the Indian Government fed and housed the continuing flow of refugees. By the end of the summer an estimated 6 million Bangladeshis had fled into India. Rather than immediate military intervention, Mrs. Gandhi began an international tour, presenting the crisis to the world community and pleading for funds for the refugees now living in India. She also called for diplomatic intervention.

Not quite diplomacy, but in August of 1971 a group of rock musicians in conjunction with the famous Indian (and Bengali) sitarist, Ravi Shankar, brought international attention to Bangladesh. Coordinated by Ravi Shankar and George Harrison – a former member of the Beatles, who had begun to practice Hinduism and had significant interest in South Asia – the 'Concert for Bangladesh' proposed to raise funds for Bangladeshi refugees. The concert blurred the various causes of disaster – the 1970 Bhola cyclone and the 1971 civil war – but the event raised a quarter of a million dollars and did more in terms of publicity. On the one hand it perpetuated an image that equated Bangladesh with starvation; on the other it set a precedent for fundraising concerts, which have continued to raise money for international causes since then. Long after the concert, sales from the 'Concert for Bangladesh' album raised fifteen million dollars for UNICEF – the United Nations Children's Fund.

Indira Gandhi's international efforts included a 20-day trip in October to Western Europe, the Soviet Union, and the United States. In Britain, on 31 October, she gave public addresses and also had a private meeting with Prime Minister Edward Heath. Her message was that India was struggling to provide resources for refugees and although she did not wish to entangle Britain in the affairs of South Asia, she hoped they would support the cause of the Bangladeshi state.

Meanwhile also in October, she began to prepare for war; Sam Manekshaw, the head of the Indian Army, recalled later that Indira Gandhi presented him with the problem of the Bangladesh crisis and asked him,

'What are you going to do about it?'

I [Manekshaw] said, 'It's got nothing to do with me.'

She said, 'I want you to do some thing. . . . I want you to march into
    East Pakistan.'

I said, 'Oh, [pause] that means war.'

'I don't mind if it is war,' [she reportedly responded.]

                                    (BBC Interview, Sam Manekshaw, 1997)

In Manekshaw's retelling, the encounter shows Mrs. Gandhi's language of
cautiousness on the one hand, and decisiveness on the other.

The decision for war brought India not only at odds with Pakistan, but
potentially with the United States as well. The USS *Enterprise*, a nuclear-
powered aircraft carrier moved into the Indian Ocean, because America,
reportedly, worried that India would march into West Pakistan as well.
Indira Gandhi, meanwhile criss-crossed the nation building up support for
her upcoming invasion.

On 3 December (one day before India planned its own strike) Pakistan
bombed Indian air bases, so when India marched into Bangladesh the next
day it claimed to be responding to provocation. The Bangladesh war took
only 13 days, ending in Pakistani surrender on 16 December 1971 [**Doc. 27,
pp. 00–00**]. Sheikh Mujib was released from jail and on 12 January 1972
became the first prime minister of Bangladesh.

Mrs. Gandhi's military victory brought her enormous popularity and
international respect. She recognized the new nation of Bangladesh and
immediately signed an agreement of mutual cooperation. For a time she was
fêted both at home and abroad.

But as the Bangladesh crisis subsided, domestic conflicts surfaced again.
In India, Mrs. Gandhi had to contend with a growing popular movement
directed against the consequences of uneven development. One manifestation
of popular dissent was a social movement organized by the veteran socialist
leader, Jaya Prakash Narayan, which attracted students and other supporters,
demanding that the government fulfill the longstanding promises of equality
and prosperity.

TOTAL REVOLUTION AND JP

There were already student protests in Bihar in 1974, when Jaya Prakash
Narayan, a Gandhian and former Freedom Fighter, returned to politics. As
a statesman who inspired great respect from many quarters, JP (as he was
known) had mediated in a number of disputes over the years in Jammu and
Kashmir and elsewhere, doing what he called service to the nation. As a
Bihari himself, he was far from disinterested as he watched the political
movement in Bihar unfold.

Along with left-wing political parties, students were protesting corruption in the educational system and in the Bihar Government. On 18 March 1974 they marched on the Legislative Assembly in Bihar's capital Patna and were met by police who forcefully pushed them back. In the clash that followed a government warehouse and a couple of other buildings were burned and several students were killed and injured. Shocked by the police tactics, JP wrote an article against the repressive use of force against protestors, which the students understood to be a sign of solidarity. As a result they approached him to take up a role of leadership in the movement. JP too was looking for signs that there were patriotic elements organizing for social change. As recorded by his colleague and biographer, Madhu Dandavate, JP described his enthusiasm for the student movement as a continuation of his own quest. 'I was groping in the darkness; but I saw a new rising force of Youth Power' (Dandavate, 2002: 172).

Narayan formed an organization called Citizens for Democracy in order to push for an end to corruption in government and equal access to the resources of the state. The main planks of Citizens for Democracy included:

- strive for free and fair elections,
- create public opinion in favour of freedom and democracy on burning issues of the day,
- create an awareness of civil liberties and defend them through peaceful and legitimate means,
- strive for clean and healthy public life by launching anti-corruption movement, aimed at higher levels of administration and government,
- involve people intelligently in anti-price rise movement,
- to become aware of the faulty machinations of corrupt officials, dishonest businessmen and beguiling politicians and to create the necessary organizations to protect the interests of the consumers.

(Citizens for Democracy, www.healthlibrary.com)

Other protests followed around the state and the police responded severely. In one police firing in Gaya, eight people were killed and others wounded. In response, JP led a silent protest in Patna, calling for restraint. He demanded that the movement remain non-violent and set up a committee to propose electoral reforms and challenge corruption in government.

On 5 June in a rally in Patna, he proclaimed the need for 'Total Revolution', the name that became associated with the movement. Its aim was redemption of the pledge of 1947, when Nehru called for a just and equitable society [**Doc. 1, pp. 134–5**]. JP argued that persisting poverty, landlessness, and soaring prices demonstrated that government had failed in its responsibility to its people [**Doc. 28, pp. 155–8**]. Even more specifically he publicly criticized Mrs. Gandhi and pointed specifically to corrupt practices in Congress governments, not just in Bihar but elsewhere.

JP's threat to Indira Gandhi's government was in part due to his moral authority among her opposition and that his movement had momentum. It inspired a number of young would-be politicians to enter politics and in fact that was one of its legacies. The idea of Total Revolution resonated with other movements taking place around the country. For example, although JP opposed the violence of the Naxalite movement, he expressed sympathy for the tribals' claims to land. He also supported existing movements to fight inflation and the rapid rise in the price of foodstuffs. In this sense, he was appealing to concurrent struggles in other states such as the Anti-Price Rise Movement in Maharashtra.

ANTI-PRICE RISE MOVEMENT

In 1972, protests against the high cost of food responded to a grain and financial crisis induced by the Bangladesh war. Although food production had increased more than 25 per cent by 1971 and the grain stores had been filled by the Green Revolution, the unexpected burden of feeding 6 million refugees had over-taxed the system. Furthermore, the war had depleted the country's financial reserves. Food prices increased and in various cities, people began mobilizing in protest.

Out of necessity and with great reluctance, Indira Gandhi approached the World Bank and International Monetary Fund (IMF). They immediately dispensed necessary funds, but demanded austerity measures in the form of retractions in social programmes and anti-inflation policies, such as freezing wages and increasing exports. The resulting pressure, especially on the urban middle and lower classes, aggravated national protests rather than alleviating them (Frankel, 1978: 515–16).

One story of women's protest against price rises, which took place in Maharashtra, illustrates the culture of mobilization that extended elsewhere. From August 1972 to June 1975 women in Maharasthra staged a series of organized protests against the government in response to prices or scarcity of specific commodities. In three years, there were protests against the level of the quota on grain purchases, the prices of milk and cooking oil, and scarcities of kerosene and other goods. Collectively, the protests came to be called the Anti-Price Rise Movement and it was especially remarkable for the diversity in tactics it comprised, from large rallies to meetings with government officials, and neighbourhood displays of solidarity.

While, even at the time, these collective protests were called a movement, they were in fact more loosely organized than the word 'movement' usually suggests and unlike most movements they were directed at a single issue: food prices. The most complete history of these protests appears in Nandita

Gandhi's book, titled *When the Rolling Pins Hit the Streets*, taking its name from the 'latni morchas,' protest marches of women carrying rolling pins, which were their hallmark (N. Gandhi, 1996). The movement began with informal gatherings that brought together various women's groups to focus on the ongoing crisis caused by inflation. Agreeing that increasing food costs hit women especially hard, leaders of a number of women's organizations, associated mainly with left-wing political parties, formed a common group which they referred to as the Mahangai Pratikar Sanyukta Mahila Andolan (which means women's movement organized against price rises). Among them, for example, was Pramila Dandavate of the Socialist Party, who later became an MP and Mrinal Gore, who was a sitting Member of the Legislative Assembly in Maharashtra and also a future parliamentarian (Jain, 1993: 526).

The nature of the early actions of the Anti-Price Rise Movement (APRM as it was known in English) shows some of the character of the movement. In a public meeting before the Maharashtra Legislative Assembly, women threatened to gherao (lock in) ministers if they did not come up with a policy to address the high price of milk. However, they also presented those ministers with bangles (bracelets) as a sign of bravery to encourage them in their efforts.

Perhaps the most remarkable aspect of the protests was their creative use of symbols. Mrinal Gore described the Samiti's complex tactics this way.

> Women and children could not usually come to morchas so we thought of the *ghanta vadan* or death knell. I announced it in a meeting and asked, 'Will you go to the street corner and beat your *thali* (metal plates) so loud that the city will resound with our noise?' For such a thing women would not have to travel but simply go up to their terraces or street corners. Middle class women preferred meetings to *morchas* (large rallies) so we would keep meetings at regular intervals. *Gheraos* had to be kept secret so we should only call those women who could be easily contacted.
>
> (Gore in Gandhi, 1996: 33)

In this way, different women could participate in ways that were the most productive for them. These were not new tactics – in peasant movements in Bihar in the 1930s, for example, women had beaten pots while men seized crops. But the APRM movement used this combination of tactics and coordination of strategies to strong effect.

The influence of the movement came in its constant pressure on the government, not only in the state, but on Indira Gandhi herself. At a meeting in January 1974 in Maharashtra, Indira Gandhi's speech was disrupted when a large section of her audience hurled shoes and sandals at the dais, shouting '*Bhashan mat do, rashan do*' (Don't give us a speech, give us food rations)' (Masani, 1976: 309).

Seen in the context of other economic protests of the period, the Anti-Price Rise Movement contributed to the environment of protest against the government that had emerged nearly simultaneously from different sections of society and different regions. In the context of women's politics, the APRM encouraged other forms of organizing among women and especially the coordination of disparate groups. This process became hijacked during the Emergency, but reappears later.

TOWARDS WOMEN'S EQUALITY

Committee on the Status of Women in India: Appointed by the government and comprised of academics, politicians, and social workers, the committee's task was to examine in broad terms the status of women in India; its far-reaching report, *Towards Equality*, published in 1974, became influential in government policy-making in the 1980s.

The publication in 1974 of *Towards Equality*, the Report of the National **Committee on the Status of Women in India**, set the stage for decades of discussion and political proposals to address women's ability to gain access to rights assured them in India's Constitution. The Report demonstrated a serious gap between the promises of gender equality enshrined in the Constitution and the women's access to all those promised benefits of citizenship. The Committee's work, coinciding with the ongoing social and political movements discussed in this chapter, and taking place during the prime ministership of an internationally recognized, powerful woman, magnified the significance of its findings.

Perhaps ironically, Indira Gandhi came to symbolize to the world the advancement both of Indian women and women in general. Under her stewardship, India entered a small club of nations in which a woman stood as the head of state. From an Indian perspective, though, her high profile position was not unique; she followed a series of women who had represented India in world affairs as ambassadors and representatives to international bodies and conventions.

At home too, she symbolized the principles of gender equality repeated throughout India's Constitution, which called for non-discrimination and at the same time acknowledged the need for remedies to achieve it. For example, Article 15 on Fundamental Rights prohibited discrimination based on caste (see Chapter 1) and also prohibited discrimination based on sex. Yet, it made clear that its declaration did not 'prevent the State from making any special provisions for women and children', something not provided for every other category of citizens mentioned in Article 15 [**Doc. 4, p. 137**], Consequently, the Indian Government established some programmes specifically to benefit women and advanced their particular interests in jobs, such as mining, in which they faced particular exploitation.

The Committee on the Status of Women in India was established by the Ministry of Education and Social Welfare in 1971. Its charge was to evaluate women's status in light of their guaranteed rights in the Constitution and to propose means to 'enable women to play their full and proper role in building up the nation' (*Toward Equality*, 1975: 2). While the impetus for forming the committee grew out of domestic concerns, it also responded to a call of the United Nations to examine the status of women worldwide. The committee, which included academics, politicians, and social workers, brought into the discussion other professionals, for example in medicine and law, to examine diverse aspects of women's lives in India. The extensive work, touring the country to interview a variety of people and holding hearings, provided benchmark data on a grand scale.

The idea of 'status', since the word was present in the title of the committee, required early definition and the committee recognized status as relational and dependent on context. So, for example, it studied women's relative power and responsibilities in families, but also the different issues relating to power and gender roles in the workforce. Given its broad remit, the committee ended the report with recommended measures to improve women's economic, political, and social status in specific but sweeping terms.

The discussion of education in the report revealed the subtlety of the committee's analysis. Using data on girls' enrolment in school in the first three decades of independence, the report showed gradual increases in girls attending school, not only in absolute terms (from 6 million to 30 million) but also relative to the number of boys – from 33 girls to each 100 boys in the 1950s to 54 to each 100 in 1971. Yet, despite these marginal gains, the report also disaggregated the data, showing that girls dropped out of school more often and earlier than boys did and that the disparities between girls and boys were greater in rural than urban areas. In this regard, the committee proposed, as a high priority, to redouble efforts to increase the access of girls and women to education (*Toward Equality*, 1975: 152).

Two areas in which the effects of the report became obvious in the following decades were in debates about sex-ratios of girls to boys and in proposals about women's political representation. The report turned greater attention to the sex-ratio issue; i.e., the decreasing number of girls in the population relative to the number of boys. Amartya Sen and other economists kept the problem in the news and subsequent studies used the report as a basis from which to begin their analysis. Second, in terms of political representation, the report lent support to arguments for mandated representation of women in governing bodies, an idea that regained popularity when Rajiv Gandhi became prime minister in 1984. Although the report did not advocate reservations for women in the manner that existed for Scheduled Castes and Tribes (see Chapter 1), it reinforced arguments about the necessity of increasing numbers of women in decision-making bodies.

The timing of the *Report of the Committee on the Status of Women in India* was both fortuitous, coinciding with international attention to women's issues and thereby promoting further study, and unfortunate, coming just at the beginning of the Emergency. Its initial influence produced an increase in ongoing research and the creation and expansion of institutions to study women's development. The Indian Council of Social Science Research (ICSSR) published a synopsis of the report in 1975 to reach a larger audience. The report was reprinted again in 1988 (ICSSR *Synopsis*, 1988). At the same time the ICSSR established an advisory committee on women's studies and the momentum increased for the establishment and support of other institutions, including the Centres for the Study of Women and Development and Centre for Advanced Research in Women's Studies (Forbes, 1996: 228).

However, during the Emergency, and the period of changing governments that followed, the proposals addressed in *Toward Equality* did not receive extensive government attention. Not until the late 1980s did the report's analysis of the issue of reservations for women in government gain active interest in the context of legislation revamping local government. The Committee did not go so far as to back reservations for women in public office, rather it provided the text for compelling arguments on both sides and decided that there was insufficient evidence to make the call [**Doc. 29, pp. 158–9**]. Therefore, it became an important resource for public debate. Finally in 1992, when legislation passed for establishing local governing bodies in all states, called the Panchayati Raj Act, it contained reservations for women in those bodies. By 2001 there were nearly two million women serving in local government.

CONCLUSION

The study of history inevitably reveals the interconnectedness of events and movements – politics, culture, and society. Here we see that agricultural change in the 1970s, the Bangladesh war, and the Anti-Price Rise Movement were in many ways linked. The war that divided Pakistan was India's history too, even before India intervened militarily, and the politics of the war and the policies of Indira Gandhi's Congress Party both effected and were affected by popular movements.

The actions of the Indian Government from 1965 to 1975 revealed a new nation, powerful and assertive in its approach to foreign policy and domestic issues. But the mirror image of Indira Gandhi's administrative boldness and real policy accomplishments was growing discontent that coalesced into mass movements. Development neither moved quickly enough, nor equitably enough, to meet the expectations of most Indians. As a result, despite the successes of the Green Revolution or the war with Pakistan (and sometimes because of these successes) popular protest accelerated toward the middle of the decade. Maoist rebels were the most extreme response to inequality in the countryside, but Jaya Prakash Narayan's followers also called for social justice and redemption of the promises of independence.

That the Green Revolution and the Total Revolution emerged concurrently signalled some of the ways in which Indira Gandhi's government had lost touch with grassroots politics in the 1970s. The government did not (at least immediately) reap political benefits from increased agricultural production. The war with Pakistan had turned Mrs. Gandhi's attention outward and her success in consolidating control within the Congress Party had quelled any voices of disagreement among her advisors. The next chapter will look more closely at the consequences of this severe disjuncture between the highest politicians in a democracy and the people who elected them to serve. In 1975, plagued by unrest and the assertion of a political opposition, Indira Gandhi declared an Emergency, suspending civil liberties and arresting opposition forces.

5

Democratic watersheds

Headline: *New York Times*, Friday 27 June 1975:

INDIA REPORTS 676 ARRESTS IN DRIVE ON THOSE OPPOSED TO
REGIME OF MRS. GANDHI; 'THREAT' IS CITED Prime Minister Says
a Conspiracy Forced New Delhi to Act NEW DELHI CITES A GRAVE
'THREAT' Disorders Around Country Said to Have Preceded State of
Emergency

So reported an American newspaper when Indira Gandhi declared a
'State of Emergency' on Thursday, 26 June 1975. 'The Emergency'
refers to a twenty-one month period of rule by decree, in which the
prime minister took on extraordinary powers, which she argued was necessary to advance economic development, increase efficiency, arrest corruption
in government, and forestall rebellions. In retrospect it is most remembered
for the grave political excesses of the government throughout its duration.

Both scholars and journalists writing about India's Emergency (1975–77)
often address it in terms of its meaning for India's democracy. This can
be seen in three ways. First of all, by declaring a state of emergency, Indira
Gandhi was not only imposing a series of decrees that suspended civil
liberties, but also suspended the democratic process; scheduled elections
were postponed and the opposition silenced. Second, as Chapter 4 demonstrated, the exuberance of democracy in the early 1970s – even peaceful
public expression of dissent, demands for accountability, and popular
mobilization – contributed to Mrs. Gandhi's sense of threat. Finally, in
retrospect, many observers claim that the way in which the Emergency
ended – with the call for new elections in January of 1977 – heralded the
ultimate victory of democracy in India.

This chapter looks at a series of watersheds in Indian politics, particularly
in relation to the Emergency, in order to understand the depth and tenacity of
democratic impulses in India. The Emergency, its justification, the experience

of authoritarianism and its end with the 1977 election, tested and redefined Indian democracy.

Some consequences included the end of the political dominance of the Congress Party. It also realigned constituencies and interest groups and tested the resilience of non-elected institutions – the Election Commission, the Supreme Court, and the Press. The second half of this chapter traces two very different political movements that benefited from this realignment and weakening of the Congress Party: the rise of the so-called Backward Classes and the rise of Hindu nationalism as a political force.

THE EMERGENCY

In modern India's political history, the Emergency is both central and ignored. As a recent book by Emma Tarlo suggests, 'so much has it slipped out of public discourse that today it is remembered if at all, for the extent to which it has been forgotten'. Tarlo, in fact, cites a newspaper essay by the sociologist Ashis Nandy, in which he says: 'Enormous political effort has gone into wiping out the Emergency as lived memory' (Tarlo, 2001: 21). In this, the Emergency shares with the Partition the desire – on the part of many of those harmed by it – to forget the past (Butalia, 2000). In each case it was national trauma with extensive and diffused ramifications of violence and personal upheaval.

However, a consequence of this non-remembrance, and of the political excesses such as censorship that characterized the Emergency, is that there are not the usual sources to elaborate it. Nevertheless, here is an attempt to summarize the period and events commonly referred to by the name: 'Emergency'.

The provisions for the 'Emergency' lay in Article 352 of the Constitution, which gave power to the President, in the case of a 'grave' threat to the nation, to issue a Proclamation of Emergency. Its effect would be to extend executive powers to the Union or any officer of the Union as necessary to meet the threat. At Indira Gandhi's request the President Fakhruddin Ali Ahmed issued such an order and Indira Gandhi took on the executive powers of the state (Constitution, Article 352–353).

During the Emergency Indira Gandhi's government jailed her opponents, muzzled dissent, and imposed draconian measures on the people in the name of development. With the assistance – and, many argue, at the instigation – of her son, Sanjay Gandhi, whose political career reached its apex at the time, Indira Gandhi implemented programmes to generate greater efficiency in government industries, stall population growth, and improve the appearance of cities. Like so much in the Emergency these positively described programmes had negative or dire consequences. They imposed arbitrary and strict timetables on workers, forced sterilization of thousands of people, and cleared slums that were home to millions of poor citizens. Further, with the opposition under arrest and the press censored, there were no checks on these excesses.

THE PROCLAMATION OF THE EMERGENCY

While Mrs. Gandhi was contending with the effects of mass political mobilizations (such as the JP Movement) and an increasingly vocal opposition, the Allahabad High Court on 12 June 1975 delivered another blow. In a long drawn-out election dispute brought by her defeated opponent, Raj Narain, the Justice Jagmohan Lal Sinha ruled that Mrs. Gandhi's election in 1971 was invalid because she had violated several election rules. Specifically, she used government workers to erect a platform for one of her speeches in her constituency. Justice Jagmohan Lal Sinha announced his judgement after a careful hearing that went to great lengths to adjust to the unusual circumstances of a prime minister in the courtroom, including special provisions for security and concerns about protocol in the court (Malhotra, in *The Hindu*, 19 March 2008).

In response to the judgement, Mrs. Gandhi refused to relinquish her seat in Parliament and in less than two weeks declared a State of Emergency in the nation. In her address to the nation on All India Radio on 26 June 1975 about the Emergency she did not mention the court case. Rather she laid out the circumstances for which Emergency measures were required as threats to the internal stability of the nation. She referred to 'false allegations' against her personally, but put the argument for the Emergency in the context of needed centralized powers, not for herself but for the institution of prime minister. She said, 'we have learned of a new programme challenging law and order throughout the country with a view to disrupt normal functioning'. Therefore, she argued that 'the nation's integrity demands firm action'. She suggested that the current climate invited the possibility of an external attack and also threatened agricultural production and the prospects of economic advancement. At the end of her address she promised to announce a new programme for economic development and asked for continued cooperation and trust in the future.

Meanwhile, she jailed her opposition, including the ailing Jaya Prakash Narayan, confirming that she found his movement for Total Revolution particularly threatening. Not only had JP called for electoral reforms and land rights, but he attracted a growing following even beyond the student movement in Bihar, from which it began. In fact, on the day he was arrested, he was set to address a rally of young people engaged in the movement.

Plate 1 Tyeb Mehta's 'Mahisasura', 1997

Plate 2 Nek Chand Garden

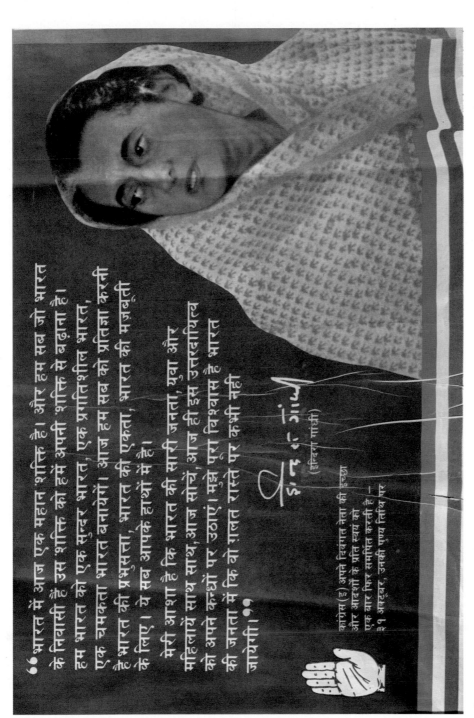

Plate 3 1984 Congress Party election poster

Plate 4a Stamp depicting Jayaprakash Narayan

Plate 4b Stamp marking 25 years of Indian independence

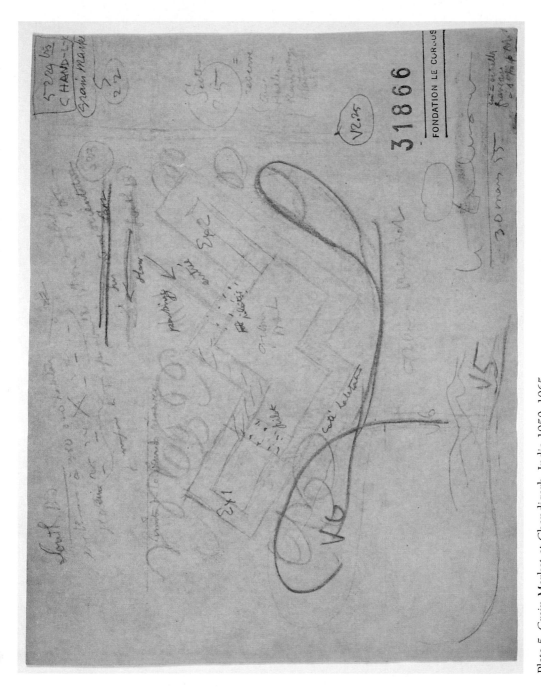

Plate 5 Grain Market at Chandigarh, India 1950–1965

© FLC/ADAGP, Paris and DACS, London 2011

The Times of India

Published Simultaneously in Bombay and Delhi — ESTABLISHED 1838

NO. 133. VOL. CXIV.   BOMBAY: TUESDAY, MAY 13, 1952   2½ ANNAS

INDIA'S PRESIDENT TO BE SWORN IN TODAY

New Cabinet To Take Charge This Evening

LIKELY ALLOCATION OF PORTFOLIOS

From Our Special Representative

NEW DELHI, May 12.

A SALUTE of 31 guns will be fired at 8-33 tomorrow morning when Dr. Rajendra Prasad is sworn in as President of the Republic, heralding a new chapter in free India's political history.

Immediately after this, Mr. Nehru will submit the resignation of his present Cabinet and, having been already elected leader of the largest party in Parliament, will be requested to form the new Government.

Mr. Nehru has almost finalised his Cabinet of 14 who will be sworn in along with other junior Ministers at Rashtrapati Bhavan in the evening. Unless an eleventh hour change is made—such a contingency must not be ruled out as the Prime Minister has not yet fully made up his mind about certain portfolios—the personnel and the portfolios of the 14 Ministers to be included in the Cabinet are expected to be as follows:

Mr. Jawaharlal Nehru—Foreign Affairs.
Maulana Abul Kalam Azad—Education and Scientific Research.
Mr. N. Gopalaswami Ayyangar—Defence.
Mr. C. D. Deshmukh—Finance.
Dr. Kailas Nath Katju—Home and States.
Mr. Gulzarilal Nanda—Planning and Natural Resources.
Mr. Rafi Ahmed Kidwai—Food and Agriculture.
Mr. T. T. Krishnamachari—Commerce and Industry.
Mr. Lal Bahadur Shastri—Transport and Railways.
Mr. Jagjivan Ram—Works, Production and Supply.
Mr. V. V. Giri—Labour.
Rajkumari Amrit Kaur—Health.
Sardar Swaran Singh—Communications.
Mr. C. C. Biswas—Law.

PARLIAMENT SESSION BEGINS TODAY

Crop Of Official Bills For 12-Week Agenda

From Our Special Representative

NEW DELHI, May 12.

LEGISLATION dealing with the rights and welfare of labour is expected to be almost the first crop of official Bills which will come up for consideration before the 12-week session of the new Parliament commencing here tomorrow.

TO-DAY'S NEWS

INDIAN

The President of the Republic of India will be sworn in at Rashtrapati Bhavan this morning the new Cabinet, headed by Mr. Nehru, will take the oath in the evening. (Page 1).

FOREIGN

It is understood that Egypt will reject the latest British proposals to solve the Anglo-Egyptian problem when the Egyptian Premier, meets British Ambassador. (Page 1).

Robbery Bid Foiled

POLICE ARREST ARMED MEN

A planned robbery in a house at Parel, Bombay, in the early hours of Monday morning was frustrated by the police, who forestalled the burglars and caught them after a brief struggle.

The armed desperadoes were surprised to encounter the police in the flat, where they were lying in wait. The alleged gangsters, however, offered resistance, but were eventually overpowered.

CONGRATULATIONS

The Prime Minister, Mr. Jawaharlal Nehru, is seen above being congratulated on his being re-elected leader of the Congress Parliamentary Party by acclamation on Sunday.

Woman Among 9 Deputy Ministers For Bombay

SWEARING-IN CEREMONY TO BE HELD ON MAY 14

BOMBAY State is to have nine Deputy Ministers, according to an announcement made by the Government on Monday. They are: Miss Indumati Chimanlal, Mr. Babubhai J. Patel, Mr. D. N. Wandrekar, Mr K. F. Patil, Mr. B. D. Jatti, Mr. B. D. Deshmukh, Dr. T. R. Naravane, Mr. M. G. Faqi and Mr. V. J. Sathe.

The first six are former Parliamentary Secretaries. The other three are trusted and old Congressmen.

PRESIDENTSHIP OF PANAMA

U. S. Anxiety

"The Manchester Guardian" and "The Times of India" Service.

LONDON, May 12.

Egypt To Reject U.K. Proposals

CANAL ZONE DISPUTE

CAIRO, May 12.

Egypt will reject the latest British proposal to solve the Anglo-Egyptian problem when the Egyptian Premier, Hilaly Pasha, meets Sir Ralph Stevenson, British Ambassador, today.—P.T.I.-Reuter.

Subsidy To Commercial Aviation Companies

NEW SCHEME POSTPONED: INTERIM ARRANGEMENT

From Our Special Representative

NEW DELHI, May 12.

THE Government of India has decided to postpone implementation of its new scheme of subsidy to commercial aviation companies until January 1, 1952, as against the original proposal to bring it into effect on October 1, 1951.

LESS INTAKE OF JUTE AND COTTON

Import-Export Budget For Half-Year

From Our Special Representative

NEW DELHI, May 12.

IN view of the comfortable position in regard to raw cotton and jute, provision for the import of these two essential commodities will be considerably reduced in the import-export budget for the next half of this year, which is being at present finalised by the Centre.

Textile Control Policy

"STATUS QUO" TILL JUNE

At an informal conference of Civil Supplies officials of the States and the Centre held in Bombay on Monday, a decision on textile control is understood to have been deferred till June, when the question is again likely to be taken up for examination at an inter-State level.

Miss Chimanlal   Mr. K. F. Patil   Mr. Wandrekar   Mr. Faqi

Mr. B. J. Patel   Mr. Deshmukh   Dr. Naravane   Mr. Jatti

Plate 6   The Times of India, 13 May, 1952

Copyright © 2011, Bennett, Coleman & Co. Ltd.

Plate 7 Meera Mukherjee's 'Spirit of Daily Work'

The Museum of Modern Art, New Delhi

Plate 8 Amul Butter advertisement, 1992

Over the time of the Emergency, opponents from left and right met the similar fate of jail and suppression. In this regard, Indira Gandhi used the Maintenance of Internal Security Act (MISA), which was manipulated to arrest politicians who attempted to advocate citizens' rights or simply opposed her. Gayatri Devi, of the royal family of Jaipur, and Vijaye Raje Scindia, of the house of Gwalior, who were both popular women politicians, whose careers advocated a multi-party system and who belong to conservative right-oriented parties, were sent to jail. George Fernandes, an MP and labour leader who presided over a massive rail strike, was also arrested. In addition, a young activist, who later became an important politician, Lalloo Prasad Yadav, was arrested as well. While in jail, his wife gave birth to a daughter, whom he named 'Misa', as a sign of defiance.

Newspapers submitted to censorship or were closed. Several papers continued to publish and brought the action of censors to their readers' attention by distributing papers with blacked out or cut out stories. Other journalists, including Raj Thapar and Romesh Thapar, of the magazine *Seminar* simply closed their papers down (Thapar, 1991). Salman Rushdie's novel *Midnight's Children*, written just after the Emergency, creates a palpable image of this silencing. The narrator, Saleem, whose life is magically linked to the history of India, because of his birth at the moment of independence, had a son, born at the moment of the Emergency. The baby, Aadam, was 'a child of a time which damaged reality so badly that nobody ever managed to put it together again'. Significant to his time of birth, Aadam, whose ears were so large and keen that he heard the history around him, did not utter a sound. His inheritance from the Emergency was that he was completely silent (Rushdie, 2006: 482).

The silencing of a free press, and censorship of other kinds, did not curtail all cultural expression. Interestingly, one of India's most popular films of all time was released during the Emergency – 'Sholay'. Although produced in 1974 before the Emergency, it portrayed an irreverent critique of authority – the government and the police. The heroes of the film, including actor Amitabh Bachchan, are kind-hearted thieves. One of their antagonists – a jailor – provides the comic role of the clown, determined to impose discipline. He says to the prisoners, 'I have been a jailer since British times and I do not believe in reform'. 'I have not changed and I know you will not change.' In Chaplinesque form, he wears a Hitler moustache and walks in goosesteps, comically tripping down the steps to the prison yard. Ultimately he is outfoxed by our jailed heroes, who are the honourable characters of the film. 'Sholay' was released on Independence Day, 15 August 1975 and for the next two years it sold out cinemas throughout the country, including the Plaza in New Delhi, not far from the centre of government.

Other films produced during the Emergency did succumb to the consequences of censorship. 'Kissa Kursi Ka' (What kind of Chair), was a political satire on the government containing fairly obvious ridicule of Sanjay Gandhi. Produced by a Congress Party MP, Amrit Nahata, the film was not only censored, but all copies destroyed. Later 'Kissa Kursi Ka' became the subject of a court suit, in which the Minister of Information and Broadcasting during the Emergency was arrested. However, Nahata disavowed the film and made amends with his party.

Meanwhile, Indira Gandhi's repressive actions converged with her pronouncement about promised economic development. On 1 July 1975, she revealed a twenty-point programme to improve the economy [**Doc. 30, pp. 159–60**]. It proposed measures to attack inflation, provide land to labourers, increase agricultural wages, and promote homespun industries. About eight months later, Sanjay Gandhi proposed a five-point programme to address social issues. He called for party workers to help transform society through increasing literacy, promoting environmental awareness, and advocating social change. His five points – which were disseminated in a variety of media – took the form of slogans for good citizenship:

1. Each one teach one;
2. Plant a tree;
3. Eliminate dowry;
4. Plan your family; and
5. Remove caste.

As a main tactic to promote these policies, Indira Gandhi advocated order and efficiency. Slogans about arriving at work on time and increasing productivity covered wall spaces, billboards, and other public areas. But the most controversial and ultimately most disastrous programmes associated with the Emergency were efforts for the beautification of Delhi and the promotion of family planning, both with innocuous names and sinister consequences. The beautification of Delhi brought destruction to slum colonies that displaced hundreds of thousands of citizens. Communities of labourers were driven out of the city to camps, while their hutments were destroyed to make room for development in Delhi. Living in camps outside the city, they now had to commute into Delhi for daily labour. And as the Shah Commission, which evaluated the consequences of the Emergency, reported, this disproportionately affected Muslim communities, especially around the Kashmiri Gate neighbourhood [**Doc. 31, pp. 160–1**].

The family planning programmes promoted sterilization, giving government workers targets for the number of sterilizations they should accomplish in a given month. As a result, the system prompted large-scale coercion. In a wide-ranging series of interviews Emma Tarlo has shown that many citizens acquiesced to sterilization in order to gain access to 'basic civic amenities, such as work, housing, hospital treatment and education' (Tarlo, 2003: 176) [**Doc. 32, pp. 161–2**]. The implementation of these programmes, especially in an atmosphere that restricted free speech and public dissent, magnified the already appalling consequences and provoked powerful resentment and frustration among the people. In moving ways, the novelist Rohinton Mistry, in *A Fine Balance*, captures the capriciousness and tragedy of these campaigns, when he untangles the roles of all the various players from political bosses to government workers to local doctors and forced patients. He shows how all of them are caught up in power struggles, corruption, and lack of access to information (Mistry, 1995).

The independence of the judiciary was also challenged. For example, the High Court in Delhi overturned the detention of the *Indian Express* journalist, Kuldip Nayar, who had been arrested during the first days of the Emergency. After a series of such rulings, Justice S. Rangarajan was transferred to Gauhati in the far northeast of the country and Justice R. N. Agarwal was made a sessions' judge.

Jaya Prakash Narayan continued to record his dissent in a diary from jail and letters to Mrs. Gandhi and other politicians. He was released after four months of imprisonment and published his diary clandestinely in 1976. A. K. Gopalan, an MP and leader of the Communist Party, was also arrested in West Bengal and later released. He immediately made his way to Delhi and reported his experiences and critique of the Emergency in a powerful speech in Parliament. However, his speech was not published outside of Parliament at the time [**Doc. 33, pp. 162–3**]. Central to his concern was the support that the Emergency seemed to have from the Soviet Union and from the CPI because of its Soviet ties. He wanted to separate himself as a Communist and a democrat from the draconian measures of the Emergency.

But the weight of censorship – that suppressed Gopalan's voice – continued to increase the anxiety produced by the Emergency itself, and the lack of open communication seemed to work in both directions. The government seemed to become more and more out of touch with the increasing dissension. Perhaps as a miscalculation, in January 1977, Indira Gandhi, convinced that a good monsoon and stable prices heralded the Emergency's success, called for fresh elections. Commentators have spent much time and print wondering what finally prompted Indira Gandhi to announce elections. Some have argued that she ultimately believed in democracy and wanted the mandate of the people. It also may have been the case that she took the advice of politicians around her, who would not have contradicted her if she anticipated winning. Another theory holds that the Intelligence Bureau's analysis gave the impression of a victory. While she may not have heard criticism from inside India, the world press certainly lambasted her policies – with titles like 'Democracy in Eclipse' or the accusation in the *Times* of a 'tinpot dictatorship'. She may have called elections because she worried about India's image abroad (*Asian Survey*, 1976, *Times*, 1976).

Whatever prompted the decision, it came suddenly on 18 January 1977 in an announcement on All India Radio. The elections were scheduled for March, according to the minimum legislated timeframe and a year ahead of the date Indira Gandhi had originally proposed. Immediately she began releasing political prisoners from jail.

THE 1977 ELECTION

Once the 1977 election was announced, election officials throughout the country set about meeting the challenge of organizing an election at such short notice. In a normal cycle, they would have been preparing electoral rolls well in advance. As the Chief Electoral Officer from Andhra Pradesh reported, 'As the elections to the Lok Sabha (the lower house of Parliament) were announced rather unexpectedly, there was a certain amount of uncertainty about the selection of candidates in the beginning and the electioneering started on a low key. It picked up gradually and was in full swing by the end of February . . .' (Andhra Pradesh, *Report*, 1977: 32).

Politicians who had been jailed by Indira Gandhi contested elections from their prison cells. The free press was restored and joined in the fray. Most spectacularly, some Congress party leaders split with Indira Gandhi and publicly opposed her. Among them was the veteran Congressman, Jagjivan Ram, a powerful Scheduled Caste politician from Bihar, who served as Minister for Agriculture and Irrigation in Indira Gandhi's government. Also, Vijayalaxmi Pandit, former ambassador and Indira Gandhi's own aunt, openly joined the campaign of the opposition. Significantly, a group of politicians called the Young Turks – who fashioned themselves the next generation of leaders of the Congress sided with JP. Among them was Chandra Shekhar, who later became prime minister.

Janata Party: When Indira Gandhi called elections in 1977, bringing to an end the Emergency, the opposition – both right and left – joined together to form the Janata or People's Party; the Janata Party won in 1977, but was soon plagued by infighting due in large part to the vast ideological differences the Emergency had temporarily allied; after Janata's defeat in 1980, a number of parties took up the Janata mantle with variations on its name.

In political terms, one of the most significant characteristics of the 1977 election was the coalescing of a disparate opposition. Left leaning and right leaning parties joined together in what they jointly called the Bharatiya Lok Dal or **Janata Party**. Though often contrasting in ideology, the members of the Janata Party cooperated to defeat Indira Gandhi's Indian National Congress and the election became a referendum on the Emergency. Despite the recent chill of martial law, 194 million people turned out to vote, i.e., 60 per cent of the electorate (Singh and Bose, 1986: 136). A documentary film called 'Voices of the People', dramatically portrays the 1977 election, incorporating underground footage from the period of the Emergency. It demonstrates the powerful rallies addressed by Janata leaders, including an ailing JP and other opposition leaders. Such election rallies served also as a cathartic release of twenty-one months of political tension.

In the end the Congress achieved only 154 seats in Parliament to the Janata's clear majority of 295 (Singh and Bose, 1986: 151). Mrs. Gandhi lost her own constituency of Rae Bareili with only 37 per cent to her old rival, Raj Narain's, 53 per cent. Sanjay Gandhi lost in Amethi constituency 34 per cent to his opponents 60 per cent (Election Commission, 1977). Across the north, voters completely routed the Indian National Congress. George Fernandes, the trade union leader, won his election by 78 per cent even though he could not campaign because he was still in jail. JP remained an important symbol of the Janata victory, though he was too ill to participate. The government issued a stamp in his memory (see Plate 4).

LEGACIES OF THE JANATA GOVERNMENT

In retrospect the Janata Party Government, which held power from 1977 to 1980, heralded the development of a successful multi-party system in India and promoted a range of interests – often, conflicting ones – among its constituent parties. However, at the time, its failings, particularly its inability to show a united front, stood out most prominently. The Janata coalition accepted Morarji Desai, as prime minister. Desai, a Gandhian, often described as spiritual and eccentric, was in fact an experienced politician. He served as deputy prime minister to Indira Gandhi in 1967 until his more conservative wing of the Congress Party was split away by Mrs. Gandhi. An outspoken opponent of her government, he was jailed during the Emergency. His 1977 campaign both in his own constituency of Surat in Gujarat and throughout the country aided the Janata victory.

Several policy shifts took place during the Janata regime. George Fernandes, as Minister of Industries, pursued an aggressive trade policy that promoted Indian corporations, through protectionist trade policies. Using the term 'swadeshi,' meaning one's own country and evoking the same word used in the Freedom Movement, the policies expelled both Coca-Cola and IBM for not relinquishing enough control to Indian partners. The government initiated a high level commission to evaluate unequal development among so-called Backward Castes – a measure designed to implement the social principles, which Desai, echoing Mahatma Gandhi, advocated. In a similar vain, Charan Singh, as Home Minister and later Finance Minister, pursued his primary interest in land reform that had been a hallmark of his whole political career. In fact, when Desai's government floundered, Charan Singh became the new prime minister.

A key issue that divided the Desai government was the prospect of giving the RSS (Rashtriya Swayamsevak Sangh) dual membership in the Janata. The RSS had been implicated in the assassination of Mahatma Gandhi; it had been banned in 1948 and again it was banned during the Emergency. It was known for its pro-Hindu stance and particularly its mobilization of Hindu youth into organized brigades. In addition, it functioned as a service organization that aided in times of disaster. It was associated with the Jan Sangh, which was part of the Janata Party in 1977 and provided a training camp for cadres – not only for their own work, but for the Jan Sangh as well. That members of an organization on the extreme (or Hindu) right were part of the Janata coalition along with the secular socialist groups demonstrated the internal challenges facing such a diverse party.

So, in July of 1978, unable to accommodate the right, left, and centre, Morarji Desai resigned. Charan Singh then formed a new coalition with a Congress faction led by Indira Gandhi (who had won an interim election to come back to Parliament), making him prime minister. Mrs. Gandhi, however, withdrew her support within six months, forcing new elections. In 1980, therefore, India held its Seventh General Election. This time the Congress Party won a majority, ending Janata rule and Mrs. Gandhi returned as Prime Minister. As a consequence of this turnabout, some scholars and politicians dismissed what they call 'the Janata interlude' as a brief exception to long-term Congress rule (*The Pioneer*, 27 May 2003). Commentator and politician, Arun Shourie, in fact, titled his book about the post-1980 period, *Mrs. Gandhi's Second Reign* (Shourie, 1984). However, there were long term consequences of the Janata Government, which emerged in state politics and national movements outlined below.

Much of the legislative and judicial efforts during the Janata regime were directed toward undoing the Emergency. For example, Parliament overhauled the 42nd Amendment that had allowed Indira Gandhi to justify Emergency Powers, such as restricting the independence of the courts and allowing wide scale detention of dissidents. The 43rd and 44th Amendments repealed those provisions and guaranteed the right of the Supreme Court and the high courts of the states to rule on the Constitutionality of legislation. These Amendments also assured that the rights of life and liberty of the individual superseded other interests of the state.

Politically as well, the Janata Government left several lasting legacies. For example, it gave opposition leaders experience in government that enhanced their ability to engage in high-level politics in the future. The constituent organizations of the coalition, including the right wing Jan Sangh, set their sights on access to future power. Atal Bihari Vajpayee, a Jan Sangh leader, who was the Foreign Minister in the Janata Government, led this group – renamed the **Bharatiya Janata Party** – to victory over a decade later. Ultimately, Vajpayee himself became prime minister in the 1990s.

Bharatiya Janata Party (BJP): A Hindu-nationalist political party that also supports small business interests; it served as the ruling party briefly in 1996 and then from 1998 to 2004.

CONSEQUENCE OF JANATA DEMOCRACY IN THE STATES

The Janata Government also initiated new state elections, on the assumption that the Centre had imposed undue pressures on state politics. Therefore, the new government reasoned, here too voters deserved the right to reconsider their government and vote again. This section will look at three examples with very different consequences – Tamil Nadu, Punjab, and Kashmir. By and large most states in the Legislative Assembly elections of 1977 overturned Congress-led governments in preference to regional and opposition parties. But these three examples demonstrate that regional movements for autonomy, perhaps exacerbated under Indira Gandhi's Congress rule, but also suppressed, became explicit in the elections of 1977. This section also traces the very different trajectories that those movements took. As a result each story begins during the Janata Government (1977–79) but demonstrates the ongoing consequences after 1980, when the Congress Party returned to power.

Tamil Nadu was an interesting case, however, because the Tamil Nadu state government controlled by the regionalist DMK – Dravida Munnetra Kazhagam Party – had been dismissed by Mrs. Gandhi in 1977 before the elections. The DMK had a long history of advocacy for regional political autonomy and the advancement of Tamil culture. It generated enthusiasm in 1967 for an anti-Hindi language platform and won state elections. In 1977 the DMK was accused of corruption by a rival party, the breakaway AIDMK – the All India Anna Dravida Munnetra Kazhagam Party (though simply called ADMK at the time). While both parties opposed the Emergency and their leaders were arrested under MISA regulations, they played off against each other using national figures – including Indira Gandhi and Janata leaders such as L. K. Advani to fight the 1977 elections. Therefore the 1977 election in Tamil Nadu focused on regional controversies, albeit with national overtones. The AIADMK benefited from the leadership of M. G. Ramachandran, a film legend, who actually was the first of several actors to rise to significant political power. The AIADMK (as the 'All India' in its name might suggest) was also less concerned with Tamil autonomy and more willing to work with first the Indian National Congress and then the Janata Government at the Centre. The extreme separatism, which worried political analysts thought would develop in Tamil Nadu, did not take place. The Tamil Nadu parties played a critical role as power-brokers in future coalition governments at the Centre.

In both Punjab and Kashmir, however, the 1977 state assembly elections represented a democratic watershed in which regional parties asserted their aspirations. In both places, separatist movements gained new force pursuing a more dangerous political path than Tamil Nadu. In Punjab the election of

1977 broke the recent lock the Congress Party held over state politics when the regional Akali Dal Party won 58 seats (out of 117) and formed a government with the support of the Janata Party, which had won 25 seats. Many people had hopes that the Akali Dal, with a strong hand and an alliance with the ruling Janata Party would bring more autonomy and development to Punjab. When this did not happen, a more militant separatist movement gained momentum in Punjab.

The Akali Dal, which means 'Eternal Party', was founded to represent the interests of Sikhs in India. An old organization with roots in the 1920s, it advocated the rights of the Sikh religious community and in the pre-independence elections, just as Muslims received separate electorates (constituencies), so did the Sikhs. Sikhism is a monotheistic faith that emerged in India from Bhakti movements – spiritual practices focused on personal devotion to the divine – in the fifteenth and sixteenth centuries. Founded by Guru Nanak (1469–1539), one of the leading Bhakti teachers, Sikhism attracted a strong following in the region of contemporary Punjab. Sikh Gurus served both as worldly and spiritual leaders, shaping the subsequent states in Punjab and later proving to be formidable foes to the British Empire. In fact, Britain failed to conquer Punjab until 1848.

In the post-independence period, Sikhs fought for increased autonomy in their region and won in 1966 a separate state, by further subdividing Punjab into a largely Sikh, Punjabi-speaking state which kept the name Punjab and a largely Hindu Hindi-speaking state, which took on the name Haryana. But issues remained unresolved, such as returning the city of Chandigarh, which now served as a union territory and capital to both Punjab and Haryana, exclusively to Punjab. There were also issues of including some additional Punjabi-speaking districts in Punjab and increased autonomy. The Akali Dal supported these efforts and other political and religious goals as outlined in what came to be known as the Anandpur Sahib Resolution (the 1978 agreement reached by Sikh leaders at the city of Anandpur Sahib, during this time the Akali Dal came to power as the largest party in a coalition government, so there was great optimism that the proposals of the Anandpur Sahib Resolution might be addressed [Doc. 34, pp. 163–4].

However, the Akali Dal government did not directly or immediately act on these interests and instead focused on internal battles among Sikh groups. Such conflict grew more assertive over time. At the same time – around 1977 – a Sikh leader, Sant Jarnail Singh Bhindrawale, called for reforms within the Sikh community or Khalsa and for a separate homeland for Sikhs – Khalistan. The disunity among Sikhs was apparent in the various organizations and factions engaged in conflict – sometimes violently – to exercise their political power. They were associated also with different political parties or branches of the Akali Dal. 'In other words', as the political scientist, Paul Brass, puts it, 'the parties in Punjab do not simply reflect basic religious and caste antagonisms, but they divide and deflect them' (Brass, 1974, 397).

The Sikh separatist movement gained momentum and, some scholars argue, support from the Congress Party, which saw division among Sikh political groups as an opening to return to power. Robin Jeffrey, for example, suggests that Congress, in fact supported Bhindranwale at first, an irony because the militant nature of the movement had dire consequences for Congress, the nation, and Indira Gandhi. By the time Congress returned to power in 1980, the unrest in Punjab was a major issue on Indira Gandhi's agenda. When in February 1980 the Congress Government declared President's rule in Punjab and dismissed the Akali Dal Government, the actions elicited widespread public sympathy. Bhindranwale's followers openly called for Khalistan and support came, not only from Sikhs in India, but many abroad as well, including large Sikh populations in Canada, Britain, and the United States.

In the 1980s three events in succession demonstrated the magnitude of the situation – Operation Blue Star, Indira Gandhi's assassination, and the explosion of an Air India flight. In March 1984, when Sant Bhindranwale perceived a threat from the government, he and his followers began occupying and fortifying the holiest of Sikh temples, the Golden Temple in Amritsar. After a three-month stand off, during which violence in the Punjab continued to escalate – attacks on Hindu civilians and targeted assassinations of the militants' opponents – Indira Gandhi sent armed troops into the Temple complex. The assault, code named Operation Blue Star, intended to quickly flush out the militants inside. However, since the followers of Bhindranwale were well-armed and many were former soldiers, the siege took three days, inflicting considerable damage and loss of life. The symbolic significance of having attacked Sikhism's holiest shrine was as considerable as the death toll, which the government estimated at 83 soldiers and 492 people in the Temple (militants or bystanders). Other estimates are much higher and in addition to the dead and injured, hundreds of people were arrested.

The consequences of the operation were broad and deep. Played out on television, the effect among Sikhs was a visual violation of their faith. It fuelled distrust in government and a sense of alienation from the Indian state. Even among those who had not supported Bhindranwale, he was now perceived with sympathy. The news of the events created a stronger bond for the considerable Sikh diaspora and served as a tool for mobilizing financial support from abroad.

For Indira Gandhi, the operation was a success. She had dealt a serious blow to the militants in the Punjab. In the mean time her intelligence officers received credible threats that her life was in danger. She too seemed to take the threats seriously and, possibly, with resignation. In a speech she delivered in October in the state of Orissa (in Eastern India) she said, 'I do not care whether I live or die . . . And when my life ends, I can say that every drop of my blood will keep India alive and strengthen it' [**Doc. 35, p. 164**]. Then prophetically, on 31 October 1984, Indira Gandhi was assassinated by two of her Sikh bodyguards.

Tragically, her death was followed by riots in Delhi in which the Sikh community were victims of the anger of her supporters and mourners. The rioting seemed to be orchestrated in some way or facilitated by Congress Party activists. Many Sikhs fled the capital and others hid. There were also rumours of broader disaster – that the Delhi water supply had been poisoned – but, if so, by whom. Rumours escalated the anxiety and violence. From rooftops, one could see fires, selectively set, where mobs had attacked Sikh homes. The government was slow to respond and estimates were of thousands dead in the two days before Rajiv Gandhi (her successor as prime minister) called out the army. In a bold political move, Rajiv Gandhi called general elections immediately to legitimize his own position as prime minister. Indira Gandhi's memory and her last speech became an important symbol of that election [**Doc. 36, pp. 164–5**].

It seemed that each action produced another painful reaction. So it was that eight months later the next tragedy occurred: the destruction of Air India Flight 182 off the coast of Ireland. The flight, having left Toronto some hours earlier, exploded from bombs packed in suitcases of non-existent passengers. The 307 passengers were primarily Canadians as well – tourists and families, Sikhs and non-Sikhs, travelling to India for holiday or to visit relatives. It was one of the largest such disasters of its time, both in terms of aviation deaths and certainly in terms of loss of civilian Canadian lives. Given evidence from the flight, the timing of events, and the fact that some potential passengers named Singh (a common Sikh surname) had made bogus reservations, authorities assumed the responsibility of Sikh militants. An investigation followed and some suspects were caught and tried, but the process took 20 years to complete and still was inconclusive. The Canadian Government launched a further Commission of Inquiry in 2006.

By the time the jetliner was attacked, Prime Minister Rajiv Gandhi was negotiating peace with Akali Dal leaders in Punjab. In fact such peace processes were tenuous and conflict in Punjab continued on and off for nearly a decade. Although Rajiv Gandhi formed a Commission to investigate anti-Sikh violence after his mother's assassination, its results, which did not set blame with any political groups, were met with scepticism. Nine more commissions were established in the next 20 years to examine aspects of the riots. What seemed to ease the violence in the long run, however, was the increasing prosperity of the region. A key beneficiary of the Green Revolution, Punjab turned the wealth of agricultural productivity into economic gain in other areas as well, such as food processing, pharmaceuticals, leather goods. Government investment in infrastructure, such as electricity and roads, facilitated families' investment in better housing and other goods. In the 1990s, it also benefited as a destination for multinational corporations, again, attracted to its prosperity.

The third example of state government change in 1977 was to Kashmir, where too there was a separatist movement as well as conflict with Pakistan. The subject or subtext of wars and conflict, Kashmir symbolized for India its multiculturalism, tolerance, and secularism, even when those concepts did not seem to thrive in Kashmir itself. All the more significant then that Morarji Desai, the Janata prime minister, insisted on free and open elections in Kashmir in 1977.

The result of the elections was that Sheikh Abdullah's National Conference Party won a very large victory. Sheikh Abdullah had once been an ally of Indira Gandhi's Congress Party, but returned in 1977 to his more independent roots. His National Conference Party won 47 of 75 in an election, for which the Centre supplied security and voter turnout was especially high. In fact the period from about 1977 to about 1989 was one of relative calm in Kashmir and the 1983 election also was characterized by little corruption (Ganguly, 1996). The violent separatist movements of the earlier period and Pakistan-supported movements for accession experienced a lull. As Stanley Widmalm, in *Kashmir in Comparative Perspective* put it, democracy seemed to mitigate violent separatism. As evidence he presents interviews with militants abroad, who found fewer recruits during this period (Widmalm, 2002).

The renewed militancy in the 1990s included tactics such as kidnappings and assassinations and the Indian armed forces and police responded with force. International conflict took a formidable turn in 1999, when infiltrators from Pakistan – some Kashmiri in origin and some not, crossed into the Kargil region. By the time the Indian Army had been alerted (by local shepherds, in fact) Pakistani troops had occupied a number of peaks overlooking the important Srinagar to Leh road. Indian and Pakistani troops once again met on the border and with the help of India air power, India recaptured 900 miles of a strategic ridge, peak by peak. The Kargil conflict ended when Pakistan's Prime Minister Nawaz Sharif withdrew, after finding a face-saving solution from the United States, which promised to look into the Kashmir situation. India lost 527 soldiers and had 1300 wounded. Pakistani estimates are more difficult to find and were not published by the government, but the range of estimates, even from among Pakistani Army officers, go from 350 to as much as 4000. Part of the question has to do with whether 'soldiers' refers to regular army or supporting militia.

In India, the end of the conflict brought a patriotic upsurge, as the returning army and the fallen soldiers were fêted and commemorated. Even the stock market rose precipitously that same week. Ramchandra Guha argues that an unintended consequence of the war was a nationalist response in

Punjab, of course, another border region. According to Guha, 'Farmers along the border insisted that if conflict became a full-fledged war, they would be on hand to assist the Indian Army, providing food and shelter' (Guha, 2007). For Kashmiris, the strategic importance of their state meant a constant pressure of army occupation that did not end with the Kargil conflict.

As the state politics of Tamil Nadu, Punjab, and Kashmir show, trends toward separatism and integration vary over time, as do the responses from the Centre. In terms of the Janata Government, one of its main contributions was not only representing the potential of democracy as a means to political and social change, but facilitating participation in that democratic process, both at the national and regional levels.

In addition to seeing this in separatist movements, several other political interests found voice and political experience through the Janata Government's brief tenure. Two particular interest groups that came to characterize Indian politics for the next decade benefited from the high profile support of key players in the Janata regime: namely, the **Other Backward Classes** **(OBC)** movement and the Hindu nationalist movement. The next sections of this chapter will discuss these two movements, which, though they had a much longer history, earned an electoral boost and new ways to articulate their politics from the Janata experience. It focuses on two particular narratives that come out of the post-Janata period – the implementation of reservations for groups called Other Backward Classes and the aggressive assertion of Hindu nationalist interests around the issue of building a temple in Ayodhya, a town in Uttar Pradesh.

OBC (Other Backward Classes): Borrowed from language in the Indian Constitution to assure social equality across class, the term has come to mean a specific set of citizens (defined by caste and class), who were underprivileged and underrepresented; OBCs have gained 'reservations' in some areas to remedy economic disadvantage; OBCs were specifically addressed and identified in the Mandal Commission Report.

BACKWARD CLASSES AND THE JANATA GOVERNMENT

In 1978, the Janata Government, which had received strong support from rural voters and other poorer constituencies, appointed a commission to examine the economic deficiencies among certain social classes. Although the Indian Census stopped categorizing people according to caste, it was clear in the 1970s that Brahmans and other upper castes dominated government service and institutions of higher education, especially in the north. The south had experienced anti-Brahman movements – in fact the DMK in Tamil Nadu had its origins in those – which had the effect of creating a broader distribution of opportunities in terms of caste. While India's Constitution established reservations and special provisions for Scheduled Castes and Scheduled Tribes and about 20 per cent of Parliament comprised members of those communities, there were no such mechanisms to incorporate various other communities into the Parliament. In the 1977 election, a number of people who identified themselves as coming from Backward Castes were elected to Parliament – by and large, these were people from non-Brahman and non-Scheduled communities.

Here the category of backward class/caste requires some definition. It returns us to the discussion begun in Chapter 1 and extends it. As the anthropologist Gail Omvedt points out, 'backward class' is a slightly misleading term that combines the interests of socially, as well as educationally, backward communities (Omvedt, 1990). In contemporary society certain jatis or castes, such as Brahmans or Kayasths associated with literate occupations, benefited from elite status. For centuries they engaged in jobs that require education and accordingly received the education necessary. Landed communities and former rulers benefited from status connected to their wealth as did some merchant communities. As Chapter 1 demonstrates these castes gained additional advantages under British imperial rule (Bayly, 2001).

Upper castes had something of a monopoly on the best service jobs – those connected to government – and were disproportionately represented in the best educational institutions. Borrowing statistics from a group that advocated the rights of Dalits (Scheduled Castes and Tribes), Omvedt extrapolated that in 1981, 82 per cent of the jobs as chief executives of government-run corporations went to Brahmans and in the civil service and elected government the number ranged from 48 to 62 per cent (Omvedt, 1999). However, Brahmans comprised about 5 per cent of the population at the time. This disparity suggested that there was a class disability experienced by certain caste groups who had insufficient access to education and job opportunities.

This kind of disparity prompted the Janata Government in 1978 to propose a commission to examine the obstacles that might impede social mobility for people who were economically (class) and socially (caste) backward. India's president selected Bindeshwari Prasad Mandal, an independent-minded politician from the state of Bihar, to chair a commission that would examine the interests and disabilities experienced by backward classes. Among the tasks of the commission was to conduct a countrywide study of 11 indicators of social, economic, and educational backwardness.

After two years of collecting a wide range of data, the commission concluded that a range of social and educational factors had indeed hindered the overall prosperity of OBCs (Other Backward Classes). The *Report*, carefully extrapolating from Census data, estimated that OBCs represented 52 per cent of the population, but had very little presence in government jobs and positions of leadership. The *Report* argued that these communities were disproportionately depressed economically and more prone to poverty than other groups because of their social and educational backwardness. Most powerfully, it stated: 'in a democratic set-up every individual and community has a legitimate right and aspiration to participate in the ruling of the country' (Mandal, 1991: 62). Thereby, it appealed to an Indian sense of social justice.

The *Report* made a series of recommendations, but most prominent and most controversial among them was its call for reservations for Other Backward Classes in government service and educational institutions along the model that existed for Scheduled Castes and Tribes. As the *Report* put it:

> When a backward class candidate becomes a Collector or a Superintendent of Police, the material benefits accruing from this position are limited to the members of his family only. But the psychological spin off of this phenomenon is tremendous; the entire community of that backward class candidate feels socially elevated.'
>
> (Mandal, 1991: 62)

Therefore, the Commission proposed reservations for OBCs in the spheres in which the government had the ability to apply them, for example, in government jobs and education [**Doc. 37, p. 165**]. However, the Commission recognized that since so many OBCs lived in rural areas, the greater disability was their insufficient control over their land. Therefore it advocated an overhaul of tenancy agreements and widespread land reform. The story of the **Mandal Commission**, however, experienced a substantial interruption in 1980. When the Congress Party returned to power, the *Report*, like all Janata initiatives, was shelved for a decade.

The *Mandal Commission Report* re-emerged in 1990 during the National Front coalition government led by Prime Minister V. P. Singh of the Janata Dal. The Janata Dal (*Dal* means party) was not literally a reincarnation of the Janata Party of 1977, but it was a successor – comprised of members of that coalition – and it claimed to carry the mantle of the 1977 government and of the JP Movement before it. The Janata Dal particularly represented lower-caste peasant cultivators. So it was perhaps not surprising that as soon as the National Front coalition gained power, it proposed to implement the reservations policy laid out by the Mandal Commission. No party was willing to oppose the *Mandal Report* publicly; but none of them wanted to enforce its recommendations either. For example, Rajiv Gandhi, former prime minister and then leader of the opposition, hedged the subject, saying 'it [would be] very difficult to implement it and his party was for a national consensus on the issue' (*Times of India*, 1991).

Immediately, anti-reservation protests emerged around the country and Mandal (which was the short-hand for the report and its controversy) became the key topic of debate among politicians and intellectuals, including

Mandal Commission and controversy: A Commission under the leadership of Parliamentarian Bindeshwari Prasad Mandal in 1978 to examine ongoing discrimination against underprivileged groups; 'Mandal' and 'mandalization' has come to mean the advocacy of certain benefits for these groups.

in editorials satirical advertising, and cartoons [**Doc. 38, pp. 165–8**]. There were some violent demonstrations, including instances of destruction of government property. Particularly disturbing were cases of self-immolation by upper caste students, at least 13 cases in Lucknow, Delhi, and other major cities. The response prompted some commentators to suggest that the Mandal issue was encouraging caste war for the sake of votes. However, Asghar Ali Engineer, a scholar of Indian politics, in a powerful essay, made an impassioned argument for the implementation of the *Mandal Report*. 'Mr. V. P. Singh while playing his politics has done something which will bring a ray of hope and sense of justice to the millions in our society which were cast at the periphery of our society' (Engineer, 1991).

Significantly members of Backward Castes had been gaining power in the Janata Dal, V. P. Singh's party, since 1977, and so the proposal for reservations recognized, rather than proposed, their growing influence. In fact, Backward Caste leaders, such as Ram Lakhan Singh Yadav, Mulayam Singh Yadav, and Laloo Prasad Yadav represented a variety of parties often competing with one another, rather than cooperating. Like every story in this book, the rise of backward class politicians stretches back before Mandal or the Janata or even independence. Many of the backward classes were among peasants who organized for land against landlords in the 1930s and again in the 1950s. What was significant in the 1990s was the confluence of the power of certain OBC politicians, the influence of their supporters, the Janata Dal commitments, and the Mandal Commission report.

In any event, V. P. Singh's proposal established new rhetoric in politics; the words *Mandal*, *Mandalization*, *OBCs*, *backward castes* and *backward classes* all became prominent terms in political debate. Mandalization became an invective from the opposition suggesting that the Janata Dal was pandering to backward caste interests. The slippage between backward caste and class was another significant issue. While the *Mandal Commission Report* focused on social disabilities based on caste as one of the obstacles OBCs had to overcome, it demonstrated that caste disabilities often coincided with class disabilities. More importantly, later court judgements required that the provisions to alleviate backwardness should especially apply to people disadvantaged by both caste and class.

The debates about the privilege of wealthy members of backward classes added another term to the political vocabulary – *the creamy layer* – and the Supreme Court ruled in 1992 that wealthy members of backward caste communities should be excluded from reservations (Indra Sawhney v. Union of India, 1992). By 1992, though, reservations were still controversial, OBCs had gained reservations in government jobs in most states, and they continued to increase their importance as a political constituency. However, because there were other political issues on the horizon, some opponents to Mandal sought to change the subject. They considered backward class rights a distraction from another more heated and violence-inducing issue over the construction of a temple to Ram on the site of a 400-year-old mosque.

THE BJP AND THE MANDIR ISSUE

If the rise of interests of Backward Classes was an issue close to the constituents of the Janata Dal, the controversy over a mosque in the town of Ayodhya became a defining feature of the politics of the BJP (the Bharatiya Janata Party), another party that descended from the Janata Government of 1977. Founded in 1980, the BJP emphasized its commitment to challenging the complacency of Congress Party politics. As the new incarnation of the Jan Sangh, a party with strong roots in *Hindutva* or Hindu nationalism – i.e., politics that emphasized the cultural unity of Hindus and Hinduism's centrality to the Indian state – the BJP sought broader appeal than its Jan Sangh antecedent. Under the leadership of Atal Bihari Vajpayee, who had been External Affairs Minister in the Janata Government, the BJP initially separated itself from the Hindu nationalist agenda of its correlated grassroots organizations; however, over time it returned to the ideology that had served as its foundation. This resulted in the BJP extending its support to the Sangh Parivar – the family of Hindu nationalist organizations, among which were the RSS (the Rashtriya Swayemsevak Sangh), the cadre base of the party, and the VHP (the Vishwa Hindu Parishad, or World Hindu Congress). The VHP focused its mobilization efforts directly on religious issues.

Hindutva: Literally 'Hindu-ness;' a term used to refer to advocating Hindu nationalism; it is the politic philosophy that puts Hindu beliefs at the centre of state interests in India.

Therefore, the rise of the BJP and especially its most potent political symbol, the movement to build a Ram temple (*mandir*) on the site on which a sixteenth century mosque currently stood, presents a chronological parallel to the Backward Class politics. Both issues – designated in the press as Mandir/Mandal – took turns gaining headlines in the daily papers and determined the fortunes of a number of politicians.

In order to understand the complexity of the BJPs political reality, we must put the Mandir issue into the context of its importance to the religious organization, the VHP. In the 1980s, the VHP had asserted a number of pro-Hindu agendas. One was a push to 're'-convert former members of Scheduled Castes, who had converted to Islam. Another campaign was to protest against Congress Government policies that it perceived as pro-Muslim, including the special status of Kashmir. Furthermore, throughout the 1980s the VHP had recruited Hindu religious leaders in an attempt to agree upon a set of principles that united all Hindus.

Hinduism – if it is an 'ism' at all – is a belief system of infinite diversity that defies the prospect of a unifying set of principles. It is not that no one had tried before. British scholars for centuries studied Sanskrit texts to make sense of the beliefs of so many of the empire's subjects. But as Wendy Doniger so intricately describes in *The Hindus: An Alternative History*, oral traditions, village rituals, local deities, and spiritual practices have continued to evolve despite British and Indian religious reform movements that have tried to tame them (Doniger, 2008). In this context, the VHP had a tall task ahead of it, so it utilized some of the most common and widely told narratives of the Hindu past, particularly the great epic Ramayana.

The Ramayana is 'told' annually through a series of popular festivals in the autumn. It is often performed in local theatre and takes on regional characteristics that adapt the story to local custom. In 1988 it was serialized for Indian television. Every week, families all over the country tuned into the programme on Sunday morning. Arvind Rajagopal, writing about politics and television, argues that this televised version of the Ramayana, like a similar one later on the Mahabharata, helped generate a common culture among Hindus, who otherwise differ even in their interpretations and telling of these epics (Rajagopal, 2001: 151). In addition, these televised versions departed from older films of the same stories, in that the actors played the divine characters more realistically and in more realistic looking settings. The story in any version is compelling. Ram, the hero, is the rightful heir to the throne of the Kingdom of Ayodhya, but is exiled for fourteen years due to palace intrigue. This is not the place for a complete retelling of the story, but what is important is that the town of Ayodhya in Uttar Pradesh is, the place that many people believe to be the Ayodhya of the Ramayana, and therefore, birthplace of Lord Ram.

In fact, the VHP believed that the actual soil of Ram's birthplace, i.e., *Ramjanambhoomi* in Hindi, lay beneath the site of a sixteenth century mosque, and in one scene in the televised version Ram reveals that he has been carrying soil from 'his birth place' in Ayodhya in his waistband. In exile, Ram sets up the soil as a shrine. The scene, therefore, underscores a sacred connection between Ram and Ayodhya and reinforces the ongoing Ram Janambhoomi movement happening at the time (Rajagopal, 2001: 109).

The mosque in Ayodhya, known as the Babri Masjid, had a narrative history of its own. It is said to have been built in 1528 in honour of the Mughal Emperor Babur. Babur was the first in the line of the dynasty that ruled India from 1526 until the British. He was known as valiant in war, elegant in writing, and merciful as a ruler; at least that is how he portrays himself in the *Baburnama*, his own memoirs, and how he is described by his sister, Gulbadan Begum, in the *Humayun Nama*, the story of his son's reign. During Babur's rule a number of mosques were built in his name, for example, to thank God for the birth of a child or success in a campaign; and tradition holds that this applied to the one in Ayodhya.

The VHP called for the destruction of the Babri mosque and for a temple to Ram to be built on the site. That claim had come before and there were clashes over the site recorded in the nineteenth century as well. In fact, the British Government of India had sealed the mosque due to this conflict. Briefly in 1949, the mosque was opened and an image of Lord Ram placed inside, though the building was then resealed. In 1986 in response to a lawsuit by Hindus who want to worship at the site, a local judge ruled that the masjid should be unsealed for the purpose of local worship.

The VHP used the temple/mosque controversy to create a common issue for Hindus, calling upon its supporters to contribute financially and to join protests calling for the building of a temple. As an example of the successful use of media, on the day that the judge's order was announced, VHP supporters charged the mosque in full view of state television, an image that reinforced their power and message.

Although the BJP attempted to broaden its constituency in 1980 by de-emphasizing its Hindu politics in order to draw into its fold politicians who were more generally frustrated with Congress rule, the pro-Hindu faction of the party, and especially, former Jan Sangh members associated with the cadres from the RSS, remained the most powerful. In fact, the BJP relied on the support of related grassroots organizations and those sympathetic to the VHP to mobilize Hindu activists for its election campaigns.

Therefore, there were obvious contradictions in the new appeal by the BJP for a broad base. From its first convocation in Bombay, traditional leaders such as Vijaya Raje Scindia, the powerful politician and former royal from Madhya Pradesh, questioned the language of the new BJP manifesto. She claimed the new party had departed from the pro-Hindu, traditional family values of the Jan Sangh (Jaffrelot, 1996: 319). If such a departure existed it was not reflected in most of the activists and many of the candidates in 1980 and 1983 who came from among the cadres trained in RSS camps.

In 1990, when V. P. Singh began promoting the Mandal issue, L. K. Advani, a stalwart of the BJP and its chief ideologue, announced that he would begin a Rath Yatra (a procession) across India from Somnath, a well-known temple city in Gujarat, west to Ayodhya in order to raise funds to build the Ram Janambhoomi Mandir, a temple to Ram. Advani admitted that Mandal influenced his decision. As an MP from Delhi (where several of the student suicides had taken place in protest against Mandal), he was under pressure from upper caste constituents to take a stand against V. P. Singh. However, backward castes made up more than 52 per cent of the voters and so he did not want to address the issue too openly. Instead he changed the subject; the temple issue shifted the focus of attention.

The Yatra proceeded and did indeed mobilize considerable support, but provoked violence and conflict as well. When it crossed the state of Bihar,

Laloo Prasad Yadav, then the Janata Dal Chief Minister of Bihar, ordered Advani arrested. Advani's arrest sparked a new round of violence, escalating the issue. By 1992, the VHP once again proceeded to Ayodhya. This time on 6 December 1992 a massive rally of 70,000 stormed the mosque and succeeded in destroying the Babri Masjid, finally and completely [**Doc. 39, p. 168**]. While the controversy over the site continued, the destruction of the 400-year-old mosque emboldened Hindu nationalists. Concomitant violence, in which the Muslim minority community comprised most of the victims, demonstrated how far beyond the symbolic the Mandir issue had gone.

CONCLUSION: MANDAL/MANDIR AND CHANGES IN GOVERNING

Both the reservations issue and the Ram temple issue sparked conflict and violence, so powerful were the ideologies they invoked or challenged. Scholars and social activists (often together) especially in the mid to late 1990s focused on the larger social costs of the resulting violence. Discussions turned to the 'communalization of politics,' which means the ways in which political parties appealed to Hindu/Muslim conflict in order to capture votes. They also use this issue to point to 'challenges to Indian secularism'. As demonstrated in Chapter 4, public intellectuals always played a role in political activism in India. The new urgency generated by communal tensions created ongoing connections between organizations that addressed the needs of victims of violence and scholars writing about that violence.

By the end of the century, the trajectory of the two narratives diverged. In some ways 1992 was a turning point. In that year Parliament passed the Panchayati Raj Act, which established a system of local self-governing bodies across India, which were charged, in part, with economic development. The next chapter discusses this in detail. Key to the OBC issue, though, is that Panchayats included reservations for Other Backward Classes, in every council, in every village, and every district. The next stage in the movement for Other Backward Classes, therefore, was reservations in private universities and perhaps in Parliament.

By the end of the century, the Ram temple had not been built, but the mandir issue continued to incite violence. Even when the BJP won parliamentary elections in 1998, the government did not sanction building the temple in Ayodhya. However, while in office, the party sought to influence the terms of historical debate by commissioning sympathetic histories and archaeological research to underpin the case for building a temple. The issue remained fore-grounded in the twenty-first century as well, when tragic riots took place in Gujarat. But that complicated story is beyond the range of this book.

The politics of both Mandal and Mandir were profoundly shaped by events and personalities from the Janata Party Government of 1977–79. Yet these were only two of the significant legacies of the moment. More broadly, the Janata Government permanently challenged the political domination of the Congress Party. In a sense then, the Emergency, the pinnacle of Congress excesses, began its transformation from the central political actor in Indian politics to one of several contenders to political power.

In 1980 and again in four of the next six parliaments, the Indian National Congress served as the ruling party. Its influence surely was not destroyed by the Emergency. However, as the political scientist Myron Weiner argued at the time, the Congress Party that won the election of 1980 was not the same party that had governed India previously, meaning that the organization had been weakened (Weiner, 1983). In fact, internally, the Congress suffered from a lack of party elections, reliance on personalities rather than service and expertise, and political interference by the Central Government in the affairs of states. Indira Gandhi's assassination in 1984 and Rajiv Gandhi's assassination in 1991 both facilitated Congress victories but challenged the resilience of the party.

The history of the interplay between political parties from 1980 until 2000, shows the development of alliances and a multi-party democracy that the Janata Party of 1977 proved could develop.

6

Social history at the crossroads of local, national, and global movements

The history of the 1990s demonstrated contradictory impulses in India to concentrate on local issues on the one hand, and globalization on the other – or even both at the same time. The government passed the Panchayati Raj Act, a law that profoundly changed how local development took place and devolved control to villages. At the same time it liberalized economic policies relating to the flow of capital that enhanced Indian companies' position in global markets. This chapter is about those contradictions and the moments in which the local, the global, and the national intersect. For example environmental movements, which began with local protests, won some villagers control over their land in Indian courts, and brought protests over dam projects to international attention. Also, Hindu nationalist politics, which benefiting from financial connections abroad, advocated *swadeshi* – India-first – at home and renamed Bombay 'Mumbai'. This chapter, therefore, looks at the wider influence of local action and the local implications of global action.

Another common thread in this period is that women's politics took centre stage. Longstanding issues about women's political representation, marriage laws, divorce, and women's inheritance gained considerable traction. Furthermore, key political players in this period were powerful women in political parties – from Uma Bharti to Mayawati – and the leaders of social movements and non-government organizations were often women as well – for example, Medha Patkar or Ella Bhatt.

It is not surprising then that scholars looking at this period have often employed gender analysis to understand the different experiences of women and men in these political arenas. The politics of the Babri mosque/Ram temple issue, as described in the previous chapter, could not be dissociated from the overwhelmingly male nature of the movement at its core. Young men from the RSS and VHP dominated the group that tore down the Babri mosque and populated demonstrations. Yet, equally important to the movements was the appeal the mandir (temple) issue elicited among women followers who provided their financial and other support.

To untangle the ways in which a variety of forces shaped Indian politics and society in the 1990s, this chapter looks at four big cases and their wider implications. The first is the Shah Bano case – a woman's legal suit for maintenance from her estranged husband. The story of Shah Bano had broader implications for Hindu/Muslim politics, competition between political parties, and the women's movement.

The second case is the establishment of a state-by-state system of local village councils through the Panchayati Raj Act of 1992. The implementation of Panchayati Raj established new systems of apportioning representation, particularly for Backward Classes and women, which had far reaching consequences. Also, given that panchayats were charged with the tasks of economic development, they functioned within a larger development process that had national and international connections through the growing Non-government Organizations (NGOs) sector.

The third case is the rise of regional parties and the BJP. The BJP traded on an assertion of male power as part of their strategy for political mobilization and did so, ironically, with some high profile women politicians often articulating the message. The Telegu Dessam Party in Andhra rose to power by advocating women's rights, but shifted its focus to technology over time. The movement for Backward Classes and Dalit rights, as expressed in several political parties, found some of its most powerful voices came from women – who then faced additional challenges in electoral politics.

The fourth case outlined in this chapter looks at some elements of environmental activism in India. Environmental causes gained international attention, influenced Indian legislation, but also experienced setbacks in the 1990s.

Perhaps best illustrating the theme of the chapter are the contradictory phenomena that characterized the decade, embracing quintessential globalization and assertion of local culture. Therefore the conclusion juxtaposes the success of the Business Process Outsourcing industry (BPOs) with the renaming of cities and cultural assertion in new Indian states. We see that even in a globalized world, or perhaps especially in a globalized world, local culture matters.

SHAH BANO – ONE WOMAN'S STORY, LARGER CONSEQUENCES

The story of the Shah Bano controversy begins with a woman's claim for maintenance from her husband in accordance with Indian law. It escalated to the Supreme Court, where her claim was upheld, and prompted new legislation passed by Parliament, exempting Muslim women from certain legislation. The implications of the case pitted Indian secular law against Muslim law, created dissension among Muslim intellectuals, rallied and divided women's organizations, and provided fuel for Hindu nationalism. Looking at the issue historically demonstrates its complexity – the winners and losers are not at all clear. To look at the various strands of the case, let us begin with the legal questions.

Initially, Shah Bano, a Muslim woman who had been married for nearly 50 years, went before a local magistrate in April 1978, charging her husband under criminal law with failure to support her. Under Section 125 of the Criminal Procedure Code, women who were destitute or deserted could claim support from their husbands.

Shah Bano's personal story, revealed in the court records, was that after more than forty years of marriage, and as a result of serious deterioration in her relationship with her husband, she had been 'turned out of the house' in 1975 (Shah Bano v. M. A. Khan 1980). Since 1975, she had lived separately from her husband, M. A. Khan, who did provide some financial support. However, when he abruptly stopped payments, Shah Bano sought relief from the local magistrate in Indore, in Madhya Pradesh, citing her husband's general obligation to maintain her (as his wife and as mother to four of his children), but also because of her significant health problems. The magistrate acknowledged her claim, but set the level of maintenance at an almost insignificant sum. She therefore appealed her case to the Madhya Pradesh High Court, which considered the fact that as a barrister her husband had a comfortable income, and increased the sum of maintenance. Meanwhile, her husband divorced her in April of 1978, using the most expedient form of divorce under Muslim law.

In November 1978 M. A. Khan appealed the ruling to the Indian Supreme Court. Central to his claim was that, especially because he had divorced Shah Bano, the case fell under the jurisdiction of Muslim Personal Law and not the criminal courts.

The Supreme Court, in a ruling composed by Chief Justice Y. V. Chandrachud, upheld Shah Bano's right to maintenance on the grounds that this was in the common interests of all those 'aspiring to create an equal society of men and women'. In addition, it suggested that the guarantee of maintenance was not only an issue of Indian Constitutional law, but also in keeping with the *Qur'an* and the Shariat. Further, the Court called for reconsideration by the Parliament, of the system of separate personal laws and the establishment of a Uniform Civil Code (The Supreme Court, Criminal Appellate Jurisdiction, 1981) [**Doc. 40, p. 168**]. This is where the ironies of the case emerged. Many women's organizations celebrated the Supreme Court verdict. In fact, women sympathetic to Shah Bano's case joined her brief before the Court. Some Muslim jurists and the Muslim Personal Law Board decried the attempt by the secular Supreme Court to interpret Shariat law and the *Qur'an*. Their argument turned, in large measure, on the issue of jurisdiction, which compelled significant support among Muslims and others interested in minority rights. In fact, Madhu Kishwar, an activist for women's rights and the editor of a major women's magazine at the time, *Manushi*, supported the verdict, but even in her support expressed concern with the language of the Court.

There were detailed and nuanced arguments in a number of circles – among Muslim reformers, for example – about the details of the verdict. But some of the most conservative views seemed to win out. On 25 February 1986, the Congress Party introduced a law undermining the Court verdict: the Muslim Women (Protection of Rights on Divorce) Bill. The Bill elicited strong criticism from opposition MPs and women's groups throughout the country. Arif Mohammad Khan, the Minister of State for Energy in then Prime Minister, Rajiv Gandhi's cabinet, resigned over the Bill. On 6 March, a large rally in Delhi brought together more than 15 different women's organizations to protest the Bill.

RESPONSES TO THE MUSLIM WOMEN'S BILL

Critics accused the Congress Party of pandering to conservative Muslim interests in hopes of gaining votes in the minority community to compensate for eroding support in other demographics. In 1986 the Congress Party was in power and Rajiv Gandhi had only been prime minister since 1984. He was still relatively new to politics and consolidating power both in the party and in the country as a whole. For example, the BJP was challenging Congress among upper caste Hindu voters, calling for unity in the context of the Babri Masjid/Ram Janambhoomi controversy, as described in the last chapter. Political scientists saw both of these issues as part of a growing phenomenon they dubbed the 'communalization' of politics, meaning that politicians were appealing to voters based on their interests as a community. This vocabulary of politics reinforced common reference in India to 'communal' as referring to the interests of a particular religious group. 'Communal violence', therefore means conflict between religious groups – Hindu and Muslim, for example.

Therefore, the language of the Shah Bano decision, the protests that followed it, and the debate over the Muslim Women's Bill, had to be seen in the context of other Hindu/Muslim issues that were part of the social consciousness of the time. Rajiv Gandhi defended the Bill as a needed assertion of India's commitment to guarantee minority rights – to show its respect for the autonomy of the Muslim community. In an interview with the columnist M. J. Akbar, he said, 'If this (Shah Bano controversy) has made [Muslims] feel threatened . . . that this is the first step toward really finishing Islam in India, I think it's a very dangerous thing. Because our intention is not to encroach on that' (Engineer, 1987).

The Shah Bano issue galvanized sections of India's diverse women's movement, creating common cause among some organizations, that otherwise had very different interests. Like many other social groups, women's organizations had been multiplying in the early 1980s, recovering from the repression of the Emergency, when they had focused on the immediate needs produced by the Emergency, such as human rights violations.

By the mid-1980s, a number of women's organizations had formed and re-formed in towns and cities across India. Older groups such as SEWA, the Self Employed Women's Association, which aided women working in the informal labour sector (especially in Gujarat and Bihar), and POW, the Progressive Organization of Women that formed out of the radical left in rural Andhra Pradesh, continued in their respective regions. Issues about women's working conditions and wages as well as social equity generated new organizations as well. In the countryside the emphasis was on issues such as labour, health conditions, and access to water.

The Shah Bano case reinforced concerns that many women's groups had been expressing for some time about domestic issues – opposing domestic violence and dowry, for example. The scholar, Rajeshwari Sundar Rajan, in an analysis of how this debate shaped the terms of the urban women's movement, argues that it was one of several examples in which women's organizations used the principles of liberal, secular government as the basis for women's rights. The debate then over the Shah Bano issue and the Muslim Women's Bill became framed in terms of religious oppression versus women's rights (Rajan, 1994). Posters for women's protest rallies at the time underscored this point. One poster literally portrays a woman muzzled by religion; a hand, extending from a graphic of a mosque/temple/church, covers her mouth (Kumar, 1993: 62). Women's organizations embraced a language that linked women's rights to modernity, as opposed to more so-called traditional terms held by religious and social authorities. The problem with this discourse, says Rajan, is that it juxtaposed women's rights against traditional values (Rajan, 1994: 137). This made many women uncomfortable.

As a social scientist, Niraja Gopal Jayal, put it, 'The Muslim woman emerged as a doubly disadvantaged citizen. She is disadvantaged both as a member of a minority community and as a woman' (Jayal, 2001: 209). As Zoya Hasan explains, the government's definition of minority rights for Muslims is based on the right to religious autonomy. In the meantime, real job discrimination, poverty and other material deficiencies that Muslims experience often remain outside the political discourse on minority rights

(Z. Hasan, 2000). So the choices for Muslim women of where to find support were not always clear.

This was true of Shah Bano herself, who on the 2 November 1985 relinquished her claim to the court settlement. In an open letter published in the Urdu paper *Inqilab* she said that now that she realized her legal appeals were in contradiction of Muslim Law she no longer wished to accept their results. She ended the letter by saying, 'I also appeal to all the Ulama (Muslim community) of India that they should establish a "Safeguard for Shariat Board" for the benefit of divorced women, through which they should be helped to get their Shariat rights' (Engineer, 1987: 213).

Some Muslims tried to change the terms of the debate, opposing the Muslim Women's Bill on grounds internal to Muslim law or supporting Shah Bano's right to continued maintenance within the context of Shariat. For example, some years later, Begum Naseem Iqtidar Ali, a member of the Muslim Personal Law Board, proposed what she considered a Shariat-based reform, a series of changes to the practice of Muslim personal law in keeping with Shariat that would benefit Muslim women's interests.

Internal debate among Muslims may have influenced the Muslim Women's (Protection of Rights on Divorce) Act, before it was finally signed into law on 20 May 1986. While the Bill did absolve ex-husbands of the responsibility for maintenance beyond the Shariat-prescribed period of *iddat*, it contained other provisions for Muslim women's maintenance after divorce. For example, there was legislation for the practice that a woman could seek support from the Waqf boards, local Muslim community-based service organizations. Also the law spelled out the obligations that those who stood to inherit family property were required to support her. As Flavia Agnes, a long time women's activist, admitted, the Act ultimately provided some rights and assurances to Muslim women that other women in India, particularly the majority, whose marriages were covered by the Hindu Code, did not enjoy (Agnes, 2001).

The Muslim Women (Protection of Rights on Divorce) Act and the Shah Bano case that inspired it had several long-term implications in Indian politics. The legislation set a general precedent for government participation in the codification of religious law within the secular framework of India's democracy. For example, in 1993 a similar case spawned legislation governing Christian marriage. In each case legislators consulted with religious leaders in producing the legislation. Among the questions this process raised is who decides which religious leaders to consult and what does it mean for the government to weigh in on issues that may be part of an evolving debate within a religious community, or even how to define the religious community.

Second, the Shah Bano case became a referent for the growing Hindu Nationalist movement and the rising BJP. Simply the name 'Shah Bano' at a BJP rally implied that the Congress Government was preoccupied with the rights of minorities. Does not democracy mean majority rule, one speaker at a BJP rally asked? If so, minorities should conform to the will of the majority, rather than carving out areas of separate law for their special interests.

The BJP ideologue and leader, L. K. Advani, used Shah Bano in his speeches to suggest that Muslims did not support their wives the way Hindus did, reinforcing prejudices among his followers, and using women as a potent symbol of his movement. The BJP relied for its political mobilization on male activists, for example on the young men trained in RSS camps (see the previous chapter). So the language of 'protecting women' was, in part, directed toward them; it portrayed women as objects of law, rather than agents of law. However, as the historian Tanika Sarkar writes in *Women and the Hindu Right*, this underscored several contradictory elements within the Hindu Right. Its rhetoric criticized Muslim Personal Law, but emulated some of its practices in advocating a conservative adherence to Hindu practices within the family (Sarkar and Butalia, 1995: 212). Furthermore, the Hindu Code had other limitations, for example, on women's inheritance rights that were more favourably spelled out for Muslim women than their Hindu counterparts.

Rhetorically, the Shah Bano case and, particularly, the political response to it, shifted the terms of another major political debate in India over what is called a Uniform Civil Code – the idea of having one law for all families and marriages. Women's organizations in the past had long agreed and advocated for a Uniform Civil Code that would grant equal rights to all women in the case of marriage, inheritance, custody, and divorce. In fact, the Supreme Court Decision in the Shah Bano case invigorated their claim because, in the judgement, Justice Chandrachud specifically called for a reconsideration of the Uniform Civil Code.

The BJP and right-wing Hindu organizations interpreted the issue differently. They too re-examined the concept of a Uniform Civil Code in the context of the Shah Bano Case. However, following from their anger over the passage of the Muslim Women Act, they now called for imposing the majority Hindu Code on a larger scale. Their claim for one – unified – code had an entirely different meaning.

Interestingly, women's organizations, which had advocated a uniform code since the time of the framing of the Constitution, now backtracked from it because of this new meaning. In other words, they accepted the change in political discourse that right wing advocates had instituted.

The transformation of the Uniform Civil Code issue was one of many instances that signalled to women activists the importance of greater participation in electoral politics. By the late 1980s some women's organizations that had avoided the electoral arena were already beginning to embrace it. This next section explores that shift and a parallel process – the development of Panchayati Raj – that created opportunities for women in local government.

WOMEN'S PARLIAMENTARY POLITICS

Women's organizations that mobilized around the Shah Bano case were largely those outside of election politics. As part of a conscious strategy to remain aloof of political party pressures, many women's organizations proclaimed themselves 'the autonomous women's movement,' meaning they would not be connected to a political party. Some, such as Karmika, a women's legal forum, required members to dissociate themselves from parties. An exception was the Mahila Dakshata Samiti (MDS), which formed initially as a consumer advocacy group, but expanded into the legal arena as well. MDS evolved from the Janata Party of 1977 and its members tended to be part of the socialist wing of that movement and the parties it developed. However, more typical were organizations such as Saheli (a women's domestic support organization), Jagori, (a women's advocacy and literacy organization) and Stree Shakti Sanghatan (a women's rights organization in Hyderabad) all of which eschewed political parties. Activists claimed that direct action was more productive than relying on parties and legislatures, in part because legislation had not always effected real change.

This pointed to a disjuncture between the politics of those women active in political parties and those in the autonomous women's movement. Some MPs, such as Renuka Ray from Bengal and Mrinal Gore from Maharashtra, devoted their careers to women's issues. But the numbers were small and the few exceptions only served to manifest for many women's organizations the difficulties they faced in accomplishing social change through legislative means. By and large, the autonomous women's movement, as diffuse as it was, considered party politics of little value and public office as corrupting and ineffective.

Nevertheless, India had a long history of women in elected and appointed positions in government. From the time of the Freedom Movement women played a major role in nationalist and national politics. Indira Gandhi, as prime minister, was not so much an exception but rather a confirmation of that tradition. There were 24 women in the first Lok Sabha in 1952 and by 1962 there were 39. Furthermore, a series of rules and customs encouraged women to run for office at the national and state levels.

Indira Gandhi herself did not particularly promote women in office. In fact, more women served in Parliament during the prime ministerships of both her father and her son, than during her own terms in office. Nor did she particularly advocate women's issues. Still, she commissioned the *Report on the Status of Women in India* in 1975 (as discussed earlier) and at critical moments stepped forward to support bills in Parliament that advocated women's rights. For example, in 1981, she established a commission on eliminating dowry and helped pass the legislation it proposed. Similarly, when women's groups in Delhi protested against plans to build a temple to honour *satis* (widows who killed themselves by self-immolation at the time of their husband's funeral) Indira Gandhi intervened to prevent the construction.

While some women in Parliament claimed that, despite Mrs. Gandhi's weak record on women's issues, her presence there served to empower other women members, other women, even in her own Congress Party, considered Indira Gandhi's leadership an obstacle to their ambitions because she prized loyalty over representation of particular groups when choosing her cabinet. Furthermore, her overwhelming power as a symbol of women's advancement may have taken some urgency out of the Congress Party's commitment to realizing palpable change.

In the 1980s and prior to then, women carved out a political arena for themselves through activism or service, demarcating a line between women's politics and election politics (Kumar, 1993, Calman, 1992) but by the mid-1990s this line began to dissolve, as the advantage of participation in elections – even the call for reservations of seats for women in legislatures – became more apparent. Several things had changed. The power of the legislature in the Shah Bano case was one inspiration and the Panchayati Raj Act, which guaranteed women representation in local governing bodies, was another.

PANCHAYATS AND RESERVATIONS

A key project for Prime Minister Rajiv Gandhi's reform agenda was a proposal to revitalize local self-government in the form of Panchayati Raj. The term *panchayat* came from an old tradition in India of village councils that settled local disputes. Many panchayats already existed. Three elements that characterized Rajiv Gandhi's proposal, however, were:

1. the creation of comparable panchayats in all states at the local and regional levels;
2. the real devolution of development – both decision-making and funds to accomplish it – to panchayats; and
3. a provision to reserve seats in panchayats for women and disadvantaged groups.

In fact, Mahatma Gandhi too had suggested that panchayats might be a model for the kind of self-sufficient villages he envisioned as part of an ideal society and there had been other proposals to revitalize panchayats after independence. Nevertheless, in the context of the 1980s, panchayats functioned in some places and not in others and often simply confirmed the will of the most powerful forces in the local countryside.

It took seven years before Rajiv Gandhi's proposal reached fruition. In the meantime, the Congress Party lost the election of 1989 and a new Janata Dal Government did not survive for a full term. When new elections were called in 1991, Rajiv Gandhi, in the midst of a campaign that looked positive for his party, was assassinated at an election rally.

Congress won the Tenth Lok Sabha elections in 1991 and the Parliament showed renewed enthusiasm for the Panchayati Raj Act; some members described it as a memorial to their slain leader. The Panchayati Raj Act required an Amendment to the Constitution and involved intense negotiations with states, which were concerned about the usurpation of states' rights. What finally became the 73rd and 74th Amendment Acts funnelled money from the Central Government directly to panchayats (as well as to similar municipal councils) to allow for decisions to be made at the local level about development priorities [**Doc. 41, pp. 168–70**]. It did not require complete uniformity in the states, but each state had to establish a three-tier system of local governing bodies and develop mechanisms to implement reservations in local elections. Village-level bodies would receive financial grants from the state and national government and also from higher-level panchayats, which could exercise the right to tax citizens.

The most obvious difference in appearance in the new panchayats lay in their composition. In addition to reservations for Scheduled Castes and Tribes, one-third of the seats were required to be reserved for women. Similarly, women also received one-third of the positions as *sarpanches* or presidents, on a rotating basis. Furthermore, states were permitted to reserve seats for Other Backward Classes (OBC) as well. Each state was required to submit a proposal for how it would comply with the new Constitutional amendment. However, states had some autonomy in terms of the specific shape of their panchayat programme.

In Andhra Pradesh, for example, where panchayats had already existed and had even required some representation of women before the 73rd Amendment, the new system was particularly complex and intricate. The Panchayati Raj Handbook described the calculations it carried out in order to achieve the right combination of reserved seats for women, OBCs, and Scheduled Castes or Tribes. Women's seats in panchayats rotated geo- graphically around the village and their access to the posts of *sarpanch* rotated throughout the state. Reservations for Backward Classes and Scheduled Castes and Tribes were distributed based on population density. This process required fine-tuning the definitions of backward classes and assuring that the total seats reserved did not surpass a legislated limit of 50 per cent.

INTERPRETING NEW PANCHAYATS

According to the Ministry of Rural Development, by the end of the twentieth century more than 721,520 women were serving in elected office in panchayats. Of those more than 150,000 held leadership roles. Some panchayats elected all women and in several places – usually those with prior experience of women in panchayats – the number of women regularly exceeded 33 per cent. This dramatic transformation countered the assumptions of some critics who had wondered if the Panchayati Raj laws could be implemented.

Sceptics of the legislation expressed concerns that women members of panchayats might serve as proxies for more powerful men. So once the 73rd Amendment passed – and it succeeded with little opposition – a number of programmes developed to anticipate this possibility. Politicians, government officers, NGOs and academics all began a process of facilitating its implementation and training new panchayat members.

The 'problem' of integrating women into panchayats took a prominent position in the newspapers. The media openly speculated on the viability of finding sufficient women to fill the seats, and articles also stressed the doubts of local men, many of whom had served in panchayat institutions. 'Men will nominate their wives, who will serve as puppets for their husband', remarked one former sarpanch. 'What will be if we cannot find women to run for positions?' questioned a party activist. (*Times of India*, 10 March 2002).

Several academic studies of panchayats have appeared since its implementation, although most are local and do not provide much opportunity to make general statements across India. Nevertheless, these studies show that women members have in fact asserted independent authority in many cases and often on issues they considered special concerns among women (Chattopadyay and Duflo, 2003). For example, there was an increase in projects to promote easier access to potable water, sanitation and indoor plumbing, better schools, and more efficient cooking stoves.

Panchayats entered a world of development, already inhabited by the Indian Administrative Service (civil service officers) and NGOs, with established protocols and customs. Still panchayats have the potential to modify or supplement the trends common among these institutions by giving villagers greater control and voice over the terms of development. NGOs, however, have played an increasingly large role in development in 1990s and garnered funding from abroad. According to the Indian *Economic Times*, in 2001–2 Indian NGOs received donations of Rs 45 billion from abroad, the equivalent of about one billion dollars at the time. In one year the amount increased by 7.4 per cent, and the range of donors continued to increase, mostly from Europe and the United States. In addition, many NGOs received funds from the Indian Government and international aid agencies. Because NGOs constitute themselves based on the interests of their organizers, their effects can be spotty and geographically arbitrary.

Ideally, panchayats, as agents of development, can reflect the needs of the community. Some levels of panchayats were permitted to levy taxes to fund development projects. Still, others, the most local, received funding from regional, state, and national government. Therefore, despite the efforts placed on democratizing and diversifying representation on panchayats they remain one sector of a complex development structure vying for government funds.

FROM PANCHAYAT TO PARLIAMENT

The success of Panchayati Raj legislation in terms of increasing representation of women encouraged a 'from panchayat to parliament' movement, demanding reservations for women in state legislatures and Parliament. However, each time such legislation reached the floor of Parliament – or sometimes in committee before reaching the floor – it failed amid heated opposition. One of the most common claims by its opponents was a demand to incorporate into the law concomitant reservations for OBCs as well.

This political manoeuvre stalled efforts for women's reservations because the Constitution of India, which allows special provisions for women's advancement and for specified Scheduled Castes does not explicitly permit discrimination – even positive discrimination – based on caste. Therefore, while provisions can be made for OBCs at the state level, and general programmes can advance socially and educationally Backward Classes, reservations for OBCs in Parliament would have required another Constitutional Amendment.

Therefore, the debate pitted community rights against gender rights and women politicians, in a way not dissimilar to the Shah Bano case. The issue of women's reservations in Parliament remained unresolved at the end of the twentieth century.

However, interestingly at the same time many of the highest profile politicians in India were women and overt appeals to women voters became a hallmark of each political campaign. For example, no party openly opposed the bill to require one-third representation for women in parliament even as they prevented it from passing on technicalities. In the BJP, several prominent women politicians dominated the scene: Rajmata Vijaye Raje Scindia, the former Maharani of Gwalior, was considered the symbolic head of the whole party until she retired from politics on health grounds in 1998. Also, Uma Bharti, the sanyasini (religious holy woman) who articulated the party's Hindu and Backward Class interests, and Sushma Swaraj, the sophisticated Delhi politician, characterized its two wings. The BJP proved to be a national party, capable of holding together the NDA (the National Democratic Alliance) in order to govern, which it did from 1998 to 2004.

Among its partners was the AIADMK (All-India Anna Dravida Munnetra Kazhagam), whose leader Jayalalithaa Jayaram played power politics in Tamil Nadu. As discussed earlier, AIADMK was founded by Tamil matinee idol M. G. Ramachandran (MGR). After his death and a brief power struggle within the party, J. Jayalalithaa, his former screen heroine and political protégé, took over as party leader. Initially, Jayalalithaa continued MGR's alliance with the Indian National Congress, but joined the BJP during its ascendancy. Her primary interests remained with strengthening Tamil Nadu's position at the Centre, whatever government was in power (though her detractors pointed to corruption in her government as a sign of less noble goals). Because of her considerable popularity and power in Tamil Nadu, Jayalalithaa became a prized ally for the Central Government, often swaying the decisions of the BJP-led government.

Political charges against Jayalalithaa often took gendered form. Her relationships with men and the elaborate wedding she financed for her godson, all served as fodder for gossip and sources of scandal. Her career on the screen both benefited her politically and made her vulnerable to scepticism about her seriousness in making policy.

In the neighbouring state of Andhra Pradesh another screen figure, often compared to MGR, rose to power with a similar message of regional identity. N. T. Rama Rao, a star of the Telegu cinema, translated his popularity to power as well when he formed the Telegu Dessam Party. And, although the Telegu Dessam Party did not prominently project a woman leader in the 1980s, it succeeded on a platform of gendered politics, portraying its leader, N. T. Rama Rao as the defender of Andhra women, or *Anna garu* (elder brother, in Telegu).

N. T. Rama Rao, who served as Chief Minister of Andhra Pradesh from 1983 to 1995, advanced Telegu language and culture, in part using his own film image, having played gods on the screen. As he explained later in an interview, his commitment to women's equality was a religious conviction. As he told it, Hindus hold women on a pedestal, giving them ultimate respect as mothers to the world. Therefore, women must be treated equally and share in the economic prosperity of society. But he added that this was all meaningless if it lay in philosophy alone; rather he insisted that legal and political intervention was necessary to secure women's rights (NTR December, 1995).

In practice, NTR took advantage of existing women's movements in Andhra Pradesh that had mobilized against alcohol consumption and high prices for rice. The anti-alcohol movement emerged from the Andhra district of Nellore, where participants associated the consumption of arrack (a local liquor) with domestic violence and household poverty. Also, the anti-price rise movement, which (as Chapter 4 demonstrated) had antecedents in other states, protested economic liberalization policies that relaxed government subsidies on basic commodities.

In response NTR banned alcohol, declaring Andhra Pradesh a dry state and subsidized rice so that the price did not exceed 2 rupees a kilo in government ration stores. Symbolically he addressed all women in Andhra as his sisters and insisted that his administration would defend their interests. As a popular and populist leader, N. T. Rama Rao was tapped as a possible prime minister if the Janata Dal Coalition succeeded in 1991.

In August 1995, however, a split in his party led by his son-in-law, Chandra Babu Naidu, forced him out of the leadership of the Telegu Dessam Party. NTR then died suddenly of a heart attack five months later. In the next election, his widow, Laxmi Parvati, carried his banner against Chandra Babu Naidu, whose platform emphasized technology and development rather than women's issues. But she had not succeeded in absorbing NTR's considerable charisma and lost by a large margin.

MAYAWATI AND PHOOLAN DEVI, LEADERS OF DEPRESSED CLASSES

The political landscape was also populated with powerful women who represented the interests of depressed groups. The competing parties of the **Bahujan** Samaj Party and the Samajwadi Party in Uttar Pradesh, prominently featured two women politicians, Mayawati and Phoolan Devi, both members of depressed castes and both unlikely politicians, sceptical of the system.

Bahujan: Literally majority; term used by the Bahujan Samaj Party to underscore that lower caste interests represent a majority in Indian politics.

Mayawati was one of the leading political agents in the 1990s. She brokered deals with a number of parties to advocate the interests of what she considered her natural constituency, Dalits across the country. Dalit is the word chosen by the political movement of Scheduled Castes, who have mobilized to remove the social disabilities of their position in society. While it had deeper roots as the translation of the British term 'depressed classes', it became prominent through use by the Dalit Panthers who, as their name suggests, were a militant group defending the rights of Scheduled Castes. Over time, the Dalit movement came to represent not only people who identified with Scheduled Castes, but other disadvantaged groups.

Mayawati, who was born into the Scheduled Caste known as Jatav or Chamar, was first trained as a lawyer and then became a teacher in a government school in Delhi. In 1984 she resigned from teaching and ran for parliament as a candidate of the newly formed Bahujan Samaj Party (BSP). Although she lost, in fact several elections in a row, the process served to help develop strategies for the BSP.

Later in Uttar Pradesh she became Chief Minister of the state, its highest elected office, demonstrating her skill both at mobilizing her base and compromising with other parties. She was elected to the Lok Sabha twice from different reserved Scheduled Caste constituencies, Bijnore (SC) in 1989 and Akbarpur (SC) in 1998.

Both educationally and politically, Mayawati benefited from reservations, which allowed her access to facilities that might have been denied her due to prejudice, a point that the BSP founder Kanshi Ram often made on the campaign trail. Mayawati was the protégé and designated successor of Kanshi Ram who, as a Dalit leader, had spent decades organizing his fellow Scheduled Caste government employees and building their union.

While the BSP was certainly associated with Dalit politics, the term *bahujan* means majority (http://www.bahujansamajparty.com). From the beginning the BSP's philosophy stated that the depressed classes – Muslims, poor peasants, and other communities that experience disabilities, including the OBCs – in fact, comprise a majority of the nation. For this reason the BSP embraced the Mandal Commission recommendations and the interests of Backward Classes. One of their slogans was 'Mandal ayog lagu karo, kursi khali karo' (Implement Mandal or vacate the seat) accusing upper caste MPs of opposing Mandal to save their positions (Jaffrelot, 1996: 38).

During the NDA government, led by the Bharatiya Janata Party, which was known for the strong support it received among upper castes, Mayawati deftly made connections with other depressed classes to gain power for the BSP. She also helped extend the popularity of the BSP, so that it encroached on traditional areas of support for another UP Party, the Samajwadi (or Socialist) Party.

The forcefulness of both Mayawati's politics and her personality drew enemies and criticism. She was accused of participating in several scandals, including shady deals that allegedly benefited her relatives with land and hotels. Several cases went to court. While some of these accusations took the form of similar charges made against male politicians, other accusations took gendered forms. For example, there were rumours about her relationship with Kanshi Ram because of assumptions about the nature of the political connection between an unmarried woman and the powerful man with whom she closely worked.

Unlike Mayawati, whose life represented a political struggle, Phoolan Devi, who became an MP on the Samajwadi ticket, endured a life characterized by armed physical struggle. Although she was elected an MP both in 1996 and 1999, Phoolan Devi entered the popular imagination earlier as the 'Bandit Queen', the woman who spent years as a bandit avenging her own violent assault by joining an armed rural gang.

Phoolan Devi's story was recorded, both in a book by the writer Mala Sen, and in a film produced by the prominent director Shekhar Kapur, and the overarching narrative of a victim fighting back helped catapult Phoolan Devi to national fame. While these representations were controversial, especially the disturbing rape scene in the movie – and Phoolan Devi briefly protested the film – she acknowledged the overall outline of the story. Specifically, Phoolan Devi, a member of the Backward Class – Mallah community – grew up in a village in Uttar Pradesh and her family arranged her marriage to a much older man. Later she ran away from the marriage and was gang-raped by upper caste Thakur men, but escaped with her life. For the next several years she joined a prominent rural bandit group and engaged in robbery and violence herself in the U.P. countryside.

The central incident for which she was convicted and jailed took place in the village of Behmai, where she took revenge, killing a number of the Thakur men, though not the same men who had raped her. After successfully evading police for four months, she finally turned herself in and spent ten years in jail. The image of her with a bandana across her forehead and a gun in her arms on the day of her surrender became something of an iconic representation of women's and lower-caste rebellion.

Having been released from jail in 1993, Phoolan Devi ran for office in the 1996 elections on the Samajwadi Party ticket. As the MP from Mirzapur constituency, she advocated the rights of Backward Classes and Dalits, so that she found supporters far beyond Uttar Pradesh. In fact, her own caste, the Mallahs, traditionally from fisher communities, celebrated her as a hero; and she found followers among other fisher communities and Backward Castes throughout India.

A journalist, Venkitesh Ramakrishnan, writing in the news magazine *Frontline*, described an incident that illustrated Phoolan Devi's commitment both to her party and to depressed class voters. During the election of 1998, she arrived at a village in Uttar Pradesh, where Thakurs had stalled polling at the booth and prevented Dalits and Backward Caste voters from exercising their franchise. Phoolan Devi calmly left her car and walked straight into the polling booth to the cheers of voters around her. She confronted the polling officers and 'beseeched' them to carry out their 'duties freely and fairly and allow everybody to vote'. She then changed her stance and made it clear that while she was appealing to them with humility she could 'speak a different language too'. Ramakrishnan reports that her display of power succeeded in opening the polls and confirmed why Dalits and Backward Caste voters had such faith in her.

In 2001, she was assassinated as she walked home for lunch following the morning session in Parliament. The main shooter, a man named Pankaj alias Sher Singh Rana, was captured and confessed to the crime, claiming (though some sources remained sceptical) that he was motivated by revenge for the Behmai killings of Thakurs.

While Phoolan Devi's relatively short political careermake broad analysis incomplete, her greatest effectiveness stemmed from her ability to translate her biography to advocate the rights of depressed classes and women. Mayawati too advocated for her Dalit constituency, but gradually expanded her base, not only to Backward Classes and Muslims, but to upper castes as well. The next section turns from the electoral arena in which Mayawati and, eventually, Phoolan Devi functioned to other forms of political action that also addressed the interests of depressed classes.

THE FOREST AND THE TREES: ENVIRONMENTAL POLITICS

The environmental movement brings together themes that have emerged in all the earlier sections of this chapter. Women have played a major role in its character and leadership and local movements have received support from NGOs, both Indian and abroad. Furthermore issues of social status are inevitably associated with the movement, which tends to involve contested forestland – populated largely by indigenous (also called Adivasi) communities, legally categorized as Scheduled Tribes.

Like all the other stories in this chapter, understanding environmental politics in the 1990s requires looking back to some earlier moments. In particular, histories of environmental movements in India usually begin with the 'Chipko' Movement as key not only to the origins of Indian environmentalism but also its particular characteristics (Guha, 2000, Khagram, 2004). The Chipko Movement in the 1970s pitted local villagers, who were members of Scheduled Tribes, against the Indian Government, whose desire it was to auction off the local lumber rights to loggers. Unlike environmental movements in the West that focus on conservation and were often supported by middle-class interests, the villagers involved in the Chipko Movement fought for control over their own forests, homes, and livelihood. In addition, although the Chipko Movement initially focused on forest rights, the mobilization it achieved helped fight a dam project soon afterward.

Briefly, the Chipko Movement took place in northern Uttar Pradesh in the forests of the foothills of the Himalayas, when the Forest Department of the state government prepared to auction off forest rights to outside companies, rather than giving local communities control over the forest. Chipko – which means hugging trees – refers to the method that local villagers used to prevent logging. Serving as human shields, they surrounded trees to prevent them being cut. After a number of protests and appeals to government that because of the special status of Scheduled Tribes, they had the right to control their own land, the situation came to a head in 1974, when the Forest

Department once again sent loggers into the forest to fell trees. The men of the village were called to an official meeting outside of the area, as a way to prevent protest. However, the women of the village of Reni gathered in the forest, hugging the trees, and despite threats from the loggers fended them off through non-violent protest. The government of Uttar Pradesh agreed to investigate forest rights and set up an inquiry committee, which by 1977 had affirmed the hill people's rights to the land. Of course, no story is quite so simple and the meaning of rights continued to be an issue of controversy – not only in this region of Uttar Pradesh, but throughout India's forests.

The legacies of the Chipko Movement can be understood in a number of ways. For example, in neighbouring forests, veterans of the Chipko Movement and their political allies fought to prevent the building of the Tehri dam, which would have displaced tens of thousands of local people and submerged 12,800 acres of forest. While many dams had been built in India up to that point, this case benefited from the publicity around the Chipko Movement. It is also an interesting example here because of its local, national, and international implications.

The Tehri dam, proposed by the national government in 1972, would have been one of the largest in Asia. It planned to provide 2400 mW of electricity, irrigation, and drinking water. But its construction was stalled by a number of processes. State approval took four years and by then the Chipko Movement and other forms of mobilization had created an energetic opposition. Local interests brought court cases, which cited among other things the fact that the area was prone to earthquakes. Working through the court system took another 10 years and so it was not until 1985 that the case was argued before the Supreme Court, on the grounds of whether or not the government had adequately considered the broad range of safety concerns and human impact of the dam. Ultimately the Supreme Court ruled in 1990 in favour of the government. In a decision that took seven years to reach and a very detailed judgement to express, the Court agreed that the government had engaged sufficient scientific study and had addressed the relevant safety factors [**Doc. 42, pp. 170–1**].

However, by 1990 there had been many changes in the world. The Soviet Union, which had initially signed on to help fund the project and provide technical support, no longer existed. The government had to start again to raise funds and, of course, protests continued, addressing successive governments both at the state and national level. While some environmental clearances took place and construction began, a nearby earthquake in 1991 brought new calls for delay.

By the end of the twentieth century, the Tehri Dam project had not been cancelled but neither had it been built. The area around the dam was now in a new state – Uttaranchal – which had been carved out of Uttar Pradesh in 2000. The creation of Uttaranchal, though not related to the dam issue, was indeed connected to the political mobilization of the hill people of the region, who felt politically alienated in the large, mostly plains state of Uttar Pradesh. As one of three new states carved out of areas covered largely by forest, and populated by Adivasi people, the state of Uttaranchal would now have to deal with the issue of the Tehri Dam construction. Uttaranchal was renamed Uttarakhand in 2007 and the state's tourist website has a paragraph on the Tehri region as a tourist destination. Ironically the paragraph on the dam both celebrates its potential achievements as well as the achievements of the opponents who have forestalled its completion (Government of Uttarakhand).

India in the twentieth century was one of the biggest builders of dams in the world. The movement to re-evaluate dam projects is associated internationally with the Sardar Sarovar Dam on the Narmada River. Despite years of protests by local Adivasis and grassroots organizers, who formed the Narmada Bachchao Andolan – Save Narmada Movement, the dam was built by 2005. A main leader of the movement, Medha Patkar, organized protests among those directly affected by the dam and lobbied the Indian Government. She also internationalized the struggle with appeals to organizations and sympathizers abroad. The government of Gujarat, which has most benefited from the dam, launched its own pro-publicity campaign heralding the benefits of the dam. The Booker prize-winning author, Arundhati Roy, publicized the issue as well, supporting the Narmada Bacchao Movement. Her high profile participation – joining protests and speaking against government rulings – brought significant international attention. She spoke about Narmada, when she received a literary award in France and refused the Sahitya Akademi Award at home, citing India's dam construction policy as one of the reasons.

Another thread connected to the Chipko Movement has been the larger question of indigenous rights to forests. The terms indigenous, tribal, or Adivasi refer to communities with their own religious, linguistic and cultural traditions, who live in forest areas and consider themselves indigenous – pre-Hindu – peoples. The Constitution protects the rights of these communities, labelled in law as 'Scheduled Tribes', through special reservations in jobs and legislatures that are similar to those for Scheduled Castes. In the late 1990s discussion began about passing a Forest Act that would guarantee Scheduled Tribes control over the forests in which they lived. The debate over the Act addressed among other things who – the government, conservation organizations, or local forest dwellers themselves – would be the best stewards of forest land. The law forced a re-examination of issue of 'rights', 'indigeneity' and 'regional autonomy'. In 2006, Parliament finally passed the

Scheduled Tribes and Other Traditional Forest Dwellers (Recognition of Forest Rights) Act with the stated objectives:

- To give rights to Scheduled Tribes and Other Traditional Forest Dwellers of land in their historical possession.
- To provide [them] rights . . . to collect, use and dispose of minor forest produce.
- To provide [them] rights on land used for community purposes.

In addition, it lays out some obligations of the government to the forest dwellers, including the building of schools, hospitals, etc.

The most controversial issue in the Act is the way it addresses the issue of conservation. It acknowledges the Indian Conservation Act of 1972 and sets out detailed provisions about the required conditions and necessary process through which forest dwellers can be relocated. But opponents of the Act, particularly among the Indian advocates of tigers, argued that it did not allow for creation of areas free of human presence, which they feel are necessary for tiger preservation. In this, Indian conservationists found support among international wildlife protection organizations.

In addition to conservation, there are other consequences of the law that will emerge in the process of implementation. It is not clear, for example, how the Act ensures the equitable distribution of rights within the forest dwelling communities. Therefore, like much legislation its implications will become clearer over time.

ONE PERSON'S OUTSOURCING AND ANOTHER'S MUMBAI

The facility through which local movements in India find international connections has increased in recent years through new communication technologies. But the most direct example of globalization in India is in the technology industry itself, an arena in which Indian software engineers have become world leaders. It is ironic though, that just as this sector embraced globalization in the 1990s, there was an equally strong assertion of regional and local culture. The two examples juxtaposed here are of the Business Process Outsourcing (BPO) industry, which has played a major role in India's recent economic boom, and some very provincial (perhaps literally) decisions to rename cities and create states that assert local/regional political interests.

To begin let us look at the BPO industry, which employed more than 200,000 workers in 1998. One company, Spectramind was adding 300 employees every month. A 1998 University of California at Berkeley study of 2000 Silicon Valley start-ups found that 40 per cent were launched by Indians, half of whom graduated from the prestigious Indian Institutes of Technology (Saxenian, 1999).

Therefore, while the technology boom in India took the world by surprise, the seeds were planted – for example the establishment of the Indian Institutes of Technology (IIT) – in the early years after independence. While many economists attribute the boom to liberalization of the economy, and specifically the loosening of government regulations, government support for IITs certainly provided the human resources that fuelled these developments. Nehru began to establish and promote IITs soon after independence. In 1963, the 'Institutes of Technology Amendment Act', established a network of such colleges (some existing and some to be built), which were declared 'Institutes of National Importance'. The result was the establishment of five IITs in Kharagpur, Kanpur, Delhi, Mumbai, and Chennai, and eventually two more were added in Guwahati and Roorkee. They now produce the most sought-after engineers in the world.

One company, Infosys, the inspiration for Thomas Friedman's book, *The World is Flat*, was established in 1981, when N. R. Narayana Murthy and six engineers in Pune, India, with an initial capital of US$ 250, began to provide technology services. By 2001, it employed over 100,000 people and represented a $4 billion company. It characterized Friedman's argument that a series of factors including technology levelled the playing field in the world so that small companies in diverse geographic areas could compete in global trade. The extent to which there is equal access to this playing field is open to question, but certain Indian industries have benefited from a more interconnected world and from Indian Government decisions in the 1990s to lessen regulations for international trade. In addition, economists argue that the period of protectionism in India in the 1970s and 1980s, may have given Indian entrepreneurs the impetus from necessity to begin developing their own technologies and products, poised for a future international market.

Infosys had advantages in a world market because it could provide customer service or technological support with a highly educated, English-speaking workforce and could even consult at hours outside the European or North American workday. Other business grew in the software-manufacturing sector – sometimes practically cottage industries – in which a few people with a computer could write new programs that transformed how a business or a scholar or a customer did his or her work.

The city of Bangalore in Karnataka, South India became a centre for this information industry. Florian Taeube argues that Bangalore was a natural place for this because it had a long history of educational institutions and a multicultural population that had always integrated newcomers from other parts of India or other parts of the world. Before 1947 Karnataka was part of the Mysore Kingdom, not British India. The semi-autonomy granted the Maharaja of Mysore had allowed him to support educational opportunities in the state and after independence the number of technical institutes continued to grow, creating as Taeube puts it a 'regional culture of learning' that always attracted outsiders. According to one study 54 per cent of IT workers came from somewhere else (Taeube, 2009) attracted by its opportunities and cosmopolitan nature.

Not just Bangalore, but Hyderabad and Delhi and other cities in India, became home to companies that helped build a technological infrastructure that fuelled global business and communication. Some international backlash to these industries has also emerged in the West. The term, 'outsourcing' suggests that the services that the Indian company offers are ones that used to be carried out inhouse, by the manufacturing firm or distributor in the West. Indian software is sometimes called 'outsourced software' along the same lines. Just as so many things have become global, it is ironic that Infosys too, the 'outsourcing' giant, opened a Boston office in 1987 and a Toronto office in 1995 and, subsequently, offices in Europe as well.

If the labelling of 'outsourcing' or 'call centres' suggests a global politics of naming, in India the maps were being redrawn – both literally and linguistically – according to local politics of language. In the case of Bombay, the move certainly had ideas about globalization in mind. In 1996 a pro-Hindu political party, the Shiv Sena, won elections in Maharasthra (the state in which Bombay was situated) and renamed Bombay after the local patron deity, Mumbai Devi. This was not the first time the argument had been made that the name 'Bombay' was an unwanted legacy of British imperialism. But the political statement in 1996 had renewed meaning, celebrating a specifically Hindu past and a Maharashtra identity in a multicultural, multi-religious, and international city.

Kolkata: The contemporary transliteration of the Bengali name for the city that the British called Calcutta and was originally the capital of British India; it became the capital of the state of West Bengal after independence and changed the spelling of its name in 1996.

The states of Tamil Nadu and West Bengal renamed their capitals as well – Madras became Chennai and Calcutta, **Kolkata**. The Tamil Nadu state assembly voted to change the name of Madras to Chennai in 1996 on the grounds that Madras was the British name for the city and they wanted to adopt an indigenous one. The names 'Chennai' and 'Madras' both had historical connections to the city, in part based on geography – Chennai in the south and Madras in the north (Chennai District Government). Also as readers of Tamil literature point out, the city was called 'Chennai' in literary contexts all along (Venkatachalapathy, 2006). The change from 'Calcutta' to 'Kolkata', on the other hand, simply reverted to a more accurate transliteration of the Bengali name for the city.

In addition three new states were created in the 1990s, carved out of Bihar, Madhya Pradesh, and Uttar Pradesh. While some analysts proposed that the BJP led government at the time presumed the new states would be areas of support for their party, people in the regions had made their own case as well. Each was largely populated by Adivasis and in that regard differed from the majority populations of the original states as a whole. A number of Indian states in the northeast of the country were, in fact, defined geographically in terms of the particular Adivasi communities that inhabited them, so there was a precedent for this. With the establishment of Jharkhand out of Bihar, Chhatisgarh out of Madhya Pradesh, and Uttarakhand (called Uttaranchal) out of Uttar Pradesh, areas rich in natural resources came into the control of people whose livelihoods depended on those environments.

CONCLUSION

This last section encapsulates the themes of the chapter as a whole. It demonstrates that in the ongoing history of contemporary India, the country has adapted to globalization, or perhaps shaped it. In addition, internal politics and local cultures continued to assert themselves – both in governmental politics and in social movements. The implications of the Shah Bano case for both Hindu/Muslim politics and women's politics show that these issues persisted and, in a secular state, the challenge remained of how to deal with religious politics. Women as political players in all movements in India, by the 1990s also advocated increased representation for themselves in Parliament. These are all inevitably unfinished stories.

Dalits and Adivasis, political groups that have on the one hand received benefits from the state in terms of reservations, also had at the end of the twentieth century exerted their own politics in increasingly successful ways. Although not addressed here, these too had global connections. For example, the international movements for indigenous rights and movements for racial equality built connections in India among organizations of Adivasis and Dalits. And those connections have been made more palpable by the technology that Indians themselves have been advancing. The world of the gated communities and urban cafes in the high tech cities of Hyderabad or Bangalore are very different from those of NGO activists and Adivasi advocates. However, the technology of the internet provided opportunities for both.

Conclusion
Democracy and activism

A common theme throughout this volume has been the vibrancy of India's democracy, which has been characterized from the beginning by the fluid relationship between activism and parliamentary politics. Perhaps an inheritance of the Freedom Movement, both legal and political debates in India have continued to incorporate mass rallies, popular protests, and even civil disobedience. The first parliamentarians all emerged from a civil disobedience movement and many were jailed during British colonial rule. When Jawaharlal Nehru walked into Parliament, he knew the effectiveness that protests outside those gates could have. The consequence was the government had to negotiate between activist politicians and parliamentary ones. Nehru did not always deal with such protests effectively. Language protests and a number of other moments of resistance provided him with difficult decisions about mass-movements – how to identify them, how to respond to them. The examples in this text included the incorporation of princely states and Goa, during which he had to confront different versions of the political will of the people.

The period before the Emergency, especially, characterized how political frustration brought large numbers of citizens into the streets – over land rights, price rises, and other issues, and the repression of that political will during the Emergency demonstrated the discomfort such politics brought to institutionalized government. The legacies of the Emergency were widespread and some of them have been illustrated in this volume. Particularly, politicians found continued political value in having defied an unjust state. Both the Janata politicians and Indira Gandhi (when she was arrested following the Emergency) celebrated their experiences in jail as a sign of their commitment to principle.

The continued effectiveness of activism, even when it did not accelerate to civil disobedience, or even when it brought destructive and tragic consequences, emerged in the Hindu nationalist movement, and backward class or women's mobilizations in the 1980s and 1990s. The difficulty along the way has been the secular government's inability to strike a balance between allowing and understanding protest and stopping the violence it can cause. The continued interplay between NGOs and government shows the resilience of India's Government when faced with grassroots mobilization and international opportunity; the government sometimes succeeded in channelling those energies. NGOs have become a powerful part of the political landscape, employed sometimes by the government itself, for example in training new members of Panchayati Raj institutions.

Writing recent history is problematic because as dynamic situations evolve, their meanings change quite rapidly. For example, the history of the Green Revolution, which was a triumph of development and self-sufficiency, has to be read now in the context of unforeseen ecological damage it caused and the failure to foresee a sustainable future.

As the last chapter showed, the end of the twentieth century was characterized by the remarkable boom in the technology service industries, call centres, and software producers. This gave India one of the largest information technology sectors in the world, with 300,000 computer engineers working inside the country and graduates from its Indian Institutes of Technology sought after in every country. Some pockets in Hyderabad, Bangalore, Delhi, Chennai, and Mumbai, rivalled the most developed countries, with a large successful middle class. At the same time India's middle class was about the size of Europe's. From the view of Gurcharan Das, an advocate of deregulation:

India thus entered the twenty-first century on the brink of the biggest transformation in its history. The changes are more fundamental than anything the country has seen, and they hold the potential to transform it into an innovative, energetic economy. . . . We realized that our great strength is our people. Our great weakness is our government. Our great hope is the Internet.

(Das, 2002: 346)

GLOBALIZATION AND ECONOMIC BOOM

India's economic boom at the end of the twentieth century, prompted an anthropologist of development to say recently, 'I don't teach India as a developing country anymore. Rather I describe it as a developed country with poverty problems' (Koenig, 2004). Even in measures of overall economic growth and poverty reduction there had been obvious change. According to the CIA Fact Book, not usually an optimistic source on India, between 1990 and 2001, India averaged a 6 per cent growth rate and a 10 per cent reduction in poverty. (http://www.cia.gov/cia/publications/factbook)

Of course there remained contradictions. The economic boom exacerbated disparities in regions and particularly between urban and rural populations. However quickly poverty was reduced, 200 million people continued to live under the poverty line in 2000 and 70 per cent of them were in the country-side. The gradual flow of wealth from cities to villages had a haphazard look. People building houses back home or investing philanthropically in their villages created spotty development. Two areas of dynamic change for the countryside did come through Panchayati Raj, a source for distributing government investment, and NGOs, sources for independent projects.

ON THE GLOBAL STAGE, NEW TERRORISM

After the United States confronted the catastrophic terrorist acts of 11 September 2001, the world began to view political violence in different terms. While separatist movements, internal conflict between communities, and Pakistani wars, had resulted in tragic loss of life, the language of terrorism had not often been used in India to describe these acts. However, when Parliament was the site of a failed attack in December 2001, the fact and language of international terrorism became part of Indian Government policy as well.

Furthermore the political scientist Martha Nussbaum argues that in the early 2000s India's Hindu-nationalist government used the rhetoric of terrorism to justify compromises in legal protection and hostility toward India's Muslim minority community. In her book *The Clash Within* she examines a horrific riot in Gujarat in 2002, in which thousands of Muslim citizens were displaced, injured, or killed in acts of what were described as 'retaliation' for another tragic act of fire in a train. As Nussbaum unravels the story, she shows the difficulty of understanding how any of these terrible acts of violence began and the failure of government to stop them and protect the citizens. Like the tragedy of the Babri Masjid described earlier, the violence in Gujarat was what once was called communal violence. Nussbaum suggests that the overlaying of terrorism and implicit fear of external complicity creates even bigger dangers. For example, it masks real security threats (which in fact did materialize in the first decades of the twenty-first century) and misdirects domestic resources (Nussbaum, 2005).

GLOBALIZATION OF CULTURE AND ART

The Indian diaspora has played a critical role in supporting and contributing to Indian arts and literature. For example, India's film industry remained the largest in the world, in part because of growing exports. Online stores for

Hindi music and film started in the 1990s in order to meet global demands, and NRIs (non-resident Indians) received a fast track from the government for opportunities within India. Therefore, there was an ongoing exchange of cultural ideas and cultural production.

Some of the best-known Indian writers lived outside the subcontinent, but at the same time there was a flourishing growth in Indian writing at home. By the end of the twentieth century, there was an increase in the numbers of published translations of Indian literature from one language to another or from regional languages to English. The curriculum at Indian universities both spurred the trend and then scrambled to catch up. English department curricula provide an interesting example. Beginning in the mid-1990s, they added papers on Indian writers in translation and moved in general away from a curriculum still wedded to a British model. As a result colleges demanding Tamil fiction or Kannada poetry created a market for those books.

Indian literary scholars also advanced the discipline of English literature. In particular, the field of post-colonial literature was dominated by Indian academics and academics with a focus on Indian writing, such as Aijaz Ahmad or Homi Bhabha. Salman Rushdie's recognition for his novel *Midnight's Children*, not only with the Booker Prize in 1981 but also with the Booker of Bookers in 1993, propelled that novel to a standard place in the English literature curriculum internationally. Of course, that itself may be both a sign of India's inclusion and of tokenism in world literary studies. In fact from Arundhati Roy and Githa Hariharan in India to Kiran Desai, Anita Desai, and Amitav Ghosh abroad there have been growing numbers of Indian writers in English available to an Indian and international audience.

Indian paintings too reached a global market due to the interest of the diaspora and its appeal to collectors. For example, a Tyeb Mehta painting of figures on a rickshaw sold at a Christie's auction for nearly $2 million dollars in 2008. This was a record for his work. But another of his paintings fetched Rs 31 million in India (about $1 million dollars), showing that Indian collectors are part of the same global market.

CONTINUING THEMES

This book has focused on key events and larger trends in India's post-independence history. Markers such as the Partition and the Emergency challenged and shaped the Indian state. Issues of social equity took on new forms both as addressed from above through legislation and from below in social movements. For example, the rights of women, minorities, and lower castes recurred as political issues.

Given the recent nature of this history, there is little historiography available, but no dearth of analytical sources. One aim here has been to look at the layers of narratives produced by political scientists, sociologists, writers, and artists over time. The most obvious result is that the view of India's past is shaped profoundly by the writer's present. For example, texts written in the wake of the Emergency explain and bemoan the end of democracy, while those written after the election of 1977 remark on democratic resilience. The view from the beginning of the twenty-first century has to be an optimistic one, both about democracy and development. Elections continue to bring about smooth transitions of power and economic growth, even in moments of broader recession. The large problems of the future – environmental, international, security – are confronted by a strong and flexible nation in which the people are its greatest resource.

As this illustrates, the salient consistency in India over time has been the ongoing interplay between social movements and democratic politics as ways of addressing challenges and adapting to a changing world. Equally important is the participation of artists and intellectuals in both. People's willingness to march in the streets or hug trees or organize for particular rights is a valuable check on the politics of representative government. The lively debates, publishing, art, and public discourse among intellectuals comments on and participates in both. That process means that there are always books and paintings and drama and the press to force a degree of transparency on the body politic and encourage government responsiveness. Citizens – in their diversity – use mass rallies and public protests in addition to official ballot boxes to express their needs and demand that the government meet them.

Part 2

DOCUMENTS

The documents in this section, not only provide illustrations for the various issues and events they describe, but also serve as illustrations of the different kinds of sources available and used to understand very recent history. These documents of the recent past include examples of popular culture, art, plans, government documents, court cases, diary entries, transcripts of oral narratives, and speeches, among others things.

Document 1 JAWAHARLAL NEHRU'S SPEECH AT INDEPENDENCE

Just before midnight on August 14/15 1947 Jawaharlal Nehru, the recognized leader of India's nationalist movement, stood before India's Constituent Assembly and called upon his fellow members to take a pledge to the service of the new nation. This speech outlined both the celebratory and solemn nature of the occasion and addressed Nehru's aspirations for the new nation. With this pledge, the Constituent Assembly became India's Provisional Parliament, until elections could be held.

'The Fifth Session of the Constituent Assembly of India commenced in the Constitution Hall, New Delhi, at Eleven p.m. Mr. President (The Honourable Rajendra Prasad) in the Chair.'

Motion Re. Pledge by Members
The Honourable President Rajendra Prasad
Pandit Jawaharlal Nehru will now move the motion, which stands in his name.

The Honourable Pandit Jawaharlal Nehru (U. P.: General)
[First read in Hindi and then in English]

Long years ago we made a tryst with destiny, and now the time comes when we shall redeem our pledge, not wholly or in full measure, but very substantially. At the stroke of the midnight hour, when the world sleeps, India will awake to life and freedom. A moment comes, which comes but rarely in history, when we step out from the old to the new, when an age ends, and when the soul of a nation, long suppressed, finds utterance. It is fitting that at this solemn moment we take the pledge of dedication to the service of India and her people and to the still larger cause of humanity.

At the dawn of history India started on her unending quest, and trackless centuries are filled with her striving and the grandeur of her successes and, her failures. Through good and ill fortune alike she has never lost sight of that quest or forgotten the ideals, which gave her strength. We end today a period of ill fortune and India discovers herself again. The achievement we celebrate today is but a step, an opening of opportunity, to the greater triumphs and achievements that await us. Are we brave enough and wise enough to grasp this opportunity and accept the challenge of the future?

Freedom and power bring responsibility. That responsibility rests upon this Assembly, a sovereign body representing the sovereign people of India. Before the birth of freedom we have endured all the pains of labour and our hearts are heavy with the memory of this sorrow. Some of those pains continue even now. Nevertheless the past is over and it is the future that beckons to us now.

That future is not one of ease or resting but of incessant striving so that we might fulfil the pledges we have so often taken and the one we shall take today. The service of India means the service of the millions who suffer. It means the ending of poverty and ignorance and disease and inequality of opportunity. The ambition of the greatest man of our generation has been to wipe every tear from every eye. That may be beyond us but as long as there are tears and suffering, so long our work will not be over. And so we have to labour and to work and work hard to give reality to our dreams. Those dreams are for India, but they are also for the world, for all the nations and peoples are too closely knit together today for any one of them to imagine that it can live apart. Peace has been said to be indivisible, so is freedom, so is prosperity now, and so also is disaster in this One World that can no longer be split into isolated fragments.

To the people of India, whose representatives we are, we make appeal to join us with faith and confidence in this great adventure. This is no time for petty and destructive criticism, no time for ill-will or blaming others. We have to build the noble mansion of free India where all her children may dwell.

I beg to move, Sir,

"That it be resolved that:

(1) After the last stroke of midnight, all members of the Constituent Assembly present on this occasion do take the following pledge:

'At this solemn moment when the people of India, through suffering and sacrifice, have secured freedom, I................................ a member of the Constituent Assembly of India, do dedicate myself in all humility to the service of India and her people to the end that this ancient-land attain her rightful place in the world and make her full and willing contribution to the promotion of world peace and the welfare of mankind.'

Source: Constituent Assembly Debates, 14 August 1947. http://parliamentofindia.nic.in/ls/debates/vol5p1.htm

Document 2   QUESTION IN THE CONSTITUENT ASSEMBLY ABOUT PARTITION

The British government did not consult the Constituent Assembly about Partition and particularly about how and where to divide Bengal and Punjab. This is the response from one member asserting the authority of the institution, which had been elected under colonial rule.

Mr. President, so far as I know it was said at the time the elections to this Constituent Assembly were held that no outside authority had any control over it. I would like to be informed whether you were consulted about the changes that have taken place in Bengal and Punjab. Have these changes taken place according to the rules made by this Assembly? So far as I am aware members of this Assembly lose their membership when they submit their resignation. I would like to know if the members for Bengal and Punjab, who are no more members, lost their membership by submitting their resignation or as a result of the Viceroy's statement, which led to new elections being held. If this is what has happened, and this appears to be the actual case, I would like to know your opinion about this matter and whether you consider all this proper and regular or not. We were told that once the Constituent Assembly was elected, neither any changes would be made in its constitution nor could any outsider have any authority or control over it. It appears to me that all these changes have taken place according to the statement of the Viceroy – a proceeding which is improper, unjust, illegal and contrary to the rules.

Source: Constituent Assembly Debates, 14 July 1947. http://164.100.24.208/ls/condeb/vol4p1.htm Parliament of India website.

Document 3   REPORT OF THE ADVISORY COMMITTEE ON THE SUBJECT OF
MINORITY RIGHTS

A committee was established with Vallabhai Patel as chair to examine the issue of minority rights in India. This part of the report discusses future elections, recommending that some provisions should be made to assure representation for minorities.

From:
    The Hon'ble Sardar VALLABHBHAI PATEL
    Chairman, Advisory Committee on Minorities, Fundamental Rights, Etc.
To:
    The President,
    Constituent Assembly of India

Dear Sir,

On behalf of the members of the Advisory Committee appointed by the Constituent Assembly on the 24th January 1947 and subsequently nominated by you, I have the honour to submit this report on minority rights. . . .

2. Our recommendations are based on exhaustive discussion both in the Sub-Committee on Minorities as well as in the main Advisory Committee. . . .

3. The first question we tackled was that of separate electorates; we considered this as being of crucial importance both to the minorities themselves and to the political life of the country as a whole. By an overwhelming majority, we came to the conclusion that the system of separate electorates must be abolished in the new constitution. In our judgment this system has in the past sharpened communal differences to a dangerous extent and has proved one of the main stumbling blocks to the development of a healthy national life. It seems specially necessary to avoid these dangers in the new political conditions that have developed in the country and from this point of view the arguments against separate electorates seem to us absolutely decisive.

4. We recommend accordingly that all elections to the Central and Provincial legislatures should be held on the basis of joint electorates. In order that minorities may not feel apprehensive about the effect of a system of un-restricted joint electorates on the quantum of their representation in the legislatures, we recommend as a general rule that seats for the different recog-nized minorities all be reserved in the various legislatures on the basis of their population . . .

Group A
1. Anglo-Indians
2. Parsees
3. Plains' tribes in Assam

Group B
4. Indian Christians
5. Sikhs

Group C
6. Muslims
7. Scheduled Castes.

Source: Constituent Assembly Debates, 27 August 1947. http://parliamentofindia.nic.in/ls/debates/vol5p8b.html

Document 4   ARTICLES 15 AND 29 OF THE CONSTITUTION OF INDIA

Articles 15 and 29 both appear in Part III of the Indian Constitution that guarantees Fundamental Rights to all citizens. These articles also provide the basis for special provisions to eliminate discrimination.

(a)

15. *Prohibition of discrimination on grounds of religion, race, caste, sex or place of birth.*

(1) The State shall not discriminate against any citizen on grounds only of religion, race, caste, sex, place of birth or any of them.

(2) No citizen shall, on grounds only of religion, race, caste, sex, place of birth or any of them, be subject to any disability, liability, restriction or condition with regard to (a) access to shops, public restaurants, hotels and places of public entertainment; or (b) the use of wells, tanks, bathing ghats, roads and places of public resort maintained wholly or partly out of State funds or dedicated to the use of the general public.

(3) Nothing in this article shall prevent the State from making any special provision for women and children.

[(4) Nothing in this article or in clause (2) of article 29 shall prevent the State from making any special provision for the advancement of any socially and educationally backward classes of citizens or for the Scheduled Castes and the Scheduled Tribes.]

ARTICLE 29 CONSTITUTION OF INDIA

(b)

Cultural and Educational Rights 29. Protection of interests of minorities.

(1) Any section of the citizens residing in the territory of India or any part thereof having a distinct language, script or culture of its own shall have the right to conserve the same.

(2) No citizen shall be denied admission into any educational institution maintained by the State or receiving aid out of State funds on grounds only of religion, race, caste, language or any of them.

Source: Constitution of India. http://indiacode.nic.in/coiweb/welcome.html

HYDERABAD AND THE UNITED NATIONS **Document 5**

In 1948 the Nizam (ruler) of Hyderabad appealed to the United Nations to prevent his state's accession to India. The following letter from Hyderabad to the Secretary-General of the United Nations expresses concern over the actions being taken by the Government of India.

H. E. H. The Nizam's Government, The Complaint of Hyderabad Against the Dominion of India Under Article 35 (2) of the Charter of the United Nations. 1948

21 August 1948

To: The Secretary-General
United Nations
Lake Success, New York

Dear Sir,
The Government of Hyderabad in reliance on Article 35(2) of the Charter of the United Nations, requests you to bring to the attention of the Security Council the grave dispute which has arisen between Hyderabad and India, and which, unless settled in accordance with international law and justice, is likely to endanger the maintenance of international peace and security. Hyderabad has been exposed in recent months to violent intimidation, to threats of invasion, and to crippling economic blockade which has inflicted cruel hardship upon the people of Hyderabad and which is intended to coerce it into a renunciation of its independence. The frontiers have been forcibly violated and Hyderabad villages have been occupied by Indian troops. The action of India threatens the existence of Hyderabad, the peace of the Indian and entire Asiatic Continent, and the principles of the United Nations. . . .

> I am, Sir
> Your most Obedient Servant
> Zahir Amed
> Secretary to the Government of the Nizam of Hyderabad
> and Berar in the Department of External Affairs

Document 6   TWO ACCOUNTS OF THE TELANGANA MOVEMENT

The Telangana Movement among peasants for land rights demonstrates the complexity of the politics within the state of Hyderabad. These accounts from women participants characterize the movement from its organized collection of data on land possession to its use of armed struggle. It also shows the way in which participants gained training and evaded capture.

(a)

[The Narrative of] Regalla Acchamamba

My name is Susheela. Our family name is Regalla. Our village is called Gollacherla and is in Manukota Taluka. My father's name is Jagga Reddy. We were poor folk. We had a little land and lived by farming it. My father could not read or write. My brother was young. We were five girls and three boys – a large family. We worked very hard.

Then the struggle against the Nizam Nawab started. Many women came into the struggle happily, singing the songs that had been written. There was so much excitement. Well, that is how I joined the movement. I was fourteen years old then; I too was caught up in the excitement. . . .

. . . There were eight or nine women who came in with me into the movement. But they left midway. Some were arrested, some were killed and some simply dropped out. One woman was killed in jail – Buchamma. She came from Pindiprolu, Khammam Taluka. She kept protesting and struggling even in jail. They knew she was dangerous and they just killed her. I do not know how . . . we were in the forest then, we just heard that she had been caught and then killed.

Soon after this we were trained to use guns. Then a doctor came and trained us. . . . We were taught to clean and bandage wounds, and give injections. I was given a doctor's responsibility. We were all given different responsibilities. One was sent to the Area Committee, another as an ordinary member, yet another was a Joint Secretary and so on. During the movement my job was dressing wounds, giving injections and medicines.

. . . . We had a meeting to decide how the squads should split – which direction each one would take. Mohan Rao [the squad leader] was running a high fever. It was very difficult looking after him and attending the meeting. Anyway I left him in one spot and sat in the meeting. We sent a courier into the village. He was to find out what the news in the village was, and come and report to us. This fellow went straight to the police.

How were we to know this? We did not even set a sentry because we had sent this man. He brought the police directly to the spot where we were. We were stunned. We just sat like that. We all had our weapons with us. Not a sound from anyone. It was such chaos . . . the man we had sent came running and jumped amidst us. . . . Actually since we were separating we had slaughtered a small goat and we were having a feast of sorts! After all we did not know who would live and who would die or when we would meet again. So we cooked a grand meal. The food was cooking just a short distance away from where we were sitting. We always cooked the food at a distance from where we sat. I had gone across to the pot to take it down from the fire when this fellow arrived. He pointed a gun at me. The bullet just whizzed past me. See this ear? I still cannot hear in this ear. A little closer and I would have been dead . . . we were all scattered. I ran some distance and that fellow followed me. I was wearing a green sari. He was hardly twenty yards away. I was running but he did not shoot. He wanted to catch me. I was determined not to be caught. I thought it was better to die. I kept running and he kept running after me. After some distance he gave up hope and joined the group of policemen. . . .

. . . Our Committee was then re-made and we moved on to another area. We went towards Tekulagudem and Miryalagudem. There all the people around called me 'Errakka, Errakka' [an affectionate reference to a village deity, literally 'Red Sister']. That is because I used to give them medicine. The koyas used to get big sores, horrible ones. I gave them medicines and cured them. Penicillin injections were so good. That, and some ointment, and keeping the sores clean would often do the trick. So they really cared for me . . . I stayed in a koya house in Miryalagudem. These koyas hid me and gave me shelter. Then the police came to their house. They used to weave baskets and trays and keep them in a hollow. They hid me in that hollow and threw baskets over me! The police searched the whole house but could not find me. They left after searching for some time.

. . . . Once we had no food to eat. There was nobody in the villages to ask for food. It was all deserted. We collected some raw paddy from the fields. Then we kept blowing on it to separate the chaff. In this way we got a handful of rice. We cooked it and ate a little each. It was as if we had come to life. Then there are some roots (alligaddalu) that grow in the water. We would go to the lake to collect them. As we bent over to collect them, a tiger came growling to drink at the pool. All of us ran away and hid in the bush. The tiger went away after drinking. Now we had the roots, but no pots to cook them! We would collect broken pots from the deserted huts and use them to cook in. Once we got some roots – like white yams; chickens eat a lot of them. The koyas used to cut them in big chunks, leave them in a basket in running water and then cook them. It was a kind of porridge.

Source: From K., Lalita., Kannabiran, Vasantha, Melkote, Rama S., Maheshwari, Uma, Shatrugna, Veena, Tharu, Susie. *We Were Making History: Life Stories of Women in the Telangana People's Struggle*. New Delhi: Zed Books, 1989. [pp. 160–171]

(b)

With the intensification of repression by the government there was a lull in the people's movement and the landlords were attempting to restore their authority in the villages by creating and manipulating disputes and getting more of our workers arrested by the police. This way they hoped to increase their strength and assert their authority. Under these circumstances the party reviewed the past struggles and the entire situation at the highest level and formulated policy and programme of action to be followed in reconstructing and revitalizing the movement. Some of the important decisions were

1. Those who collaborated with the Nizam's government and engaged or likely to engage in attacks on people should be treated as enemies. . . .
2. Small landlords who cooperated with the people's struggles be considered allies; leaving two hundred acres to them and surplus be distributed.
3. Protect the people from police raids by guarding the villages. . . .
4. Distribute all categories of government land including uncultivable forest land.
5. A programme of training in guerrilla warfare for the defence of villages and self-defence. . . .

. . . At a party camp held in Munagala Pargana, it was resolved to undertake a programme of distribution of lands belonging to landlords and government. Armed with this programme . . . I crossed over into [Huzurnagar] taluka. Two villages that I went into were Fatehpuram and Charam. In these two villages there were big landlords. With the cooperation of the local comrades a survey of the pattern of ownership of land was done; the landless agricultural labourers and poor peasants were enumerated. Estimates were prepared of the amount of land likely to be available for distribution after leaving two hundred acres to the landlords. . . . The landlords in these two villages did not offer any resistance or report the matter to the government. . . .

After staying for ten days in Huzurnagar taluka I proceeded to Bhongir walking a distance of eighty miles traversing the villages of Miryalaguda [Miryalagudem] and Nalgonda talukas. Accompanied by couriers who knew the routes in different areas we travelled only at night to avoid risk of identification by landlords and their agents, stayed at the next halt during the day where we shared the jawar soup or porridge that was the only meal which the rural poor could afford.

Source: Arutla Ramachandra Reddy, *Telangana Struggle Memoirs* (trans. B. Narsing Rao), People's Publishing House, 1984. [pp. 58–60]

LAND REVENUE ADMINISTRATION: DISTRICT GAZETEER OF CUDDAPAH,   **Document 7**
ANDHRA PRADESH

A Gazetteer is a review of the particulars of a place, with notations, statistics, and detailed description. Indian Gazetteers, first composed in the 19th Century take the district as a unit of description. Districts are administrative units of states. What follows is the description of "Land Revenue" and "Land Reform" measures in Cuddapah District of Andhra Pradesh State in the 1950s and 60s.

(a)

Land Revenue Administration (pp. 493–504)

It is difficult to give a cogent account of the history of Revenue Administration of the district. . . . In spite of various vicissitudes, the system in vogue on the eve of British occupation seemed to have been more or less democratic, based on a mutual appreciation of the fiscal needs of the state and the taxable capacity of the village. . . . In all the villages, the Ryots (peasants) are in the habit of meeting and debating upon the subject of rent but there are many villages in which they settle among themselves the exact proportion of the whole rent that each individual is to pay.

. . . [Initially under the British] the mode of [land revenue] assessment was to spread it over the villages whose cultivators were held responsible for the payment of the sums. . . . The inequity in the assessments . . . was essentially due to the fact that the total demand was first fixed for the district and then distributed among the villages. . . . Between 1821 and 1860, many attempts were made at a rational readjustment of the pattern of assessment.

. . . The fiscal measures undertaken since the last decade [since 1954] with a view to augment the sources of the State assumed the form of various legislative enactments. . . . The impact of these Acts on the Land Revenue of the district is indicated in the following . . .

Total [Land Revenue]: (1954–55) 2,561,000 rupees
                  (1958–59) 3,580,000 rupees

(b)

Land Reform (pp. 505–506)

[A] series of land reforms [in the region] . . . left their impress on the patterns of agrarian relationship in this district as well. The Estate Land Act of 1908 conferred for the first time occupancy rights on the cultivators [which] prohibited arbitrary eviction and unreasonable enhancement of rents. The tenants, however, did not derive the full benefit of the Act. . . .

The situation remained the same till 1947 when two important measures of reform were introduced to ensure the abolition of all intermediaries and to scale down the high rents obtaining in the estates, pending their abolition, by the Rent Reduction Act of 1947 and the Estate Abolition Act of 1948. The latter aimed at the abolition of the Zamindari system [landlord controlled property] and the transfer of the entire estate to Government for conversion into ryotwari tenure [peasant controlled property].

. . . Several committees have enquired into the peasant–proprietor relationship. [The] Subramanyam Committee (1950). . . . advocated a ceiling on agricultural holdings. It is in fact on the recommendation of this committee that [an] ordinance was issued in 1956 with a view to protect the tenants from unjust eviction.

. . . The fixation of ceilings on landholdings was preceded by a census conducted in the agricultural year 1953–54 according to which the total number of holdings in this district was 1,69,412 covering an area of 11,85,968 acres. . . . The Andhra Pradesh Agricultural Holding Census Ordinance of 1957 required every land holder, possessing more than 20 acres of land to declare the details of his holding. The ordinance was replaced by the Act of 1961 according to which lands were classified in eight categories and the size of a family holding ranging from six to seventy-two acres was determined. Declarations from those holding land in excess of the ceiling had to be made and the surplus surrendered to the Government on payment of compensation. The number of such declarations filed in the district exceed 1300 . . .

(c)

Law and Order (pp. 517–518)
. . . Robbery of revolvers and guns from the Police, mail robberies, thefts of agricultural produce, cattle and sheep, cloth and cash and gold and jewels were the usual inflictions of organized dacoity [robbery gangs] in this district. In recent years, however, the district seems to be comparatively free from these offences although the famine year of 1951 witnessed their incidence at its worst.

. . . Political and agrarian tensions and labour troubles are not as widespread in this district as in others.

Source: BH. SIVASANKARANARAYANA, *Andhra Pradesh District Gazetteers; Cuddapah*, Hyderabadl: Government of Andhra Pradesh Press, 1967, 493–518.

Document 8   TELEGRAM: REQUEST FROM KASHMIR

At the time of independence the Indian and Pakistani governments offered Princely States something called a Standstill Agreement, which seemed to assure the maintenance of some autonomy until a final status could be established. This telegram contains the request for such status from the Maharaja of Kashmir.

Telegram 12 August 1947
Jammu and Kashmir Government would welcome Standstill Agreement with Union of India/Pakistan on all matters on which there exists at the present

moment with outgoing British Indian government, it is suggested that existing arrangements should continue pending settlement of details and formal
execution of fresh Agreement.

ACCESSION OF KASHMIR   **Document 9**

*The following letter from the Maharaja Hari Singh to Lord Mountbatten
serves as a formal request for accession to India in light of the threats he
perceives from the Pakistani side of the border.*

Letter of Maharaja Hari Singh to Lord Mountbatten of October 26, 1947 of
Accession to India

My Dear Lord Mountbatten,

   I have to inform Your Excellency that a grave emergency has arisen in my
State and request the immediate assistance of your Government. . . . Though
we have a standstill agreement with Pakistan Government that Government
permitted a steady and increasing strangulation of supplies like food, salt,
and petrol to my State.

   Afridis, soldiers in plain clothes and desperadoes with modern weapons
have been allowed to (infiltrate) into the State at first in the Pooch area, then
in Sialkot and finally inmass in the area adjoining Hazara district on the
Ramkot side. The results have been that the limited number of troops at
the disposal of the State had to be dispersed and thus had to face the
enemy at several points simultaneously. . . . [There is a] mass infiltration
of tribesmen drawn from the distant area of the North West Frontier Province, coming regularly in motor trucks, . . . and fully armed with up-to-date
weapons. Despite repeated appeals made by my Government no attempt
has been made to check these raiders or to stop them from coming into my
state. . . .

   With the conditions obtaining at present to my State and the great emergency of the situation as it exists, I have no option but to ask for help from
the Indian Dominion. Naturally they cannot send the help asked for by me
without my State acceding to the Dominion of India. I have accordingly
decided to do so, and I attach the instruments of accession for acceptance by
your Government.

Yours Sincerely,
Hari Singh

Source: Government of India. http://india.gov.in

Document 10   PANCHSHEEL AGREEMENT, 1954

Excerpt from the Communiqué on the Agreement Between the Government of the Republic of India and the Government of the People's Republic of China on Trade and Inter-course Between Tibet Region of China and India, 29 April 1954.

The Government of the Republic of India and the Central People's Government of the People's Republic of China:
Being desirous of promoting trade and cultural intercourse between the Tibet region of China and India and of facilitating pilgrimage and travel by the people of China and India;

Have resolved to enter into the present agreement based on the following principles

1. Mutual respect for each other's territorial integrity and sovereignty;
2. Mutual non-aggression;
3. Mutual non-interference in each others internal affairs;
4. Equality and mutual benefit; and
5. Peaceful coexistence.

Document 11   TIBETAN REFUGEES AND THE DALAI LAMA ARRIVE IN INDIA

The Dalai Lama escaped to India in April 1959 after the Chinese invasion of Tibet. Nehru, serving as both Prime Minister and Minister for External Affairs, announced his arrival to an ambivalent Parliament on 3 April 1959. India also provided facilities for the influx of other Tibetan refugees, as this report from the Deputy Minister of External Affairs shows.

The Prime Minister and Minister of External Affairs (Shri Jawaharlal Nehru):
The other day, three days ago, I think, when I was speaking about recent happenings in Tibet, I mentioned that I would keep the house informed. . . . We have been receiving a number of messages . . . They were often delayed because they have had to come through a rather devious route. . . .

The facts are that on the 1st April, i.e., day before yesterday morning, we received a message via Shillong dated 31st March evening that an emissary with a message from the Dalai Lama had arrived at our border check-point at Chutangmu in the North-East Frontier Agency. He had arrived there on the 29th March, stating that the Dalai Lama requested us for political asylum and that he expected to reach the border on the 30th March. . . . The Dalai Lama with his small party of 8 had crossed into our territory on the evening of the 31st March.

Expecting that some such development might occur, we had instructed the various check-posts round about there what to do in case such a development takes place. So, when he crossed over into our territory, he was received by our Assistant Political Officer of the Tawang Division . . .

Shri Raj Braj Singh: May I ask whether we are going to give political asylum to the Dalai Lama?

Response: We have.

11 August 1959
The Deputy Minister of External Affairs (Shrimati Laxmi Menon):
Statement

The total number of Tibetan refugees who have come to India is 12,396.

Arrangements have been made for the employment of unskilled refugees in road-works in Sikkim and NEFA. Those who are old and infirm have been sent to Dalhousie and will be maintained at the expense of the Government. A number of refugees with relations in India have been permitted to join their families in Darjeeling District.

Refugees who are not being maintained by the Government and who are being dispersed for road works are being given resettlement grant of Rs 50 in addition to the cost of transportation and shelter at the work sites. Arrangements have also been made to give instructions in Hindi. . . .

Source: Parliament of India website. http://parliamentofindia.nic.in

EDICT OF CHANDIGARH   Document 12

The development of the planned city of Chandigarh was, for Prime Minister Jawaharlal Nehru, a showcase for Indian independence and modernity. The edict establishes the principles on which the city was founded and designed by the architect, Le Corbusier.

The object of this edict is to enlighten the present and future citizens of Chandigarh about the basic concepts of planning of the city so that they become its guardians and save it from whims of individuals. This edict sets out the following basic ideas underlying the planning of the city.

HUMAN SCALE:
The city of Chandigarh is planned to human scale. It puts us in touch with the infinite cosmos and nature. It provides us with places and buildings for all human activities by which the citizens can live a full and harmonious life. Here the radiance of nature and heart are within our reach. . . .

AREAS OF SPECIAL ARCHITECTURAL INTEREST:

Certain areas of Chandigarh are of special architectural interest. Where harmonized and unified construction of buildings is aimed at, absolute architectural and zoning control should remain operative. . . .

CITY CENTRE:

The central plaza in Sector 17 was designed by Le Corbusier as 'Pedestrian's Paradise'. No vehicular traffic will be permitted in the plaza.

THE LAKE:

The Lake is a gift of the creators of Chandigarh to the citizens to be at one with the lake and its environments and its tranquillity shall be guaranteed by banning noises. . . .

NO PERSONAL STATUES SHALL BE ERECTED:

The age of personal statues is gone. No personal statues shall be erected in the city or parks of Chandigarh. The city is planned to breathe the new sublimated spirit of art. Commemoration of persons shall be confined to suitably placed bronze plaques. . . .

Source: http://chandigarh.nic.in/architec.htm#arch

Document 13   LE CORBUSIER SKETCH OF GRAIN MARKET IN CHANDIGARH – See Plate 5

The development of Chandigarh took place from a very detailed artistic level. Much of the design reflected global movements in modern art. This sketch shows the artistic sense given to each element of the city.

Document 14   STATUTE OF LAND – CHANDIGARH

The Statute of Land lays out the rules, regulations, and organization of Chandigarh.

City of Chandigarh
I. Definition of use of Chandigarh

(i) Chandigarh is a city offering all amenities of life to the poorest of the poor of its citizens to lead a dignified life.

(ii) Chandigarh is a Government city with a precise goal and consequently a precise quality of inhabitants. . . .

The Sectors

The key of modern urbanism is 'the Sector' which is a container of family life (24 solar hours: night and day). The contents being from 5,000 to 20,000 inhabitants (approx.). Chandigarh has 30 sectors: each sector has its maintenance organizations, the food provisions, the schools (kindergarten and primary) the necessary artisans (repairs, etc.) the daily leisure (movies, etc.) all traversing in the middle of each sector. . . .

Appreciation of Land

When such a working has been made in a city: Obtaining the money, buying of necessary ground, first bye-laws, permitting to being construction, arriving of the first inhabitants, selling of the first plots, etc. etc.

A phenomenon is born: it is the appreciation of the land. A game, a play has begun. One can sell cheap or at a high price; it depends on the kind of 'tactic and strategy' put in this operation.

One phrase must be affirmed: 'The good urbanism makes money; the bad urbanism loses money'.

The problem is also to be vigilant: one must sell true merchandise; nothing must be allowed to provoke circumstances which will bring loss to any single inhabitant.

One has the Statute of the Land. It is like a seed. What can be grown from the seed? It is in the hands of the Administrators.

LE CORBUSIER
Chandigarh, 17 December, 1959

NEK CHAND GARDEN – See Plate 2   **Document 15**

The fanciful garden of bridges and animals and villages is a product of the imagination of Nek Chand Saini, an engineer for the Punjabi Transportation Corporation who used the remnants of building projects, including the city of Chandigarh toconstruct his own make-believe world.

PRINCIPLES OF THE FOUNDATION OF THE NATIONAL GALLERY OF   **Document 16**
MODERN ART

The National Gallery of Modern art was opened in 1954 as part of a commitment to preserve works of contemporary and modern artists. It defined its objectives in the set of principles outlined below.

Principal aims and objectives:

- To acquire and preserve works of modern art from 1850s onward
- To organize maintain and develop galleries for permanent display
- To organize special exhibitions worldwide

- To develop an education and documentation centre in order to acquire, maintain and preserve documents relating to works of modern art
- To develop a specialized library of books, periodicals, photographs and other audio visual materials
- To organize lectures, seminars and conferences, and to encourage higher studies and research in the field of art history, art criticism, art appreciation, museology and the interrelations on visual and performing arts

Source: National Gallery of Modern Art, New Delhi website. http://ngmaindia.gov.in

Document 17   'MAHISASURA' BY TYEB MEHTA – See Plate 1

The market in Indian art skyrocketed at the end of the twentieth century. This 1997 painting by the well-known Indian artist Tyeb Mehta sold at auction for $1.48 million in 2005, breaking a record at the time. Mehta struggled for success in the 1960s, but played an ongoing role influencing Indian contemporary art.

Document 18   'SPIRIT OF EVERYDAY LIFE' BY MEERA MUKHERJEE – See Plate 7

Meera Mukherjee's work characterizes the blend of traditional art forms with contemporary sculpture, having studied techniques such as wax wire sculpture from tribal communities in West Bengal. Seven of her pieces were purchased by the National Gallery of Modern Art. Among them was this assertive image of female figure with a winnowing basket. Made in a similar style to Bastar (a Tribal communitee) art, the sculpture is 180cm (5'10") tall.

Source: Meera Mukherjee, National Museum of Modern Art, New Delhi.

Document 19   RETROSPECTIVE ON NATIONAL MUSEUM OF INDIA

On the occasion of the 50th anniversary of the National Museum in 2000, I. D. Mathur, the former Assistant Director, delivered an address sponsored by the museum describing its history. The text of the lecture was published in the National Museum Bulletin in 2002.

It was not until 10 September 1945 that an Inter-Departmental meeting accepted in principle that a Central National Museum of Art, Archaeology and Anthropology ought to be established in India and located in Delhi. Thereafter the Govt. decided to appoint a small committee to frame the details for the establishment of such a Museum with special regard to:

1. The function (powers, etc.) of the Museum,
2. Its general administration,
3. Its internal organization,
4. Its site,
5. Its building (including the possibility of progressive construction).

. . . The Committee met at Shimla on the 13th and 14th of May 1946 and submitted its report recommending that the Museum should comprise five Departments, namely

1. Art,
2. Pre-historic Archaeology,
3. Historic Archaeology,
4. Numismatics and Epigraphy, and
5. Anthropology, besides a
6. Circulating Department,
7. a Library, and
8. Chemical Laboratory.

Emphasis was laid on the importance of the role of the Librarian in guiding research.

. . . Its beginnings, however, go back to the great Exhibition of Indian Art that was shown in the Burlington House in London in 1947–48 organized by the Royal Academy, London with the cooperation of the Government of India and the British Government. The Exhibition was perhaps the richest collection of Indian Art that had been brought together until then. Many of the museums of undivided India had loaned some of their finest exhibits and in addition private collectors had sent art objects of exquisite workmanship and inestimable value.

. . . The nucleus of the National Museum was thus built with gifts or loans by State Government, Museum authorities and individual donors.

. . . Collections alone do not make a Museum in contemporary opinion, but they remain its heart, its reason for existence and its ambition. With comprehensive collections in its charge and the prospect of their steady increase in size, variety, breadth and importance, the National Museum, during the course of the last 50 years, has the sound foundations on which depend the other aspects of museum development. Collections are always the beginning. Caring for the objects collected is the next step. They must be studied, described and catalogued, they must if necessary, have conservative treatment, they must be placed on exhibition in a way to bring out their maximum quality and importance, as individual items, and in relation to other materials exhibited; or they must be stored away safely according to methods that will make them readily available for study. Finally they must be made to contribute effectively to the education, cultural growth and intelligent enjoyment of the citizens of all ages, as well as to the research and publication of scholars.

Source: *National Museum Bulletin No. 9*, National Museum of India (Mathur, D.), 2002, pp. 7–10.

Document 20   ON HARAPPA: DEPICTIONS OF ANCIENT PASTS

A key purpose of the National Museum was the presentation of national history. The excavations of the Indus valley civilization, important to India's historical identity, lay primarily in Pakistani territory. The sharing of artifacts was part of the exchange during Partition. This discussion of Harrapan terracottas illustrates their significance and the controversies of history in which museums participate.

(a)

p. 9

During the third millennium BC a highly developed civilization, known as the Harappan Civilization or the Indus Civilization now also called the Saraswati Civilization, existed along the rivers Indus and Saraswati. Nothing of this civilization was known until the early part of the twentieth century, when two archaeologists – R. D. Banerji and D. R. Sahni – discovered Mohenjodaro in Sind and Harappa in Punjab (both in Pakistan now), in 1920–21. So far about 200 Harappan and its associated sites have been excavated.

. . . The National Museum has a collection of about 3800 artefacts collected from the various towns of the Harappan Civilization. Besides these, 1025 objects from Indian sites have been recently received as temporary loan from the Archaeological Survey of India. These objects and the photographs of the archaeological remains in the gallery show the developed facets of the Harappan civilization. These towns were well planned after the grid or chessboard pattern in which major roads, running north–south and east–west were intersecting each other at right angles . . . They had built houses of bricks and stones with stairs; bathrooms and a well laid drainage system, both covered and open. . . . Among the artefacts from the Harappan Civilization in the National Museum are seals, fishhooks, pottery, weights, measures, jewellery, figurines, toys, tools and weapons, etc.

(b)

p. 47

. . . There is a controversy about the existence of horse (Eques cabulusoinn) during the mature Harappan period (Bokonyi: 1996, Sharma A. K.: 1993). Terracotta figurines of horses are reported from Harappan sites like Mohenjodaro, Banawali, Nausharo, Rakhigarhi, Lothal, Rangpur, and Surkotada. Mackay has identified one terracotta horse from Mohenjodaro which is now exhibited in the National Museum, New Delhi.

Source: Deo Prakash Sharma. *Harappan Terracottas in the Collection of the National Museum*, New Delhi: National Museum, 2003.

FOUNDING OF SAHITYA AKADEMI   **Document 21**

The founding of Sahitya Akademi signaled both India's dedication to promoting literary expression but also the recognition that in a multi-lingual country a national literature would have to be diverse and promoted through translation.

The mission of the Sahitya Akademi is to work actively for the development of Indian letters and to set high literary standards, to foster and co-ordinate literary activities in all the Indian languages and to promote through them all, the cultural unity of the country.

Source: Ministry of Education Report, 1971.

LANGUAGES RECOGNISED IN THE CONSTITUTION   **Document 22**

The Eight Schedule of the Constitution of India listed the languages that would be recognized by the state. Initially 14 languages were included on the list, but over time more languages were inserted. This list reflects the constitution as of 2000. Four more languages were added in 2003.

[Eighth Schedule [Articles 344(1) And 351]
With dates for additions

1. Assamese.
2. Bengali
3. Gujarati
4. Hindi
5. Kannada
6. Kashmiri

7. Konkoni (Inserted in 1992)
8. Malayalam
9. Manipuri (Inserted in 1992)
10. Marathi
11. Nepali (inserted in 1992)
12. Oriya
13. Punjabi
14. Sanskrit
15. Sindhi (inserted in 1962)
16. Tamil
17. Telegu
18. Urdu

Document 23   THE OFFICIAL LANGUAGE ISSUE

A commission was established to examine the issue of a national language for India. Reporting in 1956, the Official Language Commission recommended that the state move toward Hindi as a national language with broader influences from other regions of the country. However, the dissenting voices within the Commission raised important objections, which had lasting influence, and are included here.

Minute of Dissent
By Dr P. Subbarayan

Introduction

I regret I cannot accept the recommendations as presented in the Report. When I was invited to serve on the Official Language Commission I thought that it would be possible for us to submit a unanimous report in the interest of the country after considering the different points of view within the country. I feel sorry that after having worked together for many months for the common purpose of making such recommendations to the President as will ultimately conduce to the well-being of the nation, I should find myself at ultimate variance with many of my colleagues. . . .

In light of recent happenings and trends of events in India, my views have become strengthened and consequently my reading of the nature of the linguistic situation and the linguistic problem has been different on many matters from that finally presented in the Report. . . .

. . . The Report has been prepared on the assumption that under the present Constitution Hindi has been already voluntarily accepted by the whole of India, that non-Hindi-speaking peoples are eager for it as speakers of Hindi, and that it will be something anti-national not to try to replace English by Hindi. It might appear to some people that the report represents the view of the Hindi speakers, who alone benefit immediately, and for a long time to come, if not for ever. I fear that in the entire report there is very little evidence of understanding, imagination and sympathy for the non-Hindi-speaking people of India. There is hardly any serious consideration of the fact that great languages more ancient and more developed in every way than Hindi do exist and do flourish vigorously in the country, claiming the passionate homage of their speakers . . .

Suniti Kumar Chatterji (Another Dissent)

The wisest attitude in my opinion should be, considering the prevalence of Hindi and the ultimate possibility of a much wider group of people becoming acquainted with Hindi, that it would be worthwhile to propagate it and to persuade non-Hindi speaking peoples to acquire it. But as said before, Hindi speaking peoples should also as a gesture of friendliness and a real desire to make some sacrifices themselves for the Unity of India – if taking up the burden of learning one of the great languages of the country can be describes as a 'sacrifice' – take upon themselves voluntarily the study of some one of the other of the Modern non-Hindi languages . . .

English has virtually become one of the languages of India, as it is the home language of an influential and advanced minority group, the Anglo-Indians and some Indian Christians of both Indian and Foreign Origin, and Indian Jews in many cases; and (what is more important) it is still serving us as a modernizing and unifying leaven for the whole of India. Let Hindi develop with the other languages of the Union . . .

Some Definitive Suggestions

. . .* The choice of Hindi as a language to replace English in our pan-Indian affairs has been hasty . . . This is giving rise to a growing Linguistic Chauvinism and ('Hindi Imperialism' as it has been called) on the one hand and to passionate and jealous Linguism on the other hand in non-Hindi States. This is a menace to Indian Unity . . .

*. . . English side by side with the Indian languages, great and small – this is the only solution for a polyglot state which strives to retain its basic unity while developing its own modern languages without special favour for any one of them in particular.

* English should be given a place in the 8th Schedule [which lists the prescribed languages used for official purposes] as the language of an important community in India. This will be an act of belated justice to a small but advanced community of Indian citizens; and English has besides a special

claim for being regarded as one of the Languages of Modern India, in spite of its foreign origin because of its great implications and its service in helping to maintain the Unity of India, politically, intellectually, and culturally.

Peroration: the Views of the Prime Minister of India.

Sri Nehru said that the question of languages must be kept out of the domain of politics. The languages should be considered on their own merits. 'We have therefore to recognize the importance of English to us, for at least two reasons.

'One is that even now it does help in our understanding each other, more especially the people from the North and the South and other parts of India. We should keep this link.

'The other reason is that it provides a link between us in India and the outside world, and it is of the utmost importance that we should maintain that link with the outside world and not try to cut off ourselves from it and isolate ourselves. . . .'

Suniti Kumar Chatterji
4 July 1956

Source: Subbarayan, P. 1956. 'Minute of Dissent' and Suniti Kumar Chatterji. In *Report of the Official Language Commission*, 315–30. New Delhi: Government of India.

Document 24   REGULATION OF THE FILM INDUSTRY

The Cinematograph Act of 1052 established standards for the evolving film industry. Section 5B included below laid out principles for certifying films.

5B. Principles for guidance in certifying films.

(1) A film shall not be certified for public exhibition if, in the opinion of the authority competent to grant the certificate, the film or any part of it is against the interests of [the sovereignty and integrity of India] the security of the State, friendly relation with foreign States, public order, decency or morality, or involves defamation or contempt of court or is likely to incite the commission of any offence.

(2) Subject to the provisions contained in sub-section (1), the Central Government may issue such directions as it may think fit setting out the principles which shall guide the authority competent to grant certificates under this Act in sanctioning films for public exhibition.

Source: Act 37 of 1952, the cinematograph act, 1952.

POLITICAL CALLS FOR LAND REFORM **Document 25**

Such a major proportion of the population remained in the agricultural sector that calls for land reform were a high priority for all political parties. When the government seemed slow to respond, opposition parties, such as the Praja Socialist Party, emphasized the needs of peasants in their political platforms. This Report from the Second National Conference of the party set out the argument.

Chapter VIII: Kisan

. . . This National Conference of the Praja Socialist Party is gravely concerned over the continuation of injustice, instability and disorder in the agricultural sector of our economy. The fluctuation in the prices of agricultural produce, enhancement of irrigation rates, imposition of betterment levy and such other new and old taxes have deteriorated the lot of our already impoverished peasantry. The Government have not paid adequate attention to the problem of increasing the produce of agriculture per acre. The peasantry is suffering great hardship owing to the lack of sufficient credit facilities and no encouragement is forthcoming to foster the growth of sale, purchase and such other co-operative institutions in the rural areas.

All over the country evictions of tenants are being effected on a large scale in spite of the tall talk about abolition of landlordism and progressive tenancy legislations. In the absence of firm determination to help the tenants, the unwillingness to implement effectively the laws enacted, and the hostile attitude of the bureaucracy, the Congress governments have failed to put an end to evictions that are on the increase every day. . . .

Source: Conference Report, Second National Conference, 26–30 December, 1955, p. 144.

AGRICULTURAL STATISTICS **Document 26**

India functioned to various degrees as a planned economy. Each five year plan proposed a course of action and set of goals in various industries, including agriculture. To measure the success of agricultural programs, the government kept careful statistics on yield in various crops. Unlike some socialist states, where officers charged with producing high yields were the same people keeping records and therefore had a tendency to inflate results, Indian bureaucrats had no such incentives. These agricultural statistics show change over time due to temporary weather set backs, on the one hand, and the benefits of the green revolution, on the other.

Crop Yields in Kilograms/Hectare

Crop	Pre-Plan	First Five-Year Plan					Second Five-Year Plan				
Year	'50–1	'51–2	'52–3	'53–4	'54–5	'55–6	'56–7	'57–8	'58–9	'59–60	'60–1
Paddy	1032	1071	1146	1353	1230	1311	1349	1185	1395	1405	1520
Wheat	663	653	763	750	803	708	695	682	789	772	851

Crop	Third Five-Year Plan					Annual	Annual	Annual
Year	'61–2	62–3	63–4	64–5	65–6	66–7	67–8	68–9
Paddy	1542	1396	1550	1617	1294	1295	1548	1613
Wheat	890	793	730	913	827	887	1103	1169

Crop	Fourth Five-Year Plan				
Year	'69–70	'70–1	'71–2	'72–3	'73–4
Paddy	1609	1685	1711	1605	1726
Wheat	1209	1307	1380	1271	1172

Source: Government of India, Ministry of Agriculture Statistics.

Document 27   SURRENDER OF PAKISTAN IN BANGLADESH WAR

The following document, signed by General A. A. K. Niazi in Dhaka on 16 December 1971 ended the Pakistani War and surrendered the Pakistani army to Indian and Bangladeshi leaders.

Signed by Lieutenant General A. A. K. Niazi, Commander of the Pakistani Eastern Army

Presented to Lieutenant General Jagjit Singh Aurora, General Officer Commanding-in-Chief of India's Eastern Command

Excerpt

Pakistani Eastern Command agree to surrender all Pakistani armed forces in Bangla Desh to Lt-General Jagjit Singh Aurora, GOC-in-C of the Indian and Bangla Desh Forces in the Eastern theatre.

This surrender includes all Pakistani land, air and naval forces as also all para-military forces and civil armed forces.

These forces will lay down their arms and surrender at the place where they are currently located to the nearest regular troops in the command of Lt-Gen Jagjit Singh Aurora. . . .

Lt-Gen. Jagjit Singh Aurora gives his solemn assurance that personnel who surrender shall be treated with dignity and respect that soldiers are entitled to in accordance with the provisions of the Geneva Convention and guarantees safety and well-being of all Pakistani Military and para-military forces who surrender.

Source: *Asian Recorder*, 15–21 January 1972, p. 10565.

JAYAPRAKASH NARAYAN AND "TOTAL REVOLUTION"   **Document 28**

Jayaprakash Narayan, a senior Gandhian freedom fighter, agreed to support and lead the student movement in 1973. Arrested by Indira Gandhi during the Emergency he kept a diary in prison. Excerpts from the diary are available below. In addition see the following letter that JP (as he was known) wrote to Indira Gandhi condemning the Emergency.

(a)

Picking up the thread after a lapse of three days the students' movement gave me an opportunity to turn it into a peaceful people's movement for larger ends: total revolution. Here two points should be made clear. One, I had no specific or direct hand in starting the Bihar movement. Though since the publication of 'Appeal to Youth' in December 1973 I had specially concentrated on university students . . .

Two. When I declared on 5th June 1974 at the Gandhi Maidan (Patna) before a vast audience of students and citizens of Patna . . . that the Bihar movement was no longer a students' movement restricted to the 12 original demands . . . but that the movement's or struggle's ultimate aims were nothing less than total revolution, thunderous applause greeted my declaration, thus putting on it the imprimatur of the students' as well as the public's enthusiastic approval.

. . . . [T]here was insistent demand from my students and other colleagues for clarification and elaboration. This I did in many discussions and public speeches, which were published in a pamphlet entitled *Sampoorna Kranti* (Total Revolution).

Source: Jayaprakash Narayan, *Prison Diary*. Bombay: Popular Prakashan, 1977 [pp. 23, 31–34], August 21, 1975.

(b)

Letters from Jail
To Indira Gandhi
July 21, 1975
Chandigarh

Dear Prime Minister

I am appalled at press reports of your speeches and interviews. (The very fact that you have to say something every day to justify your action implies a guilty conscience.) Having muzzled the press and every kind of public dissent, you continue with your distortions and untruths without fear of criticism or contradiction. If you think that in this way you will be able to justify yourself in the public eye and damn the Opposition to political perdition, you are sorely mistaken. If you doubt this, you may test it by revoking the emergency, restoring to the people their fundamental rights, restoring the freedom of the press, releasing all those whom you have imprisoned or detained for no other crime than performing their patriotic duty. Nine years, madam, is not a short period of time for the people, who are gifted with a sixth sense, to have found you out.

The burden of your song, as I have been able to discover is that (a) there was a plan to paralyse the government, and (b) that one person had been trying to spread disaffection among the ranks of the civil and military forces. These seem to be your major notes. But there have been also minor notes. Every now and then you have been doing out your *obiter dictae* such as the nation being more important than democracy and about the suitability of social democracy to India, and more in the same vein.

As a villain of the piece, let me put the record straight. This may be of no interest to you for all your distortions and untruths are willful and deliberate – but at least the truth would have been recorded.

About the plan to paralyse the government there was no such plan and you know it. Let me state the facts.

Of all the States of India it was in Bihar alone where there was a people's movement. But there too, according to the Chief Minister's many statements it had fizzled out long ago, if it had ever existed. But the truth is – and you know if your ubiquitous Intelligence has served you right – that it was spreading and percolating deep down in the countryside. Until the time of my arrest janata sarkars were being formed from the village upwards to the block level. Later on, the process was to be taken up, hopefully, to the district and State level.

If you have cared to look into the programme of the janata sarkars [people's governments], you would have found that for the most part it was constructive, such as regulating the public system, checking corruption at the lower levels of administration, implementing the land reform laws, settling disputes through the age-old custom of conciliation and arbitration, assuring a fair deal to Harijans, curbing such social evils as talak [a very quick form of divorce] and dahez [dowry], etc. There was nothing in all this that by any stretch of the imagination could be called subversive. Only where the janata sarkars were solidly organized were such programmes as non-payment of taxes taken up. At the peak of the movement in the urban areas an attempt was made for some days, through dharna and picketing to stop the working of government offices. At Patna whenever the Assembly opened attempts were made to persuade the members to resign and to prevent them peacefully from going in. All these were calculated programmes of civil disobedience and thousands of men and women were arrested all over the State. If all this adds up to an attempt to paralyse the Bihar Government, well, it was the same kind of attempt as was made during the freedom struggle through non-cooperation and satyagraha to paralyse the British Government. But that was a government established by force, whereas the Bihar Government and leg-islature are both constitutionally established bodies. What right has anyone to ask an elected government and elected legislature to go? This is one of your favourite questions. But it has been answered umpteen times by com-petent persons, including well-known constitutional lawyers. The answer is that in a democracy the people do have the right to ask for the resignation of an elected government if it has gone corrupt and has been misruling. And if there is a legislature that persists in supporting such a government it too must go, so that the people might choose better representatives. . . .

. . . I have pondered over this riddle: why did not those governments act wisely? The conclusion I have arrived at is that the main hurdle has been cor-ruption. Somehow the government have been unable to deal with corruption in their ranks, particularly corruption in the government and the administration.

Be that as it may, except for Bihar, there was no movement of its kind in any other State of India. In U. P. though satyagraha and started in April, it was far from becoming a people's movement. . . .

. . . In a democracy the citizen has an inalienable right to civil disobedi-ence when he finds that other channels of redress or reform have dried up. It goes without saying that the satyagrahi willingly invites and accepts his lawful punishment. This is the new dimension added to democracy by Gandhi. What an irony that it should be obliterated in Gandhi's own India!

. . . You have accused the Opposition and me of every kind of villainy. But let me assure you that if you do the right things, for instance, your 20 points, tackling corruption at the Ministerial levels, electoral reform, etc., take the Opposition in to confidence and heed its advice, you will receive the willing cooperation of every one of us. For that you need not destroy democracy. The ball is in your court. It is for you to decide.

With these parting words, let me bid you farewell. May God be with you.

Jayaprakash

Source: Jaya Prakash Narayan, *J. P.'s Jail Life (A Collection of Personal Letters)* New Delhi; Arnold-Heinemann, 1977, pp. 67–69.

THE COMMITTEE ON THE STATUS OF WOMEN IN INDIA   **Document 29**

The Committee on the Status of Women in India was established by the government to determine areas in which women's development required greater support and improvement. The committee's report, published as it was in 1974 just before the Emergency, did not fully receive attention for another six years . . . The Committee examined women's education, employment, property rights, as well as political rights. The excerpt below focuses on arguments for and against political reservations for women. On this issue the committee chose not to take a single position.

Summarizing arguments for reservations

7.105 (C) A system of reservation of a proportion of seats for women in these bodies would provide an impetus for both the women as well as the political parties to give a fairer deal to nearly half the population in the various units of government. If women enter these bodies in larger numbers the present inhibitions that result from their minority position in these institutions may disappear faster and give them greater freedom to articulate their views. . . .

7.109 (b) The failure of Indian society to 'look upon women's participation with sympathy and understanding' is an exceedingly retarding factor in political socialisation of both men and women. A 30% reservation of seats in the legislative bodies for women will alter the very character of our legislature and will compel the political parties to change their strategies and tactics and induce them to give women their due. Reservation of seats for women cannot lead to their becoming 'isolated pockets in the nation' because 'women are not marginal to society as a minority group might be'. It could, instead lead to increase in women's participation and motivate them to shoulder their political responsibilities.

7.110 If 'access to policy making powers and facilities is a component of social status' then the presence of more women in the legislatures will help to direct the rate and type of changes in the position of women. Only a system of reservations, increasing the number of women representatives will help to broaden the base of women's representation in the legislative bodies.

Summarizing arguments opposed to reservations

7.112 We however received a strong opposition to the suggestion from representatives of political parties and most women legislators. They felt that any system of special representation would be a retrograde step from the equality conferred by the Constitution. There was also some resistance to women being equated with socially backward communities as all women do not suffer from the same disabilities as these under-privileged groups. The representatives of some parties however did not have any strong objections to reservation of seats for women in local bodies for which certain precedents were already existing.

7.113 There is a fallacy in the entire argument for separate representation for such a system of special representation may precipitate similar demands from various other interests and communities and threaten national integration. . . .

(a) Women have been competing as equals with men since 1952. They must continue to do so and stand on their own merits and intensify their political and social life. A departure from this equality now will be a retrograde step.

(b) The minority argument cannot be applied to women. Women are not a community; they are a category. Though they have some real problems of their own they share with men the problems of their groups, locality, and community. Women are not concentrated in certain areas confined to particular fields of activity. Under these circumstances, there can be no rational basis for reservations for women.

Source: Excerpt from the *Report of the Committee on the Status of Women in India*, 1975, pp. 176–180, Government of India.

THE EMERGENCY: TWENTY-POINT PROGRAMME   **Document 30**

Indira Gandhi announced a 20-point programme of development both to justify the Emergency (retroactively) and to mollify some critics.

1. Continuance of steps to bring down prices of essential commodities. Streamline production, procurement and distribution of essential commodities. Strict economy in Government expenditure.
2. Implementation of agricultural land ceilings and speedy distribution of surplus. In addition, land and compilation of land records.
3. Stepping up of provision of house-sites for landless and weaker sections.
4. Bonded labour wherever it exists will be declared illegal.
5. Plea for liquidation of rural indebtedness. Legislation for moratorium on recovery of debt from landless labourers, small farmers and artisans.
6. Review of laws on minimum agricultural wages.
7. Five million more hectares to be brought under irrigation. National programme for use of underground water.
8. An accelerated power programme. Super thermal stations under Central control.
9. New development plan for development of the handloom sector.
10. Improvement in quality of supply of people's cloth.
11. Socialisation of urban and urbanisable land. Ceiling on ownership and possession of vacant land and on the plinth area of new dwelling units.
12. Special squads for valuation of conspicuous construction and prevention of tax evasion. Summary trials and deterrent punishment to economic offenders.
13. Special legislation for confiscation of smugglers' properties.

14. Liberalization of investment procedures. Action against misuse of import licences.
15. New schemes for workers' association in industry.
16. National permit scheme for road transport.
17. Income-tax relief to the middle-class – exemption-limit raised to Rs 8,000.
18. Essential commodities at controlled prices to students in hostels.
19. Books and stationery at controlled prices.
20. New apprenticeship scheme to enlarge employment and training especially of weaker sections.

Source: ASIAN RECORDER, 30 July–5 August, 1975, p. 12711.

Document 31   *ECONOMIC AND POLITICAL WEEKLY* ON THE SHAH COMMISSION FINDINGS

The Shah Commission investigated excesses and violations of human rights during the Emergency. It published a report in 1978. The following excerpt is an analysis of the Shah Commission's findings as it appeared in the Economic and Political Weekly (EPW). The source here is also important. The EPW is a weekly periodical that publishes timely analyses by respected academics. It demonstrates the important role that intellectuals play in the discussion of contemporary issues.

Next only to the forcible sterilization of hundreds of thousands of women and men all over the country, the large-scale demolition of hutments, houses and shops in different parts of Delhi and in nearby villages during the Emergency perhaps wreaked havoc on the lives of the largest number of common people. The demolitions, which are the subject of Chapter XIII of the Shah Commission's Interim Report II, were carried through on the false pretext of removing unauthorized constructions and beautifying the capital city. Compared to 1800 structures demolished in the two-and-a-half years preceding the imposition of the Emergency, in the next 20 months no less than 150, 105 structures were pulled down by the Delhi Development Authority (DDA), the Municipal Corporation of Delhi (MCD) and the New Delhi Municipal Committee (NDMC).

. . . .

Anti-Muslim Prejudice

The demolition operations in the Jama Masjid were quite plainly directed against Muslims. . . . The late President, Fakhruddin Ali Ahmed, himself intervened with Indira Gandhi in an attempt to prevent the demolitions in the Jama Masjid area, but to no avail.

In a fortnight from April 13–27, 1976, nearly 850 pucca structures were razed to the ground in this area with the help of bulldozers and motor graders. The ferociousness of the authorities is reflected in the fact that the resistance put up by the people, which was ruthlessly put down by the police, actually caused the DDA to sharply step up the tempo of the demolitions and press into service a larger number of bulldozers so that 457 pucca structures were demolished in just six days between April 19 and 24, 1976.

. . . The Shah Commission concludes that 'on the basis of evidence on record, it appears that among other considerations the political affiliations of the shopkeepers to a party opposed to the Congress was one of the deciding factors which impelled Shri Sanjay Gandhi to order the demolition of the structures in Karol Bagh'. [A neighbourhood where a market was destroyed.]
. . .

The Shah Commission's conclusions about the demolitions in Delhi during the Emergency are categoric – they were illegal, the procedures laid down under the relevant laws were not observed and even court orders staying the demolitions were disregarded. . . .

If prosecutions are not launched even in cases in which the Shah Commission has been able to pinpoint responsibility for illegal and criminal actions as clearly as it has done in regard to the demolitions in Delhi, the conclusion is inescapable that the fulminations of the Janata party leaders from Morarji Desai down, against the excesses of the Emergency are intended to mislead the people and conceal from them the fact that there is a deliberate conspiracy afoot at various levels to shield the criminals of the Emergency.

Source: Economic and Political Weekly, 24 June 1978.

ORAL ACCOUNTS OF THE EMERGENCY   **Document 32**

The following two paragraphs come from interviews carried out by anthropologist Emma Tarlo with citizens recalling the Emergency. The first interview is with a pradhan a low-level government worker, whose home was one of those targeted for demolition. The second interview is with an Older Muslim Woman.

Interview with a *pradhan*, a low-level government worker, whose home was one of those targeted for demolition.

'The pressure was on all of us. We had to get sterilized in order to get the plots [to build a new house] No one was happy with that but no one had any choice either . . . Initially I had a lot of difficulty persuading people to get sterilized, but then I told them that I myself had had the operation and that I had not suffered any problems, physical or otherwise. After that people gradually started following.' . . .

Interview with an Older Muslim Woman

'Let me tell you how I was forced . . . Initially we women were prevented from going for sterilization by the men of the family who were immediately opposed to the idea. But then Ruksana's workers would come to the house when all the men were out. They tried to entice us by offering various things like money, blankets, and ghee. We women got tempted by such offers and gave out names for sterilization. I was promised a blanket and Rs. 500, but all they actually gave me was Rs 70. I was forced.' (p. 175)

Source: Tarlo, E. *Unsettled Memories: Narratives of the Emergency in Delhi*. London: Hurst and Company, 2003, pp. 169, 175.

Document 33   SPEECH BY A. K. GOPALAN, A MEMBER OF PARLIAMENT, ARRESTED DURING THE EMERGENCY

A. K. Gopalan was a member of the political opposition who had been detained without trial during the initial arrests at the time of the Emergency. After his release, he stood before Parliament on 21 July 1975 and gave a speech about this violation of democracy. The speech was suppressed from the political record at the time but later published by his own Communist Party of India-Marxist in a volume of collected documents.

'I rise to speak in an extraordinary and most distressing situation in which 34 members of Parliament are not here, not of their own volition but because they have been detained without trial, and Parliament itself has been reduced to a farce and an object of contempt by Srimati Gandhi and her party. I have to say that I myself had been arrested and kept in jail for one week and Jyotirmoy Basu, you know him very well, with Noorul Huda, another member of our Party. I am an old man who cannot speak loudly now. I was released and both of them were kept inside the jail. The reasons are very clear. I am not afraid of jails because during the period of the last 45 years, for 17 years I have been in jail . . .

On behalf of the Communist Party of India (Marxist), I totally oppose the new declaration of Emergency and its ratification in the House. We know full well that in the present situation no one is immune from arrest and detention.

We cannot betray the interests of the people and give our assent to the obliteration of all vestiges of democracy in India – freedom of the person, freedom of speech, freedom to form associations, freedom to approach the Courts, freedom of the press, freedom to criticize the government and work for its replacement by a government of the people's choice . . .

The people cannot be deceived for long by the rulers and people are on the move and calling the bluff of 'garibi hatao' [eliminate poverty] and "bekari hatao' [eliminate forced labour].

It is this background that the movement led by Shri Jaya Prakash Narayan gathered momentum. Our Party has clearly stated our differences with Shri Narayan, but at the same time given our support to the democratic demands, which he has championed. Whatever our differences with the movement, we have defended and will defend the right to organize satyagraha, strikes, bandhs, etc., which are all legitimate weapons in the hands of the people.

Whatever be the price we may have to pay our Party has no other interest apart from the interests of the people. The interest of the people demand that the Emergency, the all pervasive measures taken under it, the total denial of democracy be fought and the broad based united struggle against the exploiters be carried on with the strength of the people.

We will never surrender ourselves to the ruling classes, we will never betray the toiling people and democratic forces of our country. History will vindicate us. Thank you.

Source: Speech by A. K. Gopalan in Lok Sabha, 21 July 1975, published by the Communist Party of India (Marxist). Jyoti Basu, Sailen Das Gupta, Buddhadev Bhattacharya, Anil Biswas, Shanti Shekhar Bose. *Documents of the Communist Movement in India, Vol XVII.* Calcutta: National Book Agency, 1998, pp. 77–91.

ANANDPUR SAHIB AGREEMENT OF THE SHIROMANI AKALI DAL **Document 34**

At the height of the political movement in Punjab for greater autonomy, the Shiromani Akali Dal (a major political party in Punjab) came to an agreement of principles that both united factions within the Akali Dal and set out some of the issues the party wanted to address with the Indian government. The agreement took place in the Anandpur Sahib, one of the holiest cities to the Sikh religion in 1978.

Resolution No. 1
The Shiromani Akali Dal realizes that India is a federal and republican geographical entity of different languages, religions and cultures. To safeguard

the fundamental rights of the religious and linguistic minorities, to fulfill the demands of the democratic traditions and to pave the way for economic progress, it has become imperative that the Indian constitutional infrastructure should be given a real federal shape by redefining the Central and State relation and rights on the lines of the aforesaid principles and objectives. The concept of total revolution given by Lok Naik Jaya Parkash Narain is also based upon the progressive decentralization of powers. The climax of the process of centralization of powers of the states through repeated amendments of the Constitution during the Congress regime came before the countrymen in the form of the Emergency (1975), when all fundamental rights of all citizens was usurped. It was then that the programme of decentralization of powers ever advocated by Shiromani Akali Dal was openly accepted and adopted by other political parties including Janata Party, C.P.I. (M), D.M.K., etc. Shiromani Akali Dal has ever stood firm on this principle and that is why after a very careful consideration it unanimously adopted a resolution to this effect first at the All India Akali Conference, Batala, then at Anandpur Sahib which has endorsed the principle of State autonomy in keeping with the concept of federalism. As such, the Shiromani Akali Dal emphatically urges upon the Janata Government to take cognizance of the different linguistic and cultural sections, religious minorities as also the voice of millions of people and recast the constitutional structure of the country on real and meaningful federal principles to obviate the possibility of any danger to the unity and integrity of the country and, further, to enable the states to play a useful role for the progress and prosperity of the Indian people in their respective areas by a meaningful exercise of their powers.

Resolution No. 2
This momentous meeting of the Shiromani Akali Dal calls upon the Government of India to examine carefully the long tale of the excesses, wrongs, and illegal actions committed against the Sikhs by the previous Congress Government, more particularly during the Emergency, and try to find an early solution to the following problems:

(a) Chandigarh originally raised as a Capital for Punjab should be handed over to Punjab.
(b) The long-standing demand of the Shiromani Akali Dal for the merger in Punjab of the Punjabi-speaking areas, to be identified by linguistic experts with village as a unit, should be conceded.
(c) The control of headworks should continue to be vested in Punjab and, if need be, the Reorganization Act should be amended.
(d) The arbitrary and unjust Award given by Mrs. Indira Gandhi during the Emergency on the distributions of Ravi-Beas waters should be revised on the universally accepted norms and principles, and justice be done to Punjab.

(e) Keeping in view the special aptitude and martial qualities of the Sikhs, the present ratio of their strength in the Army should be maintained.

(f) The excesses being committed on the settlers in the Tarai region of the Uttar Pradesh in the name of Land Reforms should be vacated by making suitable amendments in the ceiling law on the Central guidelines.

Resolution No. 3

(Economic Policy Resolution)

The chief sources of inspiration of the economic policies and programme of the Shiromani Akali Dal are the secular, democratic and socialistic concepts of Guru Nanak and Guru Gobind Singh. Our economic programme is based on three principles:

(a) Dignity of labour.

(b) An economic and social structure, which provides for the uplift of the poor and depressed sections of society.

(c) Unabated opposition to concentration of economic and political power in the hands of the capitalists.

While drafting its economic policies and programme, the Shiromani Akali Dal in its historic Anandpur Sahib Resolution has laid particular stress on the need to break the monopolistic hold of the capitalists foisted on the Indian economy by 30 years of Congress rule in India. This capitalist hold enabled the Central Government to assume all powers in its hands after the manner of Mughal imperialism. This was bound to thwart the economic progress of the states and injure the social and economic interests of the people. The Shiromani Akali Dal once again reiterates the Sikh way of life by resolving to fulfil the holy words of Guru Nanak Dev: 'He alone realizes the true path who labours honestly and shares with others the fruits of that labor.'

This way of life is based upon three basic principles:

i.   Doing honest labour,
ii. Sharing with others the fruits of this labor, and
iii. Meditation on the Lord's Name.

The Shiromani Akali Dal calls upon the Central and the State governments to eradicate unemployment during the next ten years. While pursuing this aim, special emphasis should be laid on ameliorating the lot of the weaker sections, scheduled and depressed classes, workers, landless and poor farmers and urban poor farmers and urban poor. Minimum wages must be fixed for all of them.

The Shiromani Akali Dal urges Punjab government to draw up such an economic plan for the state as would turn it into the leading state during the next ten years by raising per capita income to Rs. 3,000 and by generating an economic growth rate of 7% per annum as against 4% at the national level. . . .

Source: Moved by Sardar Gurcharan Singh Tohra, President, Shiromani Gurdwara Parbandhak Committee, and endorsed by Sardar Parkash Singh Badal, Chief Minister, Punjab.

Document 35   INDIRA GANDHI'S LAST SPEECH

This is a portion of the text of Indira Gandhi's last speech delivered in Orissa on 30 October 1984. (She was assassinated the next day, having returned to New Delhi.) The speech took place in the parade ground in Bhubaneshwar, which later became a park in Indira Gandhi's memory.

I do not care whether I live or die. I have lived a long life. And if I am proud of anything it is that my whole life has been spent in service. I am proud of this as of nothing else. And as long as there is breath in me, my life will be spent in service. And when my life ends, I can say that every drop of my blood will keep India alive and strengthen it. It is my hope that people, specially the youth and women, will think about this and take the responsibility on their own shoulders. I have full confidence in the people of India that they will never take the wrong path.
Orissa, October 1984,

Source: *Sandesh*, Congress Party Newsletter.

Document 36   1984 ELECTION POSTER – See Plate 3

After Indira Gandhi's assassination, Rajiv Gandhi, her successor as leader of the Congress Party and Prime Minister, called elections. During the campaign Indira Gandhi's memory played an important role as indicated in a Congress Poster containing her picture and some of her last words (see plate 4). Its translation is below.

There is great strength in India today. And we all citizens of India have to make that stronger with our own force. We will make India, a beautiful India, a developed India, a shining India. We must take a vow today for India's sovereignty, India's unity, India's strength. All these are in your hands.

My wish is that all people of India, youth and women together, should think today – today itself – and take the responsibility on their shoulders. I have

full faith in the people of India that they will never go in the wrong path.
(translation: Kailash Chandra Jha and Wendy Singer)

MANDAL COMMISSION REPORT ON BACKWARD CLASSES   **Document 37**

*The Mandal Commission was established by the Janata government in 1978
to examine the obstacles that might impede social mobility for people who
were economically (class) and socially (caste) backward. The Commission
was named after its chair, Bindeshwari Prasad Mandal and played a critical
role in Indian politics over the next several decades.*

Recommendations:
Reservations for SCs and STs are in proportion to their population, i.e.,
22.5%. But as there is a legal obligation to keep reservations under Articles
15 (4) and 16 (4) of the Constitution below 50% the Commission recom-
mends a reservation of 27% for OBCs. This reservation should apply to all
Government services as well as technical and professional institutions, both
in the Centre and the State.

Special educational facilities designed at upgrading the cultural environment
of the students should be created in a phased manner in selected areas containing high concentrations of OBCs. Special emphasis should be placed on
vocational training. Separate coaching facilities should be provided in technical
and professional institutions to OBC students to enable them to catch up
with the students from the open quota.

Special programmes for upgrading the skills of village artisans should be
prepared and subsidized loans from financial institutions granted to them for
setting up small scale industries.

At present no Central assistance is available to any State for implementing
any welfare measures for other Backward Classes. Several State Governments
expressed their helplessness in undertaking more purposeful development
programmes for backward classes in view of lack of resources. It is, therefore,
recommended that welfare programmes specially designed for OBC should
be financed by the Central Government in the same manner and to the same
extent as done in the case of SCs and STs.

Source: Reservations for Backward Classes: Mandal Commission Report of the Backward Classes Commission, 1980. Delhi: Akalank Publications, 1991.

Document 38   AMUL BUTTER ADVERTISEMENT – See Plate 8

The Amul Butter (and cheese) company regularly put up topical ads on bill-boards across India. Taking on the Mandal Commission controversy in 1992, Amul Butter poked fun at the concept of reserving seats. The ad also plays with language by building into the joke the different meanings of words in Hindi and English. This is reminiscent of the use of language in some contemporary Indian fiction. See plate

"Caste No Bar"
"Class No Bar"
"Amul Butter Bar Bar"

"Caste no bar, class no bar" in the Mandal context means anyone is eligible for the post. It is also a phrase used in marriage ads that suggests the advertiser is open to partners no matter their jati. "Bar bar" is a Hindi phrase meaning "again and again." So Amul butter bar bar" means "Amul butter everytime."

Document 39   DESTRUCTION OF THE BABRI MASJID

Following is the speech that the Prime Minister P. V. Narasimha Rao delivered upon hearing the news on 6 December 1992 that the 16th century mosque (the Babri Masjid) had been destroyed by Hindu activists in Ayodhya. In the speech he both tried to unravel how this could happen without the successful intervention of law and order and also to condemn the act.

Initial reports from Ayodhya in the beginning of the day on 6 December indicated an air of normalcy. About 70,000 persons had assembled in the Ram Katha Kunj [complex near Babri Masjid built by Temple supporters] for public meetings with some 500 sadhus [Hindu renouncers] and sants [Hindu holy figures] gathered on the foundation terrace for performing pooja [worship]. Everything seemed to be going according to the plan announced by the organizers for doing a symbolic *kar seva* [doing service, in this case for the 'Ram Temple' not yet built and observing other formalities of *kar seva* not involving violation of the Court orders]. As the crowd was being addressed by leaders of the BJP, VHP, RSS and Bajrang Dal, roughly 150 persons in a sudden move broke through the cordon on the terrace, regrouped and started pelting stones at the police personnel. All this happened in a few minutes before noon and within a very little time around a thousand persons broke into the RJB-BM [Ram Janambhoomi-Babri Masjid] structure. Around 12:20 about 80 persons had managed to climb onto the RJB-BM structure and started damaging the domes. At this time, the crowd inside the complex was around 25,000 with larger numbers milling around outside. By 2:40 p.m. the crowd had increased to about 75,000.

The U.P. police moved away as the *kar sevaks* scaled barricades and clambered on to the domes of the mosque where saffron flags were hoisted. Then began a frenzied demolition with shovels iron rods and pickaxes.

While this was going on, the local authorities and the police appeared to be standing as mute spectators. This dismal picture of inaction and dereliction of duty was because of orders from the Chief Minister of U.P. not to use force. Even the small contingent of CRPF [Central Reserve Police Force] was rendered inactive and powerless by express directions given to them by the local magistrate and higher State Government authorities. pp. 155–156

159
. . . Until late in the evening of 6 December, the Supreme Court was reviewing the happenings at Ayodhya. When the final news of the demolition reached the Court, they expressed their extreme annoyance and distress at the unfortunate turn of events. The State Government had deliberately misled the Supreme Court over the past few days and when the ultimate vandalism took place, the Court called the senior counsel of the State Government and called for an explanation. To this, the counsel replied, 'I was misled by the party and my head hangs in shame'.

165
. . . In the context the Supreme Court held that 'the demolition of Babri Masjid in brazen defiance of the order of this Court is indeed a challenge to the majesty of law and the Constitution. This act of defiance is indeed a defiance of the Constitution and also of the powers of the Constitutional authorities of the Centre and the State. The Demolition is an unprecedented attack on the secular foundation of democracy, the authority and dignity of this Court. The Court thus stands betrayed as never before'.

Source: P. V. Narasimha Rao, Prime Minister of India, Ayodhya 6 December 1992. New Delhi: Viking, 2006.

THE SHAH BANO MAINTENANCE IN MARRIAGE CASE   **Document 40**

The following document comes from the Appeal brought in 1985 by M. A. Khan the former husband of Shah Bano concerning his obligation to pay maintenance to her. The case rested on issues that addressed the relationship between Muslim personal law and the Indian courts. In this excerpt from the appeal, the lawyers address the potential conflict in law.

Appeal, by M. A. Khan, 1985

There is no conflict between the provisions of Section 125 and those of the Muslim personal law on the question of the Muslim husband's obligation to provide maintenance for a divorced wife who is unable to maintain herself . . .

Whether the spouses are Hindus or Muslims, Christians or Parsis, pagans or heathens, is wholly irrelevant in the application of these provisions.

Document 41   KERALA'S EXPERIENCE WITH ADAPTING PANCHAYATS

When the Panchayati Raj Amendment Act came into force in 1993, each state created a legal structure to implement its provisions. Kerala, like many states, had an earlier system of local self government. This document from the Kerala Assembly based on legislation passed in 1999 described the necessary changes that would take place with the implementation of this new system.

The amendments to the Panchayat Raj/Municipal Act passed by the Legislative Assembly in February 1999 were intended to strengthen the power of the decentralization process and to expand the powers and responsibilities given to the three-tier system as per the 73rd and 74th amendments in the Constitution. It is to smooth the decentralization of power based on the amended Act that the Government tried to amend 35 more acts which have inseparable relation with the functioning of the local self governments. With these amendments, the power of the decentralization process is attaining perfection to a great extent.

. . . The Government do not target simple decentralization of power. What we want is democratic and corruption-free decentralization of power and the power thus conferred should be utilized for the *summum bonum* of the people. Such local self-government bodies are the need of the hour. A style of administration in which the officials and the representatives of the people go shoulder to shoulder and work for the local development should emerge. On the part of the Government steps are being taken to reach this goal.

People's planning – aims and achievements

Five years have elapsed since the local self-government bodies as part of people's planning movement, formulated their schemes and implemented them with people's co-operation. Regarding the qualitative changes the movement brought about in the power decentralization sector in general and development sector in particular, a consensus has come out. People's planning has more or less acquired by now the ability to cut and clear its own path and forge ahead. The people's planning has become the urgent obligation of the local self-government bodies of the state . . . To ensure balanced development in the environmental sector of the State is the fourth aim of the people's planning. To deliver the womenfolk who constitute more than half of the society from the different kinds of exploitation they face today and take them to the mainstream of development is again another important aim of this movement.

The reflections of change

It cannot be claimed that with activities of the movement, all the aims and objectives were achieved. In the place of a sense of pessimism that nothing would improve, a sense of optimism developed among the people, the optimism that if worked on the basis of people's participation with will power and determination, a lot of things could be implemented. Objectives and transparent style of taking decisions based on distinct priorities and norms have come to stay in the majority of the local self-government bodies.

The large participation in the village assemblies

The most important achievement of the village assemblies is that they could prove that they have a very crucial role in the planning-decentralization activities. As part of people's planning activities village assemblies were organized and public interest was generated in the planning-decentralization activities. The village assemblies could prove to be the most suitable practical local unit for these activities.

Source: Government website: http://www.kerala.gov.in/dept_panchayat/index.htm Power Decentralization Act.

TEHRI DAM JUDGMENT IN THE SUPREME COURT **Document 42**

The following is the court document giving the decision on the Tehri Dam project. It dismisses the objections of the petitioners – a citizens' group against the dam – which had claimed the government did not adequately consider the dangers and risks of the project. The court said that it could not rule on the merit of the dam, but that it agreed with the government that the government had carried out sufficient study and taken the advice of experts.

PETITIONER:
TEHRI BANDH VIRODHI SANGARSH SAMITI AND ORS.

     vs.

RESPONDENT:

STATE OF U.P AND ORS.

DATE OF JUDGMENT 07/11/1990

BENCH:
SINGH, K.N. (J)
KULDIP SINGH (J)

CITATION:
1990 SCR Supl. (2) 606 1992 SCC Supl. (1) 44
JT 1990 (4) 59 1990 SCALE (2) 1003 ACT:
Constitution of India, 1950: Article 32 – Tehri Dam Construction of – Safety aspect – Consideration of – Court can only investigate and adjudicate the question whether the Government applied its mind.

Environmental Law: Tehri Dam – Construction of – Tehri Hydron Power Project – Implementation of – Safety aspect – Consideration of – Held UOI considered question in various details and relevant aspects.

HEADNOTE:

The petitioners have filed this petition in public interest under Article 32 of the Constitution praying that the respondents be restrained from constructing and implementing the Tehri Hydro Power Project and the Tehri Dam. They allege that in preparing the plan for Tehri Dam Project the safety aspect has not been taking into consideration; that the dam, if allowed to be constructed, will pose a serious threat to the life, ecology and the environments of the entire northern India as the site of the dam is prone to earthquake; and that the Government of India had not applied its mind to this very important aspect in preparing the project. The respondents, on the other hand, assert that the Government of India, through its various departments and ministries has at every stage considered all relevant data and fully applied its mind to the safety and various other aspects of the project.

Dismissing the petition, this Court,

HELD:

(1) The Union of India considered the question of safety of the project in various details more than once. It satisfied itself by obtaining the reports of experts and also took into consideration the dissenting view of Dr.V.K. Gaur. The project has been finalised after obtaining the expert report of Prof. Jai Krishna. In the circumstances, it is not possible to hold that the Union of India has not applied its mind or has not considered the relevant aspects of the safety of the Dam. [613C-D]

(2) The questions relating to the design of the dam, the seismic potential of site where the dam is proposed to be constructed, and the various steps which have been taken for ensuring the safety of the dam are highly intricate questions relating to science and engineering. This Court does not possess the requisite expertise to render any final opinion on the rival contentions of the experts. The Court can only investigate and adjudicate the question as to whether the Government was conscious to the inherent danger as pointed out by the petitioners and applied its mind to the safety of the dam.

Source: Government of India website. http://indiacode.nic.in/coiweb/welcome.html

Further reading

A number of surveys of Indian history have been published in recent years and many of them include a small section on the post-independence period, usually ending in the 1960s. However, because they include the nationalist movement before independence, they might provide additional contexts for further reading. For example, see Barbara Metcalf and Thomas Metcalf, *A Concise History of India* and Peter Robb, *A History of India*. Sugata Bose and Ayesha Jalal, *Modern South Asia*, pay special attention to the issues of Partition.

Partition

India's Partition has recently become a topic of interest across disciplines in South Asia. While there has always been a rich body of literary works on the subject, social scientists are now analyzing it from different perspectives. Among the most important works of literature on Partition are the stories of Sadaat Hasan Manto, available in a variety of translated collections – 'Toba Tek Singh' and 'Kol Do' – are particularly powerful. Bapsi Sidwa, *Cracking India*, Attia Hosain, *Sunlight on a Broken Column*, New York: Penguin Books–Virago Press, 1989) and Mukul Kesavan, *Looking Through Glass* treat the moment through the experiences of characters from different communities.

Urvashi Butalia's oral history/memoir/sociological study, *The Other Side of Silence* is important both because of its unique genre and the perspective it provides on the experiences of women. Mushirul Hasan's *Inventing Boundaries: Gender, Politics, and the Partition of India*, is a valuable collection of primary sources and analysis, New Delhi: Oxford University Press, 2000. Another collection, by Suvir Kaul, *The Partitions of Memory: the afterlife of the division of India*, Bloomington: Indiana University Press, 2002, is more specifically focused on literary criticism. Much of the scholarship does focus on the issue of 'remembering'. See for example, Gyanendra Pandey, *Remembering Partition: violence, nationalism*, New York: Cambridge University

Press, 2001. For further analysis Hasan, Mushirul, *India's Partition: Process, Strategy, Mobilization*, New Delhi: Oxford University Press, 1994.

Reconsidering Nehru

Nehru's vision of India as a modern, socialist, secular state infused not only much of India's political culture, but also post-independence scholarship. Therefore, there is a vigorous current debate about the meaning of Nehru's legacy. Sunil Khilnani's critique in *The Idea of India*, New York: Farrar, Straus and Giroux, 1999 gets something of a response in Shashi Tharoor's *Nehru: the Invention of India*, New Delhi: Penguin, 2003. Gucharan Das, *India Unbound: the social and Economic Revolution from Independence to the Global Age*, New York: Anchor Books, 2002 and Bimal Jalan, *The Future of India*, New Delhi: Penguin, 2005 provide an economic view. Das was at one time CEO of Proctor and Gamble and Jalan was the Governor of the Reserve Bank of India.

However, the complex interplay of a variety of sources is probably too detailed to discuss here. The political scientist, Paul Brass, lays out some of the most salient arguments and major participants in an essay, 'India, Myron Weiner, and the Political Science of Development' in *Economic and Political Weekly (EPW)* 20 July 2002. That essay raises another issue worth further reading: development.

Agricultural development

The book by Francine Frankel, *India's Green Revolution, Economic Gains and Political Costs*, Princeton: Princeton University Press, 1971, historically speaking is an important discussion of what that movement looked like at the time. For larger contemporary context, see her *India's Political Economy 1947–2004: The Gradual Revolution*, Francine R. Frankel, New Delhi, Oxford University Press, 2005, an updated version of one written in 1977. A collection of essays edited by Arun Agarwal and K. Sivaramakrishnan, called *Agrarian Environments: Resources, Representations, and Rule in India*, Durham: Duke University Press, 2000, contains essays covering a variety of different development concerns and in a place as diverse as India that is a very useful approach. However, one of the most influential books on agrarian development is Bina Agarwal, *A Field of One's* Own: *Gender and Land Rights*, Cambridge: Cambridge University Press, 1994, which examines in detail the history of women's access to land and its implication on development and prosperity. The book has helped shaped and encourage reform in inheritance laws. Finally, although it is not solely about India, Amartya Sen, *Development as Freedom* contains a number of examples drawn from India and puts the agriculture, economic, and social development into a useful context.

Because the new panchayats have become a major vehicle for development, the literature on panchayats would be useful reading on this subject as well. The Institute of Social Sciences has supported a number studies, for example the overview by George Mathew, *Status of Panchayati Raj in the States and Union Territories of India, 2000*, New Delhi: Institute of Social Sciences, 2000. Also see *Decentralisation and Local Governance*: *Essays for George Mathew* edited by L. C. Jain, New Delhi: Orient Longman, 2005.

The Emergency

On the Emergency, *Unsettled Memories: Narratives of the Emergency in India* by Emma Tarlo, Berkeley: University of California Press, 2001, uses oral histories to test some of the dominant assumptions about that understudied historical moment. The most powerful images of the Emergency appear in fiction. Rohinton Mistry, *A Fine Balance*, not only contains characters who experienced the Emergency but, even more unusually, they are slum dwellers and street people and yet fully realized and three-dimensional. Perhaps the most obvious narrative of the Emergency in fiction is *Midnight's Children* by Salman Rushdie, New York: Viking, 1980.

Hindu nationalism

The politics of Hindu Nationalism is a complex subject with many nuances. Some sources that address these issues are Peter Van der Veer, *Religious Nationalism*, Delhi: Oxford University Press, 1996, Tanika Sarkar and Urvashi Butalia's edited volume – *Women and the Hindu Right*, New Delhi: Kali Press, 1995, Christopher Jaffrelot's *The Hindu Nationalist Movement in India*, New Delhi: Viking, 1996 and Mushirul Hasan's collection of essays under the title *Will Secular India Survive?* Gurgaon: ImprintOne, 2004, addresses some of these same issues from a different perspective.

Other social movements

Although it is difficult to find, *Why I am not a Hindu: A Sudra Critique of Hindutva, Philosophy, Culture, and Political Economy*, Calcutta: Samya; Bombay: distributed by Bhatkal Books International, 1996, by Kancha Ilaiah examines contemporary politics from a perspective that addresses issues of depressed classes. The rich material on the women's movement includes the following overviews: Radha Kumar, *The History of Doing: An Illustrated Account of Movement for Women's Rights and Feminism in India, 1800–1900*, New Delhi: Kali, 1993; Leslie Calman, *Toward Empowerment: Women and Movement Politics in India*, Boulder: Westview Press, 1992 and Geraldine

Forbes, *Women in Modern India*, Cambridge: Cambridge University Press, 1996. On gender issues, Rajeshwari Sunder Rajan, *The Scandal of the State,* Durham, NC: Duke University Press, 2003, includes a number of interesting cases. Also see Kirin Kapadia, *The Violence of Development: The Politics of Identity, Gender and Social Inequalities In India*, London: Zed Books, 2002.

References

Agnes, Flavia (2001) *Law and Gender Inequality: The Politics of Women's Rights in India*, New Delhi, Oxford University Press.

Ahmad, Aijaz (1992) *In Theory: Classes, Nations, Literatures*, New Delhi: Oxford University Press.

Ahmed, Akbar (1992) 'Bombay Films: The Cinema as Metaphor for Indian Society and Politics', *Modern Asian Studies*, 26:2.

Aiyar, Swarna (1995) '"August anarchy": the partition massacres in Punjab, 1947', *South Asia*, 18, 13–35.

Anderson, Robert G. W. (2005) 'To thrive or survive? The state and status of research in Museums', *Museum Management and Curatorship*, 20, 297–311.

Asaduddin (2001) '"Against forgetting": memory as metaphor in "dream images"', in Ravikant Saint and Tarun K. Saint (eds), *Translating Partition*, New Delhi: Katha.

Banerjee, Ashish (1990) '"Comparative curfew": changing dimensions of communal politics in India', in Veena Das (ed.), *Mirrors of Violence: Communities, Riots and Survivors in South Asia*, Delhi: Oxford University Press.

Banerjee, Bibhutibhushan (1990) *Pather Panchali* (Song of the Road), trs. T. W. Clark and Tarapada Mukherji, Calcutta: Rupa.

Banerjee, Shampa (1985) *Profiles: Five Film-Makers from India*, New Delhi: National Film Development.

Banerjee, Sumanta (1984) *India's Simmering Revolution: The Naxalite Uprising*, London: Zed Books.

Bansil, P. C. (1975) *Agricultural Problems of India*, Delhi: Vikas.

Barnouw, Erik and S. Krishnaswamy (1980) *Indian Film*, New York: Oxford University Press.

Bayly, Susan (1999) *Caste, Society, and Politics in India from the Eighteenth Century to the Modern Age*, Cambridge: Cambridge University Press.

BBC/WGBH-TV/Canal (1997) In addition, Production, 'The Dynasty – The Nehru Gandhi Story'.

Benegal, Shyam (2000) 'Indian cinema: a perspective', in Vinita Damodaran and Maya Unnithan-Kumar, *Post Colonial India: History, Politics, Culture*, New Delhi: Manohar.

Bhalla, R. P. (1973) *Elections in India*, New Delhi: S. Chand.

Bose, Ajoy (2008) *Behenji: A Political Biography of Mayawati*, Delhi: Penguin.

Bose, Sugata and Ayesha Jalal (1997) *Modern South Asia*, London: Routledge.

Brass, Paul (1974) *Language, Religion and Politics in North India*, Cambridge: Cambridge University Press.

Brass, Paul (1994) *The Politics of India Since Independence*, Cambridge: Cambridge University Press.

Butalia, Urvashi (1993) 'Community, state, and gender: on women's agency during Partition', *Economic and Political Weekly*, 28:17, pp. WS12–24.

Butalia, Urvashi (1998) *The Other Side of Silence: Voices from the Partition of India*, Durham: Duke University Press.

Calman, Leslie J. (1992) *Toward Empowerment: Women and Movement Politics in India*, Boulder: Westview Press.

Chakravarty, Sumita (1993) *National Identity in Indian Popular Cinema, 1917–1987*, Austin: University of Texas Press.

Chandigarh: Government of Chandigarh Official Website. http://sampark.chd.nic.in/pls/esampark_web/le_corbusier_plan

Chandra, Bipan, Mridula Mukherjee and Adhitya Mukherjee (1999) *India after Independence (1947–2000)*, Delhi: Penguin Press.

Chatterji, Suniti Kumar (1956) 'Dissent', in *Report of the Official Language Commission*, New Delhi: Government of India.

Chattopadhyay, Raghabendra and Esther Duflo (2003) 'The impact of reservation in the Panchayati Raj: evidence from a nationwide randomized experiment', in *Natural Field Experiments*, 0027, online: http://karlan.yale.edu/fieldexperiments/pdf/Chattopadhyay%20and%20Duflo_2003.pdf

Churchill, Winston (1896) Letter to Lady Randolph Churchill (Trimulgherry, Deccan) November 4, Churchill Archive Chartwell Collection, Churchill College, Cambridge, CHAR 29/22/18-23.

Cinematography Act of 1952, (Act 38 of 1952).

Cohen, Stephen P. (2001) *India: Emerging Power*, Washington, DC: Brookings Institution Press.

Constituent Assembly Debates, 14 July 1947. http://164.100.24.208/ls/condeb/vol4p1.htm (Parliament of India Website)

Constituent Assembly Debates, 17 July 1947. http://164.100.24.208/ls/condeb/vol4p1.htm (Parliament of India Website)

Constitution of India, Parliament of India Website, http://164.100.10.12/coiweb/coifiles/amendment.htm

CPI (M-L) Document (1986) *Report from the Flaming Fields of Bihar*, Calcutta: Pobodh Bhattacharya.

Craven, Roy (Spring, 1965) 'A Short Report on Contemporary Painting in India', *Art Journal*, 24:3.

Damodaran Vinita and Maya Unnithan-Kumar (2000) *Post Colonial India: History, Politics, Culture*, New Delhi: Manoha.

Dandavate, Madhu (2002) *Jayaprakash Narayan*, Mumbai: Allied Publishers.

Das, Arvind (1983) *Agrarian Unrest and Socio-economic Change, 1900–1980*, Delhi: Manohar Books.

Das, Gurcharan (2002) *India Unbound: The Social and Economic Revolution from Independence to the Global Age*, New York: Anchor Books.

Das, Tarkanath (June 1950) 'The Kashmir issue and the United Nations', *Political Science Quarterly*, 65:2, 164–186.

Dehejia, Vidya (1997) *Indian Art*, New York: Phaidon.

Doniger, Wendy (2008) *The Hindus*, New York: Penguin.

Dwyer, Rachel and Divia Patel (2002) *Cinema India: The Visual Culture of Hindi Film*, London: Reakton Books.

Engineer, Asghar Ali (ed.) (1987) *The Shah Bano Controversy*, New Delhi: Orient Longman.

Engineer, Asghar Ali (ed.) (1991) *Mandal Commission Controversy*, New Delhi: Ajanta.

Engineer, Asghar Ali and Pradeep Nayar (eds) (1993) *Communalisation of Politics and the 10th Lok Sabha Elections*, New Delhi: Ajanta.

Forbes, Geraldine (1994) *Women in Modern India, The New Cambridge History of India, Vol. IV-2*, Cambridge: Cambridge University Press.

Franda, Marcus (1971) *Radical Politics in West Bengal*, Boston: Massachusetts Institute of Technology Press.

Frankel, Francine (1978) *India's Political Economy, 1947–1977: The Gradual Revolution*, Princeton: Princeton University Press.

Friedman, Thomas (2006) *The World Is Flat [Updated and Expanded]: A Brief History of the Twenty-first Century*, New York: Farrar, Straus and Giroux.

Gandhi, Nandita (1996) *When the Rolling Pins Hit the Streets: Women in the Anti-Price Rise Movement in Maharashtra*, New Delhi: Kali.

Ganguly, Sumit (Fall 1996) 'Explaining the Kashmiri insurgency: political mobilization and institutional decay', *International Security*, 21:2.

Gilmartin, David (November, 1998) 'Partition, Pakistan, and South Asian History: In search of a narrative', *Journal of Asian Studies*, 57:4.

Government of Andhra Pradesh (1977) *Report on the Sixth General Elections (House of the People) in Andhra Pradesh*, Vol I, General.

Guha, Ramachandra (2000) *The Unquiet Woods: Ecological Change and Peasant Resistance in the Himalaya,* expanded edition, Berkeley: University of California Press.

Guha, Ramachandra (2007) *India after Gandhi: The History of the World's Largest Democracy,* New York: HarperCollins.

Guide to the National Museum, A (1977) National Museum, Delhi: Government of India Press.

Hardgrave, Robert (October 1993) 'The dilemmas of diversity', *Journal of Democracy,* 4:4, 54–68.

Hasan, Mushirul (1994) *India's Partition: Process, Strategy, Mobilization,* New Delhi: Oxford University Press.

Hasan, Mushirul (2000) *Inventing Boundaries: Gender, Politics, and the Partition of India,* New Delhi: Oxford University Press.

Hasan, Zoya (2000) 'More equal but still not equal: state and inter-group equality in contemporary India', in Imtiaz Ahmad *et al.* (eds) *Pluralism and Equality: Values Indian Society and Politics,* Delhi: Sage.

H. E. H. The Nizam (1948) *The Complaint of Hyderabad Against the Dominion of India Under Article 35(2) of the charter of the United Nations.*

Irish, Sharon (Summer, 2004) 'Intimacy and monumentality in Chandigarh, North India: Le Corbusier's Capitol Complex and Nek Chand Saini's Rock Garden', *The Journal of Aesthetic Education,* 38:2.

Jaffrelot, Christopher (1996) *The Hindu Nationalist Movement in India,* New Delhi: Viking.

Jain, C. K. (1993) *Women Parliamentarians in India,* New Delhi: Lok Sabha Secretariat.

Jalal, Ayesha (1995) *Democracy and Authoritarianism in South Asia,* Cambridge: Cambridge University Press.

Jalal, Ayesha (8 August 1998) 'Nation, reason and religion: the Punjab's role in the partition of India', *Economic and Political Weekly,* 33:12.

Jayal, Niraja Gopal (2001) 'The state and democracy in India or whatever happened to welfare, secularism and development, N. G. Jayal (ed.) *Democracy in India,* New Delhi: Oxford University Press.

Jeffrey, Robin (1986) *What's Happening to India? Ethnic Conflict, Mrs. Gandhi's Death and the Test of Federalism,* London: Macmillan.

Jencks, Charles (2000) *Le Corbusier and the Continual Revolution of Architecture,* New York: Monacelli Press.

Kapoor, Raj (1954) Director 'Boot Polish'.

Kapoor, Raj (1955) Director 'Shree 420'.

Kesavan, Mukul (1995) *Looking Through Glass*, New Delhi: Ravi Dayal.

Khagram, Sanjeev (2004) *Dams and Development: National Struggles for Water and Power*, Ithaca: Cornell University Press.

Khan, M. A. Apellant *v.* Shah Bano Begum and Others, Respondent. Criminal Appeal No. 103 of 1981.

Khan, Mehboob (1957) Director 'Mother India'.

Khanna, Balraj and Aziz Kurtha (1998) *Art of Modern India*, London: Thames and Hudson.

Khilnani, Sunil (1999) *The Idea of India*, New York: Farrar, Straus and Giroux.

Kripilani, Sucheta (1995) [Article title], in Verinder Grover and Ranjana Arora (eds), *Sucheta Kripalanii: Her Contribution to Political, Economic and Social Development*, Delhi: Deep and Deep.

Kumar, Radha (1993) *The History of Doing. An Illustrated Account of Movements for Women's Rights and Feminism in India, 1800–1990*, London: Verso Books.

Kumar, R. Siva (Autumn, 1999) 'Modern Indian art: a brief overview', *Art Journal*, 58:3.

Kumari, Abhilasha and Sabina Kidwai (1999) *Crossing the Sacred Line*, New Delhi: Friedrich Ebert Stiftung.

Lang, Jon (2002) *A Concise History of Indian Architecture*, New Delhi: Permanent Black.

Laxman, R. K. (2000) *The Best of Laxman: The Common Man Balances His Budget*, New Delhi: Penguin.

Mallick, Ross (1994) *Indian Communism: Opposition, Collaboration and Institutionalization*, New York: Oxford University Press.

Mandal, B. P. (1991) *Reservations for Backward Classes: Mandal Commission Report of the Backward Classes Commission, 1980*, New Delhi: Akalank Publication, p. 131.

Manto, Sadaat Hasan (1990) *Kingdom's End and Other Stories*, New York: Penguin.

Masani, Zareer (1976) *A Biography of Indira Gandhi*, New York: Thomas V. Crowell.

Mathur, I. D. (2002) 'On retrospective', *National Museum*, Bulletin No. 9.

Maxwell, Neville (1970) *India's China War*, New York: Pantheon.

Mehta, Deepa (2002) Director 'Hollywood, Bollywood'.

Menon, Ritu and Kamla Bhasin (1998) *Borders & Boundaries: Women in India's Partition*, New Brunswick, NJ: Rutgers University Press.

Metcalf, Barbara and Thomas Metcalf (2002) *A Concise History of India*, Cambridge: Cambridge University Press.

Mistry, Rohinton (1995) *A Fine Balance: A Novel*, New York: Vintage Books.

Moraes, Frank (1960) *India Today*, New York: MacMillan.

Muslim Women (Protection of Rights on Divorce) Act, 1986 (Act 25 of 1986).

Nahata, Amrit (1976) Director, 'Kissa Kursi ka'.

Noorani, A. G. (9 September, 2003) 'India and China: facts of history', *Frontline*, 20:18.

Nussbaum, Martha (2005) *The Clash Within: Democracy, Religious Violence, and India's Future*, New York: Belknap Press.

Omvedt, Gail (29 September, 1990), '"Twice-Born" riot against democracy', *Economic and Political Weekly*, 25:39, 2195–2197, 2199–2201.

Panchayati Raj Act, 1992, Constitutional Amendment Acts 73 and 74.

'Platform of Citizens for Democracy', Jaya Prakash Narayan Movement, www.healthlibary.com.

Prakash, Vikramaditya (2002) *Chandigarh's Le Corbusier*, Seattle: University of Washington Press.

Rajagopal, Arvind (2001) *Politics after Television: Hindu Nationalism and the Reshaping of the Public in India*, Cambridge: Cambridge University Press.

Rajagopal, M. V., I. A. S. (1967–83) *Andhra Pradesh District Gazetteers*, Hyderabad: Government Central Press, Karimnagar, Guntur, Kurnool.

Rajan, Rajeshwari Sundar (1994) *Real and Imagined Women: Gender, Culture and Postcolonialism*, London: Routledge.

Ramakrishnan, E. V. (2000) *Indian Short Stories* (1900–2000), New Delhi: Sahitya Akademi, pp. 515–529.

Ramusack, Barbara (2004) *The Indian Princes and the States: Cambridge History of India. Vol III: 6*, Cambridge: Cambridge University Press.

Ray, Satyajit (1955) Director, 'Pather Panchali' (Song of the Road).

Report of the Official Language Commission (1956), New Delhi: Government of India.

Report of the Advisory Committee on the Subject of Minority Rights (1947), New Delhi: Government of India,

Robb, Peter (2002) *A History of India*, London: Palgrave.

Roy, Arundhati (1997) *The God of Small Things*, London: Flamingo.

Roy, Parama (1998) *Indian Traffic: Identities in Question in Colonial and Post Colonial India*, Berkeley: University of California Press.

Rushdie, Salman (2005) *Shalimar the Clown*, New York: Random House.

Rushdie, Salman (2006) *Midnight's Children*, New York: Avon Books.

Sahgal, Manmohini Zutshi and Geraldine Forbes (eds) (1994) *An Indian Freedom Fighter Recalls Her Life*, New York: M. E. Sharpe.

Sahitya Akademi. http://www.sahitya-akademi.gov.in/old_version/home.htm

Saint, Ravikant and Tarun K. Saint (eds) (2001) *Translating Partition*, New Delhi: Katha.

Sarkar, Tanika and Urvashi Butalia (eds) (1995) *Women and the Hindu Right: A Collection of Essays*, New Delhi: Kali Press.

Satyamurti, S. T. (ed.) (1964) *Handbook of the Madras Government Museum*, Madras: Government of Madras Press.

Saxenian, AnnaLee (1999) *Silicon Valley's New Immigrant Entrepreneurs*, San Francisco: Public Policy Institute of California.

Sen, Sukumar (1955) *Report of the First General Election in India (1951–522)*, New Delhi: Government of India Press.

Sen, Sukumar (1958) *Report of the Second General Election in India (1957)*, New Delhi: Government of India Press.

Sharrod, Robert (9 January, 1963) 'Nehru: his crisis with China', *The Saturday Evening Post*.

Shourie, Arun (1984) *Mrs Gandhi's Second Reign*, New Delhi: Vikas.

Shukla, V. N. (2003) *Constitution of India*, Lucknow: Easter Book.

Sidwa, Bapsi (1991) *Cracking India*, Minneapolis: Milkweed.

Singh, Kushwant (2011) *Train to Pakistan*, New York: Penguin.

Singh, Prakash (1995) *The Naxalbari Movement in India*, Delhi: Rupa.

Singh, Y. B. and Shankar Bose (1986) *Elections in India: Data Handbook on the Lok Sabha Elections (1952–1985)*, New Delhi: Sage.

Sinha, Arun (2002) *Goa Indica: A Critical Portrait of Postcolonial Goa*, New Delhi: Bibliophile South Asia.

Sippy, Ramesh (1997) Director., 'Sholay' (Flames).

Stein, Burton (1998) *A History of India*, London: Blackwell Press.

Subrahmanyam, K. (1976) 'Nehru and the India–China conflict', in B. R. Nanda (ed.) *Indian Foreign Policy: The Nehru Years*, Honolulu: University of Hawaii Press.

Subramanyam, K. G. (1978) *Focus: Essays on Indian Art*, New Delhi: Lalit Kala Akademi.

Subramanyam, K. G. (1987) *The Living Tradition: Perspectives on Modern Indian Art*, Calcutta: Seagull Books.

Sunder Rajan, Rajeshwari (1993) *Real and Imagined Women: Gender Culture and Postcolonialism*, London: Routledge.

Taeube, Florian (2009) 'The Indian software industry: cultural factors underpinning its evolution', in K. Moti Gokulsing and Wimal Dissanayake (eds), *Popular Culture in Globalised India*, London: Routledge, pp. 223–237.

Talbot, Philips (1949) 'Kashmir and Hyderabad', *World Politics*, I:3.

Tarlo, Emma (2001) *Unsettled Memories: Narratives of the Emergency in India*, Berkeley: University of California Press.

Thapar, Raj (1991) *All These Years*, New Delhi: Seminar Publications.
Times of India. Online. http://timesofindia.indiatimes.com/
Toward Equality: The Report of the Committee on the Status of Women in India (1975) New Delhi: Department of Social Welfare, Government of India.
Tuli, Neville (1998) *Indian Contemporary Painting*, New York: Harry N. Abrams.

United States Government. CIA Report, *The Sino-Indian Border Dispute: Part I (1950–59)* 2 March 1963. Declassified and Released May 2007.

Van der Veer, Peter (1996) *Religious Nationalism*, Delhi: Oxford University Press.
Venkatachalapathy, R. (ed.) (2006) *Chennai not Madras: Perspectives on the City*, Mumbai: Marg Publications.

Weiner, Myron (1983) *India at the Polls, 1980: A Study of the Parliamentary Elections*, Washington: American Enterprise Institute.
Widmalm, Sten (2002) *Kashmir in Comparative Perspective: Democracy and Violent Separatism in India*, London: Routledge.

Index